Tree & Shrub
Gardening
for
Washington
and
Oregon

Alison Beck
Marianne Binetti

Principal Photography by Tim Matheson

Lone Pine Publishing

The Publisher: Lone Pine Publishing

10145 – 81 Avenue
Edmonton, AB T6E 1W9
Canada

202A, 1110 Seymour St.
Vancouver, BC V6B 3N3
Canada

1901 Raymond Ave. SW
Suite C, Renton, WA 98055
USA

Website: www.lonepinepublishing.com

Canadian Cataloguing in Publication Data

Beck, Alison, 1971-
    Tree and shrub gardening for Washington and Oregon

    Includes bibliographical references and index.
    ISBN 1-55105-271-7

    1. Ornamental trees—Washington (State). 2. Ornamental trees—Oregon. 3. Ornamental shrubs—Washington (State) 4. Ornamental shrubs—Oregon. I. Binetti, Marianne, 1956- II. Title.
SB435.52.W2B42 2001   635.9'77'09795   C00-911177-8

Editorial Director: Nancy Foulds
Project Editor: Dawn Loewen
Editorial: Dawn Loewen, Shelagh Kubish
Illustrations Coordinator: Carol Woo
Photo Editor & Research: Don Williamson
Research Assistant: Allison Penko
Production Manager: Jody Reekie
Book Design, Layout & Production: Heather Markham
Production Support: Elliot Engley
Cover Design: Robert Weidemann
Image Editing: Elliot Engley, Arlana Hale-Anderson, Ian Dawe, Monica Triska

Photography: all photographs are by Tim Matheson (with field identification by Dawna Ehman), except: Agriculture & Agri-Food Canada (Morden Research Centre) 171b; Alison Beck 329b; Tamara Eder 16a, 23c, 33, 36, 39, 40, 49, 62a, 63, 66, 67, 76, 77a, 84b, 85a, 179i, 201a, 237a, 239a, 245a, 247c, 249a, 253, 255a, 257b, 295a, 298b, 301b, 315, 316, 317b, 319b; Janet Davis 140; Don Doucette 77b, 182, 282, 283a, 320, 321a; Erich Haber 271a; Linda Kershaw 28, 98, 99, 129a; Colin Laroque 29a, 112, 322; Dawn Loewen 170, 173, 242a, 275b, 279a, 323; David McDonald/Photo-Garden 97, 141; Heather Markham 277a, 307b; Allison Penko 27b, 116, 117a, 119a, 145a, 167b, 187, 236, 243a, 249b, 285a, 296, 299, 314, 321b, 326, 338a, 343a, 343b.

Front cover photos (clockwise from top left) by Tim Matheson: beech, viburnum, redbud, maple

Illustrations: Ian Sheldon

We acknowledge the financial support of the Government of Canada through the Book Publishing Industry Development Program (BPIDP) for our publishing activities.

Toxicity information in this book is for interest only. In case of suspected poisoning, consult qualified medical personnel.

CONTENTS

ACKNOWLEDGMENTS

We express our appreciation to all who were involved in this project. Special thanks are extended to the following individuals and organizations: Mark Carfae, Brenda Costanzo, Linda Kershaw, Margaret Lockett, Todd Major and Pension Fund Realty at Park and Tilford Gardens, Heather Markham, Tim Matheson and assistant Dawna Ehman, Nancy Matheson, Betty Miller, Paul Montpellier and the Vancouver Board of Parks and Recreation, Bill Stephen, Butchart Gardens, City of Bellevue (Bellevue Botanical Border), Free Spirit Nursery, Gibbs Nurseryland and Florist, Minter Gardens, Queen Elizabeth Park, Riverview Arboretum, Stanley Park, UBC Arboretum, Van Dusen Botanical Garden.

Additional thanks to Peter Thompstone for his generous contribution and involvement in preparing this book.

THE TREES & SHRUBS AT A GLANCE

A Pictorial Guide in Alphabetical Order, by Common Name

Abelia
p. 72

Aralia
p. 74

Barberry
p. 82

Arborvitae (Cedar)
p. 76

Arbutus
p. 80

Beautyberry
p. 86

Beech
p. 88

Birch
p. 92

Bluebeard
p. 96

Bog Rosemary
p. 98

Boxwood
p. 100

Broom (Woadwaxen)
p. 104

California Lilac
p. 110

Clethra
p. 114

Butterfly Bush
p. 106

Cedar
p. 112

Cotoneaster
p. 116

Daphne
p. 120

Dawn Redwood
p. 124

Deutzia
p. 126

Dogwood
p. 128

Douglas-Fir
p. 132

Dove Tree
p. 134

English Ivy
p. 138

Enkianthus
p. 140

Euonymus
p. 142

Elder
p. 136

False Cypress
p. 146

Fir
p. 150

Firethorn
p. 154

Flowering Cherry, Plum & Almond
p. 158

Flowering Crabapple
p. 164

Flowering Quince
p. 168

Forsythia
p. 170

Fothergilla
p. 174

Fringe Tree
p. 176

Ginkgo
p. 178

Goldenchain Tree
p. 180

Grape
p. 182

Hazel (Filbert)
p. 188

Hawthorn
p. 184

Heather (Heath)
p. 190

Hemlock
p. 192

Holly
p. 196

Horsechestnut
p. 200

Huckleberry
p. 202

Hydrangea
p. 204

Japanese Kerria
p. 214

Incense-Cedar
p. 210

Japanese Acuba
p. 212

Jasmine
p. 216

Juniper
p. 218

Kalmia (Mountain Laurel)
p. 224

Katsura-Tree
p. 226

Kinnikinnick
p. 228

Kiwi
p. 230

Larch
p. 232

Leucothoe
p. 234

Lilac
p. 236

Magnolia
p. 240

Mock-Orange
p. 250

Oak
p. 254

Maple
p. 244

Ninebark
p. 252

Oregon-Grape
p. 256

Pieris (Lily-of-the-Valley Shrub)
p. 258

Pine
p. 260

Plane-Tree (London
Plane), p. 264

Potentilla (Shrubby
Cinquefoil), p. 266

Redbud
p. 270

Redwood
p. 272

Rhododendron, Azalea
p. 274

Rockrose
p. 280

Rose-of-Sharon
p. 282

Russian Olive
p. 284

Silverbell
p. 286

Skimmia
p. 288

Smoketree
p. 290

Snowbell
p. 292

Snowberry (Coralberry)
p. 294

Spirea
p. 296

Spruce
p. 300

Stewartia
p. 304

Sumac
p. 306

Sunrose
p. 308

Sweetbox
p. 310

Thornless Honeylocust
p. 312

Viburnum
p. 314

Weigela
p. 320

Virginia Creeper (Boston Ivy)
p. 318

Winter Currant
p. 322

Winterhazel
p. 324

Wisteria
p. 326

Witch-Hazel
p. 328

Yew
p. 332

Yucca (Adam's Needle)
p. 336

Introduction

Trees and shrubs are woody perennials. Their life cycles take three or often many more years to complete, and they maintain a permanent live structure above ground all year. In cold climates, a few shrubs die back to the ground each winter. The root system, protected by the soil over winter, sends up new shoots in spring, and if the shrub forms flowers on new wood it will bloom that same year. Such shrubs act like herbaceous perennials, but because they are woody in their native climates they are still treated as shrubs. Some hydrangeas fall into this category.

A tree is generally defined as a woody plant having a single trunk and growing greater than 15' (4.5 m) tall. A shrub is multi-stemmed and no taller than 15' (4.5 m). These definitions are not absolute because some tall trees are multi-stemmed and some short shrubs have single trunks. Even the height definitions are open to interpretation. For example, a Japanese Maple may be multi-stemmed and may grow about 10' (3 m) tall, but it is often still referred to as a tree. To make matters more complicated, a given species may grow as a tree in favorable conditions and as a shrub in harsher sites. It is always best to simply look at the expected mature size of a tree or shrub and judge its suitability for your garden based on this. If you have a small garden, a large, tree-like shrub, such as a Smoketree or Rose-of-Sharon, may be all you have room for.

Vines are also included in this guide. Like trees and shrubs, these plants maintain living woody stems above ground over winter, but they generally require a supporting structure to grow upon. Again, the definition is not absolute, because some vines, such as wisteria, can be trained to

grow as free-standing shrubs with proper pruning. Similarly, certain shrubs, such as some of the California lilacs, can be trained to grow up and over walls and other structures.

Woody plants are characterized by leaf type, whether decidous or evergreen, needled or broad-leaved. Deciduous plants lose all their leaves each fall or winter. They can be needled, like Dawn Redwood and larches, or broad-leaved, like the maples and dogwoods. Evergreen trees and shrubs do not lose their leaves in the winter and can also be needled or broad-leaved, like pines and rhododendrons, respectively. Some plants are semi-evergreen; these are generally evergreens that in cold climates lose some or all of their leaves. Some viburnums fall into this category.

Trailing cotoneaster

Variety of textures and colors

The Pacific Northwest is famous for the magnificent trees that thrive in the moderate and often damp climate near the Pacific coast. The cool summers and mild winters, with often plentiful rainfall, provide growing conditions among the best in the world for magnificent stands of evergreen trees such as Douglas-fir and Western Redcedar. These moderate growing conditions are also ideal for a wide variety of shrubs.

Areas of eastern Washington and Oregon offer more growing challenges; summers can be hot and dry, and winters present below-freezing temperatures. Wind protection and winter mulching may be necessary in these areas in order to grow the wide array of species that so easily thrive

Purple Weeping Beech

Elder (above), hemlock (below)

along the coast. On the other hand, certain species grow better here than west of the Cascades.

These are of course broad generalizations; the region exhibits a wide diversity of ecological zones and each presents its own unique challenges. Higher elevations, for example, have a shorter growing season, colder winter temperatures and abundant snow.

Because the maritime climate in some areas of the Pacific Northwest is similar to England's, gardeners here can take advantage of the rich garden legacy that Great Britain has to offer. Imported and unusual species of rhododendrons, azaleas, dogwoods and brilliant blooming trees can thrive here, and plant lovers can also take full advantage of the varieties of trees and shrubs discovered and developed in China and Japan.

Gardeners in our region are supported by an active and hospitable gardening population with many horticulture clubs throughout the states. Outstanding garden shows, public gardens and arboretums in Seattle, Portland and elsewhere attract gardeners and growers from all over the world and are sources of inspiration as well as information. The chief resources of any gardener, however, are imagination and enthusiasm.

HARDINESS ZONES MAP

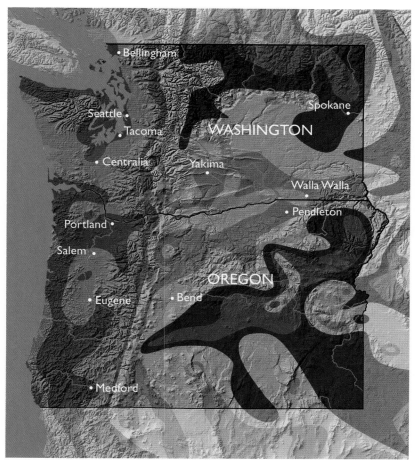

Average Annual Minimum Temperature

TEMPERATURE (°C)	ZONE	TEMPERATURE (°F)	TEMPERATURE (°C)	ZONE	TEMPERATURE (°F)
−28.9 to −31.6	4b	−20 to −25	−15.1 to −17.7	7a	5 to 0
−26.2 to −28.8	5a	−15 to −20	−12.3 to −15.0	7b	10 to 5
−23.4 to −26.1	5b	−10 to −15	−9.5 to −12.2	8a	15 to 10
−20.6 to −23.3	6a	−5 to −10	−6.7 to −9.4	8b	20 to 15
−17.8 to −20.5	6b	0 to −5	−3.9 to −6.6	9a	25 to 20
			−1.2 to −3.8	9b	30 to 25

WOODY PLANTS IN THE GARDEN

rees and shrubs create a framework around which a garden is designed. These permanent features anchor the landscape, and in a well-designed garden they create interest all year round. In spring and summer, woody plants provide shade and beauty with flowers and foliage. In the fall, leaves of many tree and shrub species change color, and brightly colored fruits attract attention and birds. In winter, the true backbone of the garden is revealed; the branches of deciduous trees and shrubs are laid bare, perhaps dusted with silvery frost, and evergreens take precedence to keep color in the garden.

Carefully selected and placed, woody plants are a vital and vibrant element of any garden, from the smallest city lot to the largest country acreage. They can provide privacy and keep unattractive views hidden from sight. Conversely, they can frame an attractive view and draw attention to particular features or areas of the garden. Trees and shrubs soften hard lines in the landscape created by structures such as buildings, fences, walls and driveways. Well-positioned plants create an attractive background against which other plants will shine. Trees and shrubs can be used in groups for spectacular flower or fall color shows, and a truly exceptional species, with year-round appeal, can stand alone as a specimen plant in a prime location.

Woody plants help moderate the climate in your home and garden. As a windbreak, trees provide shelter from the winter cold, reducing heating costs and protecting tender plants in the garden. A well-placed deciduous tree keeps the house cool and shaded in summer but allows the sun through in winter, when the warmth and light are appreciated. Woody plants also prevent soil erosion, retain soil moisture, reduce noise and filter the air.

Attracting wildlife is an often overlooked benefit of gardening. As cities expand, our living space encroaches on more and more wildlife habitat. By choosing plants, especially native plants, that are beneficial to the local wildlife, we provide food and shelter to birds and other animals and at the same time fulfill our obligation as stewards of the environment. We can bring nature closer to home. The unfortunate difficulty is that the local wildlife may so enjoy a garden that they consume it. It is possible, though, to find a balance and attract wildlife but at the same time protect the garden from ruin.

When the time comes to select woody plants, give careful thought to the various physical constraints of

Beech in fall color (above)

A large horsechestnut provides shade.

your garden and the purposes you wish the plants to serve. First and foremost, consider the size of your garden in relation to the mature size of the plants in question. Very large plants are always a bad idea in a small garden. Remember, too, that trees and shrubs not only grow up, they also grow out. Within a few years what started as a small plant may become a large, spreading tree. Redwoods, often sold as cute seedlings, are an example of fast-growing, potentially huge trees not suitable for many gardens.

Another consideration that relates to size is placement. Don't plant trees and shrubs too close to houses, walkways, entryways or driveways. A tree planted right next to a house may hit the overhang of the roof, and trying to fix the problem by pruning will only spoil the natural appearance of the tree. Plants placed too close to paths, doors and driveways may eventually block access completely and will give an unkempt appearance.

Bad placement (above), good placement and variety (below)

Consider, too, the various features of trees and shrub species. A feature is an outstanding element, such as flowers, bark or shape, that attracts you to the plant. Decide which of the following features are most important to you and which will best enhance your garden. Many plants have more than one feature, providing interest for a longer period of time. Whether you are looking for showy flowers, fall color, fast growth or a beautiful fragrance, you can find trees or shrubs with features to suit your design; consult the individual accounts and the Quick Reference Chart at the back of the book.

Form is the general shape and growth habit of the plant. From tall and columnar to wide and gracefully weeping, trees come in a wide variety of shapes. Similarly, shrubs may be rounded and bushy or low and ground hugging. Form can also vary as the year progresses. Often an interesting winter habit makes a tree or shrub truly outstanding.

You should be familiar with some growth form terminology when considering a purchase. A 'shade tree' commonly refers to a large, deciduous tree but can be any tree that provides shade. An 'upright,' 'fastigiate' or 'columnar' plant has the main branches and stems pointing upward and is often quite narrow. 'Dwarf' properly refers to any variety, cultivar or hybrid that is smaller than the species, but the term is sometimes mistakenly used to mean a small, slow-growing plant. The crucial statistic is the expected size at maturity;

Juniper 'Skyrocket' (above), Weeping Beech (center)

Dwarf arborvitae

if a species grows to 100' (30 m), then a 50' (15 m) variety would be a dwarf but might still be too big for your garden. 'Prostrate' and 'procumbent' plants are low growing, bearing branches and stems that spread horizontally across the ground. These forms are sometimes grafted onto upright stems to create interesting, often weeping, plant forms.

Foliage is one of the most enduring and important features a plant will provide in the garden. Leaves come in myriad colors, shapes, sizes, textures and arrangements. You can find shades of green, blue, red, purple, yellow, white or silver; variegated types have two or more colors combined on a single leaf. The variety of shapes is even more astounding, from short, sharply pointed needles to broad, rounded leaves the size of dinner plates. Leaf margins can be smooth, like those of many rhododendrons, or so finely divided the foliage appears fern-like, as with some Japanese Maple cultivars. Foliage often varies seasonally, progressing from tiny, pale green spring buds to the vibrant colors of fall. Evergreen trees provide welcome greenery even when winter is at its wettest and coldest.

An entire garden can be designed based on varied foliage. Whether it forms a neutral backdrop or stands out in sharp contrast with the plants around it, foliage is a vital consideration in any garden.

Top to bottom: Japanese Acuba, Euonymus, English Ivy, Virginia Creeper

Flowers are such an influential feature that they may be enough reason to grow trees or shrubs that are dull or even unattractive the rest of the year, such as the Goldenchain Tree. Flowering generally takes place over a few weeks or occasionally a month; only a few woody plants flower for the entire summer. Keep this limitation in mind when selecting woody plants. If you choose species with staggered flowering periods, you will always have something in bloom. You can achieve different but equally striking effects by grouping plants that flower at the same time, or by spreading them out around the garden.

Fruit comes in many forms, including winged maple samaras, dangling birch catkins, spiny horsechestnut capsules and the more obviously 'fruity' Oregon-grape berries and apple pomes. This feature can be a double-edged sword. It is often very attractive and provides interest in the garden in late summer and fall, when most plants are past their prime. When the fruit drops, however, it can create quite a mess and even odor if allowed to rot on the ground. Choose the location of your fruiting tree carefully. If you know the fruit can be messy, don't plant near a patio or a sidewalk. Most fruit isn't all that troublesome, but keep in mind that there may be some clean-up required during fruiting season.

Top to bottom: Goldenchain Tree,
Flowering Cherry,
Amur Maple samaras,
Flowering Crabapple

Arbutus (above), magnolia (center)

Corkscrew Hazel (below)

Bark is one of the most overlooked features of trees and shrubs. Species with interesting bark will greatly enhance your landscape, particularly in winter. Bark can be furrowed, smooth, ridged, papery, scaly, exfoliating or colorful. A few trees valued for their interesting bark are birches, Plane-tree, stewartias and Paperbark Maple.

Fragrance, though usually associated with flowers, is also a potential feature of the leaves, fruit and even wood of trees and shrubs. The flowering quinces, winterhazels, cedars, sweetboxes and of course lilacs are examples of plants with appealing scents. Try to plant a species whose fragrance you enjoy where the scent will waft into an open window.

Branches as a feature fall somewhere between form and bark, and, like those two features, they can be an important winter attribute for the garden. Branches may have an unusual gnarled or twisted shape, like those of the Corkscrew Hazel, or they may bear protective spines or thorns, like those of Firethorn.

Growth rate and **life span,** though not really aesthetic features of woody plants, are nonetheless important aspects to consider. A fast-growing tree or shrub that grows 24" (60 cm) or more a year will mature quickly and can be used to fill in space in a new garden. A slow-growing species that grows less than 12" (30 cm) a year may be more suitable in a space-limited garden. A short-lived plant appeals to some people because they enjoy changing their garden design or aren't sure exactly what they want in their garden. Short-lived plants, such as Rockrose, usually mature quickly and therefore reach flowering age quickly as well. A long-lived tree, such as a Redwood, on the other hand, is an investment in time. Some trees can take a human lifetime to reach their mature size, and some may not flower for ten years after you plant them. You can enjoy a long-lived tree as it develops, and you will also leave a legacy for future generations, because the tree may very well outlive you.

Katsura-tree 'Pendula' (above)

Yew hedges are slow to develop.

FAST-GROWING TREES & SHRUBS

Butterfly Bush
Dawn Redwood
Elder
Forsythia
Holly
Hydrangea (except *H. quercifolia*)
Jasmine
Katsura-Tree
Redwood (on coast)
Snowberry
Staghorn Sumac
Thornless Honeylocust
Virginia Creeper
Wisteria

SLOW-GROWING TREES & SHRUBS

Arbutus
Bog Rosemary
Boxwood
Enkianthus
Euonymus
Fothergilla
Japanese Acuba
Kalmia
Kinnikinnick
Pieris
Rhododendron
Skimmia
Yew

GETTING STARTED

*B*efore you fall in love with the idea of having a certain tree or shrub in your garden, it's important to consider the type of environment the species needs and whether any areas of your garden are appropriate for it. Your plant will need to not only survive, but thrive, in order for its flowers or other features to reach their potential.

All plants are adapted to certain growing conditions in which they do best. Choosing plants to match your garden conditions is far more practical than trying to alter your garden to match the plants. Yet it is through the very use of trees and shrubs that we can best alter the conditions in a garden. Over time a tree can change a sunny, exposed garden into a shaded one, and a hedge can turn a wind-swept area into a sheltered one. The woody plants you choose must be able to thrive in the garden as it exists now or they may not live long enough to produce these changes.

Light, soil conditions and exposure are all factors that will guide your selection. As you plan, look at your garden as it exists now, but keep in mind the changes trees and shrubs will bring.

LIGHT

Buildings, trees, fences, the time of day and the time of year influence the amount of light that gets into your garden. There are four basic levels of light in the garden: full sun, partial shade (partial sun), light shade and full shade. Some plants are adapted to a variety of light levels, but most have a preference for a narrower range.

Ginkgo likes full sun.

Full sun locations receive direct sunlight most of the day. An example would be a location along a south-facing wall. *Partial shade* locations receive direct sun for part of the day and shade for the rest. An east- or west-facing wall gets only partial shade. *Light shade* locations receive shade most or all of the day, but with some sun getting through to ground level. The ground under a small-leaved tree is often lightly shaded, with dappled light visible on the ground beneath the tree. *Full shade* locations receive no direct sunlight. The north wall of a house is considered to be in full shade.

It is important to remember that exposure to sun may mean more intense heat in some regions than in others. On the coast, where the heat is generally more moderate, many trees and shrubs thrive in full sun, but inland those same plants may need

Flowering crabapple provides light shade.

Bog Rosemary likes moist, organic soil.

largest. Water drains quickly from a sandy soil and nutrients are quickly washed away. Sand has lots of air spaces and doesn't compact easily. Clay particles are the smallest, visible only through a microscope. Water penetrates clay very slowly and drains away even more slowly. Clay holds the most nutrients, but there is very little room for air and a clay soil compacts quite easily. Most soils are made up of a combination of different particle sizes and are called loams.

Particle size is one influence on the drainage and moisture-holding properties of your soil; slope is another. Knowing how quickly the water drains out of your soil will help you decide whether you should plant moisture-loving or drought-tolerant plants. Rocky soil on a hillside will probably drain very quickly and should be reserved for those plants that prefer a very well-drained soil. Low-lying areas tend to retain water longer, and some areas may rarely drain at all. Moist areas suit plants that require a consistent water supply; constantly wet areas suit plants that are adapted to boggy conditions. Drainage can be improved in very wet areas by adding sand or gravel to the soil or by building raised beds. (If the soil is a heavy clay, add gravel rather than sand or you may end up with concrete.) Water retention in sandy or rocky soil can be improved by adding organic matter.

partial or light shade to protect them from the summer heat. Additionally, the shady side of a building may shelter plants in the heat of summer but can cause a longer, harder freeze in winter than some plants can tolerate. You may actually be able to use this situation to your advantage if, for example, you live on the coast and are trying to grow shrubs (such as lilacs) that need a good freeze in order to flower the following summer.

Soil

Plants have a unique relationship with the soil they grow in. Many important plant functions take place underground. Soil holds air, water, nutrients and organic matter. Plant roots depend upon these resources for growth, while using the soil to hold the plant body upright.

Soil is made up of particles of different sizes. Sand particles are the

Another aspect of soil that is important to consider is the pH, a measure of acidity or alkalinity. Soil pH influences the availability of nutrients for plants. A pH of 7 is neutral, values lower than 7 are acidic and values higher than 7 are alkaline. Most plants prefer a neutral soil pH, between 6.5 and 7.5. Many soils in coastal areas tend to be acidic, whereas in other areas soils may be more alkaline. You can test your soil if you plan to amend it. Soil can be made more alkaline with the addition of horticultural lime. It is more difficult to acidify soil, but you can try adding composted bark, leaves or needles. It is much easier to amend soil in a small area rather than in an entire garden. The soil in a raised bed or planter can easily be adjusted to suit a few plants whose soil requirements vary greatly from the conditions in your garden.

EXPOSURE

Exposure is a very important consideration in all gardens that include woody plants. Wind, heat, cold, rain and snow are the elements to which your garden may be exposed, and some plants are more tolerant than others of the potential damage these forces can cause. Buildings, walls, fences, hills and existing hedges or other shrubs and trees can all influence your garden's exposure.

Wind can cause extensive damage to woody plants, particularly to evergreens in winter. Plants can become too dehydrated in windy locations because they may not be able to draw water out of the soil fast enough to replace that lost through the leaves. Evergreens in areas where the ground freezes often face this problem because they are unable to draw any

Exposed Douglas-fir

Sheltering Firethorn hedge

water out of the frozen ground. The broad-leaved evergreens, such as rhododendrons and Oregon-grape, are most at risk from winter dehydration, so a sheltered site is often suggested for them. Strong winds can cause even bigger problems if large trees may be blown over by them. However, woody plants often make excellent windbreaks that will shelter other plants in the garden. Hedges and trees temper the effect of the wind without the turbulence that is created on the leeward side of a more solid structure like a wall or fence. Windbreak trees should be flexible in the wind or planted far enough from any buildings to avoid extensive damage should they blow over.

Oregon-grape

Hardiness zones (see map, p. 17, and Quick Reference Chart, p. 344) indicate whether species will tolerate conditions in your area, but they are only guidelines. Daphnes are listed as Zone 4 plants but can thrive in Zone 3. Don't be afraid to try species that are not listed as hardy for your area. Plants are incredibly adaptable and just might surprise you.

Here are some tips for growing out-of-zone plants.

• Before planting, observe your garden on a frosty morning. Are there areas that escape frost? These are potential sites for tender plants.

• Shelter tender plants from the prevailing wind.

• Mulch young plants in fall with a thick layer of clean organic mulch, such as bark chips, bark dust, composted leaves or compost mixed with peat moss, or with special insulating blankets you can find at garden centers. Ensure that organic mulches have a minimum depth of 12" (30 cm) for good winter protection. Mulch for at least the first two winters.

• In regions where the ground freezes, water thoroughly before freeze-up.

• In regions with snow, cover an entire frost-tender shrub with salt-free snow for the winter. You can also cover or wrap it with burlap or horticultural cloth, or, if in a container or planter, place it under shelter or against a house for protection.

Purchasing Woody Plants

Now that you have thought about what sorts of features you like and what range of growing conditions your garden offers, you can select the plants. Any reputable garden center should have a good selection of popular woody plants. Finding more unusual specimens may require a few phone calls and a trip to a more specialized nursery.

Many garden centers and nurseries offer a one-year warranty on trees and shrubs, but because trees take a long time to mature it is always in your best interest to choose the healthiest plants. Never purchase weak, damaged or diseased plants, even if they cost less. Examine the bark and avoid plants with visible damage. Observe the leaf and flower buds. If they are dry and fall off easily, the plant has been deprived of moisture. The stem or stems should be strong, supple and unbroken. The rootball should be soft and moist when touched. Do not buy a plant with a dry rootball. The growth should be even and appropriate for the species. Shrubs should be bushy and branched to the ground. Trees should have a strong leader. Selecting a healthy tree or shrub will give it the best chance in your garden.

Woody plants are available for purchase in three forms.

Bare-root stock has roots surrounded by nothing but moist sawdust or peat moss within a plastic wrapping. The roots must be kept moist and cool, and planting should take place as soon as possible in spring. You should avoid stock that has been frozen during shipping, but unfortunately it is hard to tell if a plant has been frozen. Bare-root stock is the least expensive of the three forms. Shrubs from mail-order companies usually come this way.

Balled-and-burlapped (B & B) stock comes with the roots surrounded by soil and wrapped in burlap, often secured with a wire cage for larger plants. The plants are usually field grown and then balled and burlapped the year they are sold. It is essential that the rootball remain moist. Large trees are available in this form; be aware that the soil and rootball are often very heavy and there may be an extra expense for delivery and planting. Balled-and-burlapped stock is usually less expensive to purchase than container-grown stock.

Container plants are grown in pots filled with potting soil and have established root systems. This form is the most common at garden centers and nurseries. It is the most expensive way to buy plants because the plants have been cared for over months or years in the container. Be aware that some field-grown stock may be placed in plastic or other containers instead of burlap; ask if you are not sure. Such plants must be treated like balled-and-burlapped stock. Container stock establishes very quickly after planting and can be planted almost any time during the growing season. It is also easy to transplant. When choosing a plant, make sure it hasn't been in the container too long. If the roots are encircling the inside of the pot, then the plant has become root-bound. A root-bound tree or shrub will not establish well, and as the roots mature and thicken, they can choke and kill the plant.

Bigger is not always better when it comes to choosing woody plants. Research and observation have shown that smaller stock oftens ends up healthier and more robust than larger stock, particularly for field-grown (as opposed to container-grown) plants. When a plant is dug up out of the field, the roots are severely cut back. The smaller the plant, the more quickly it can recover from the shock of being uprooted.

Root-bound specimen

Plants can be damaged by improper transportation and handling. You can lift bare-root stock by the stem, but do not lift any other trees or shrubs by the trunk or branches. Rather, lift by the rootball or container, or if the plant is too large to lift, place it on a tarp or mat and drag it. Remember, too, that the heat produced inside a car can quickly dehydrate a plant. If you are using a truck for transport, lay the plant down or cover it to shield it from the wind. Even a short trip home from the nursery can be traumatic for a plant. Avoid mechanical damage such as rubbing or breakage of the plant during transport.

At home, water the plant if it is dry and keep it in a sheltered location until you plant it. Remove damaged growth and broken branches, but do no other pruning. Plant your tree or shrub as soon as possible. A bare-root tree or shrub should be planted in a large container of potting soil if it will not be planted outdoors immediately. If you must store container plants over a cold winter before planting, bury the entire container until spring.

Fall selection is often limited (above); temporary winter storage (below)

PLANTING TREES & SHRUBS

*B*efore you pick up a shovel and start digging, step back for a moment and make sure the site you're considering is appropriate. The most important thing to check is the location of any underground wires or pipes. Even if you don't damage anything by digging, the tree roots may in the future cause trouble, or if there is a problem with the pipes or wires you may have to cut down the tree in order to service them. Most utility companies will, at no charge, come to your house and locate any underground lines. Prevent injury and save time and money by locating utilities before you dig.

Check also the mature plant size. The plant you have in front of you is most likely pretty small. Once it reaches its mature height and spread, will it still fit in the space you have chosen? Is it far enough away from the house, the driveway and the sidewalk? Will it hit the overhang of the house? Are there any overhead power lines? If you are planting several shrubs, make sure they won't grow too close together once they are mature. The rule of thumb for spacing: add the mature spreads together and divide by two. For example, when planting a shrub with an expected spread of 4' (1.2 m) and another shrub with an expected spread of 6' (1.8 m), you would plant them 5' (1.5 m) apart. For hedges and windbreaks, the spacing should be one-half to two-thirds the spread of the mature plant to ensure there is no observable space between plants when they are fully grown.

Finally, double-check the conditions. Will the soil drainage be adequate? Will the plant get the right amount of light? Is the site very windy? Remember, it's easier to start with the plant in the right spot and in the best conditions you can give it. Planning ahead saves time and money in the long run.

WHEN TO PLANT

For the most part, trees and shrubs can be planted at any time of year, though some seasons are better for the plants and more convenient than others. Spring is the best time to plant because it gives the tree or shrub an entire growing season to become established. Bare-root stock must be planted in spring because it is available only at that time, and it must be planted as soon as possible to avoid moisture loss. Balled-and-burlapped and container stock can be planted at any time, as long as you can get a shovel into the ground. They can even be planted in frozen ground if you had the foresight to dig the hole before the ground froze. Keep the backfill (the dirt that came out of the hole) in a warm place so it won't be frozen when you need to use it. Most plants will benefit, especially in cold winter regions, from having some time to become established before winter sets in. Many gardeners

also avoid planting during the hottest and driest part of summer, mainly because of the extra work that may be involved in terms of supplemental watering.

The time of day to plant is also a consideration. Avoid planting during the heat of the day. Planting in the mornings, in the evenings or on cloudy days will be easier on both you and the plant. It is a good idea to plant as soon as possible after you bring your specimen home. If you have to store the tree or shrub for a short time before planting, keep it out of the direct sun and ensure the rootball remains moist.

PREPARING THE HOLE

Trees and shrubs should always be planted at the depth at which they were growing, or just above the roots if you are unsure where this was for bare-root stock. The depth in the center of the hole should be equal to the depth of the rootball or container, whereas the depth around the edges should be one and one-half times the depth of the rootball or container. Making the center higher will prevent the plant from sinking as the soil settles and will encourage excess water to drain away from the new plant.

Be sure that the plants are not set too deep, particularly in a moist climate, because bark problems are likely if plants are even a few inches (8 cm) too deep. Most potted field-grown trees are planted too deep in the pot in order to help keep the freshly dug tree from tipping over, and there may

Sizing up the hole

Digging the hole

Adding organic matter to backfill

be mulch on top of the soil as well. Planting such a tree to the same depth as the level in the pot may not be a good idea. Scrape off the soil until you find the root mass, and then plant to just above it.

The diameter of the hole for balled-and-burlapped and container stock should be about twice the width of the rootball or container. The hole for bare-root stock should be big enough to completely contain the expanded roots with a little extra room on the sides.

The soil around the rootball or in the container is not likely to be the same as the soil you just removed from the hole. The extra size of the hole allows the new roots an easier medium (backfill) to grow into than undisturbed soil, providing a transition zone from the rootball soil to the existing on-site soil. It is good practice to rough up the sides and bottom of the hole to aid in root transition.

A handful or so of organic matter can be mixed into the backfill. This small amount will encourage the plant to become established, but too much will create a pocket of soil that the roots are reluctant to move beyond. If the roots do not venture beyond the immediate area of the hole, the tree or shrub will be weaker and much more susceptible to problems, and the encircling roots could eventually choke the plant. Such a tree will also be more vulnerable to blowdown in a strong wind.

PLANTING BALLED-AND-BURLAPPED STOCK

Burlap was originally made of natural fibers. It could be left wrapped around the rootball and would eventually decompose. Modern burlap may or may not be made of natural fibers, and it can be very difficult to tell the difference. Synthetic fibers will not decompose and will eventually choke the roots. To be sure your new plant has a healthy future, it is always best to remove the burlap from around the rootball. If there is a wire basket holding the burlap in place, it should be removed as well. Strong wire cutters may be needed to get the basket off.

With the basket removed, sit the still-burlapped plant on the center mound in the hole. Lean the plant to one side and roll the burlap down to the ground. When you lean the plant in the opposite direction, you should be able to pull the burlap out from under the roots. If you know the burlap is natural and decide to leave it in place, be sure to cut it back so that none shows above ground level. Exposed burlap can wick moisture out of the soil and prevent your new plant from getting enough water.

If possible, plants should be oriented so that they face the same direction that they have always grown in. Don't worry if you aren't sure—the plant will just take a little longer to get established. As a general rule, the most leafy side was probably facing south.

Past horticultural wisdom suggested removing some of the top branches when planting to make up for the roots lost when the plant was dug out of the field. The theory was that the roots could not provide enough water to the leaves, so top growth should be removed to achieve 'balance.' We now know that the top growth—where photosynthesis occurs and thus where energy is produced—is necessary for root development. The new tree or shrub might drop some leaves but don't be alarmed; the plant is doing its own balancing. A very light pruning will not adversely affect the plant, but remove only those branches that have been damaged during transportation and planting. Leave the new plant to settle in for a year before you start any formative pruning.

treewell

rootball with burlap removed

central mound

PLANTING CONTAINER STOCK

Containers are usually made of plastic or pressed fiber. All should be removed before planting. Although some containers appear to be made of peat moss, they do not decompose well. The roots will be unable to penetrate the pot sides and the fiber will wick moisture away from the roots.

Container stock is very easy to plant. Gently remove or cut off the container and observe the root mass to see if the plant is root-bound. If roots are circling around the inside of the container, they should be loosened or sliced. Any large roots encircling the soil or growing into the center of the root mass instead of outward should be removed before planting. A sharp pair of hand pruners (secateurs) or a pocket knife will work well.

Place the plant on the central mound. Orientation is less important with container-grown stock than with balled-and-burlapped stock because container plants may have been moved around during their development.

PLANTING BARE-ROOT STOCK

Remove the plastic and sawdust from the roots. Fan out the roots and center the plant over the central mound in the hole. The central mound for bare-root stock is often made cone-shaped and larger than the mound for other types of plants. Use the cone to help spread out and support the roots. Make sure the hole is big enough so the roots can be fully extended.

BACKFILL

With the plant in the hole and standing straight up, it is time to replace the soil. Backfill should reach the same depth the plant was grown at previously, or just above the rootball. If planting into a heavier soil, raise the plant about 1" (2.5 cm) to help improve surface drainage away from the crown and roots. Keep graft unions above ground if your plant is grafted stock. If you have amended the soil, ensure it is well mixed before putting it into the hole.

When backfilling, it is important to have good root-to-soil contact for initial stability and good establishment. Large air pockets remaining after backfilling could result in unwanted settling. The old method was to tamp or step down the backfilled soil, but the risk of soil compaction and root damage has made this practice fall out of favor. Use water to settle the soil gently around the roots and in the hole, taking care not to drown the plant. It is a good idea to backfill in small amounts rather than all at once. Add some soil, then water it down, repeating until the hole is full. Stockpile any remaining soil after backfilling and use it to top up the soil level around the plant after the backfill settles.

Ensure good surface drainage away from the new transplant. Do not allow the plant to sit in a puddle, but do not allow it to dry out, either.

1. Gently remove container.

2. Ensure proper planting depth.

3. Backfill with amended soil.

4. Settle backfilled soil with water.

5. Ensure newly planted shrub is well watered.

6. Add mulch.

Russian Olive in its new home

Staking

Staking provides support to a plant while the roots establish. It is no longer recommended, unless it is absolutely necessary, because unstaked trees develop more roots and stronger trunks. Generally, newly planted trees will be able to stand on their own without staking. Do not stake to keep a weak-stemmed tree upright. In windy locations, trees over 5' (1.5 m) tall will need some support, until the roots establish, to prevent them from blowing over.

There are two common methods for staking newly planted trees. For both methods you can use either wood or metal stakes.

The **two-stake** method is used for small trees, about 5–6' (1.5–1.8 m) tall, and for trees in low-wind areas. Drive stakes into the undisturbed soil just outside the planting hole on opposite sides of the tree, 180° apart. Driving stakes in right beside the

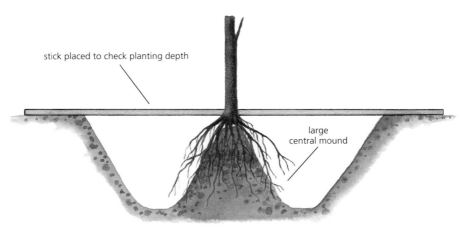

stick placed to check planting depth

large
central mound

Planting bare-root stock

newly planted tree can damage the roots and will not provide adequate support. Tie string, rope, cable or wire to the stakes and attach to the tree about 3–4' (0.9–1.2 m) above the ground.

The **three-stake** method is used for larger trees and trees in areas subject to strong or shifting winds. The technique is much the same as the two-stake method, but with three stakes evenly spaced around the tree.

Here are a few points to keep in mind, regardless of the staking method used:

• Never wrap a tie or cable directly around a tree trunk. Thread it through an old piece of garden hose or use some other buffer to protect the trunk from being cut or worn.

• Never tie trees so firmly that they can't move. Young trees need to be able to move in the wind so that the trunk strengthens and so that roots develop more thickly in appropriate places to compensate for the prevailing wind.

• Don't leave the stakes in place too long. One year is sufficient for almost all trees. The stake should be there only long enough to allow the roots some time to fill in. The tree will actually be weaker if the stake is left for too long, and over time the ties can damage the trunk and weaken or kill the tree.

stake in undisturbed soil

treewell

Two-stake method

TREEWELLS

A treewell is a low mound of soil built up in a ring around the outer edge of the filled-in planting hole. When you water your tree, this ring will keep the water from running away before it soaks down to the roots. Though a treewell is not necessary, it can make it easier to keep your new plant well watered until it becomes established. The treewell will be most useful during dry periods and should be removed during rainy periods to prevent the roots from becoming waterlogged.

TRANSPLANTING

If you plan your garden carefully, you should only rarely need to move trees or shrubs. Some woody plants (indicated as such in the individual species entries) resent being moved once established, and for these species transplanting should be avoided wherever possible. For all species, the younger the tree or shrub, the more likely it is to re-establish successfully when moved to a new location.

Woody plants inevitably lose most of their root mass when they are transplanted. The size of the tree or shrub will determine the minimum size of the rootball that must be dug out in order for the plant to survive. As a general guideline, for every 1" (2.5 cm) of main stem width, which is measured 6–12" (15–30 cm) above the ground, you need to excavate a rootball a *minimum* of 12" (30 cm) wide, and preferably larger. Trees with stems more than 2" (5 cm) wide should be moved by professionals with heavy equipment.

Follow these steps to transplant a shrub or small tree:

1) Calculate the width of the rootball to be removed (see above).

2) Water the proposed rootball area to a depth of 12" (30 cm) and allow excess water to drain away. The moist soil will help hold the rootball together.

3) Wrap or tie the branches together to minimize branch damage and to ease transport from the old to the new site.

4) Slice down vertically with a shovel or long spade in a circle around the plant; the circle should be as wide as the calculated rootball width. Cut down to 12" (30 cm) or more. (This depth probably contains most of the roots for the size of tree or shrub you should contemplate moving.)

5) Cut another circle one shovel-width outside the first circle, to the same depth.

6) Excavate the soil between the two cut circles.

7) When the appropriate rootball depth is reached, cut horizontally through the bottom of the rootball to free it from the surrounding soil.

8) Lift the rootball out of the hole *by the rootball,* not by the stem or branches. Place the freed plant on a tarp.

9) Lift or drag the tarp to the new location and plant immediately. See planting instructions given in preceding sections for information on when to plant, how to plant, staking, etc. Transplanted trees and shrubs can be treated as balled-and-burlapped stock.

Some older sources may recommend pruning the roots of a tree or shrub a year or so before transplanting. This practice should be strongly discouraged. It adds an additional, unnecessary stress before the major trauma of transplanting, making the plant more vulnerable to pests and diseases and reducing the likelihood that it will re-establish successfully.

treewell

Three-stake method

CARING FOR WOODY PLANTS

The care you give your new tree or shrub in the first year or two after planting is the most important. During this period of establishment, it is critical to keep the plant well watered and fed (but not overfed), to remove competing weeds and to avoid all mechanical damage. Be careful with lawn mowers and string trimmers, which can quickly girdle the base of the tree and cut off the flow of food and water between roots and branches. Remember that whatever you do to the top of the plant affects the roots, and vice versa.

Once trees and shrubs are established, they generally require minimal care. A few basic maintenance tasks, performed on a regular basis, will save time and trouble in the long run.

WEEDING

Weeding is a consideration for trees and shrubs in a garden bed. Weeds compete with plants for space, light and nutrients, so keep them under control and give your garden ornamentals the upper hand. When pulling weeds or scuffing the soil with a hoe, avoid damaging the delicate feeder roots of shallow-rooted shrubs and trees. Weed killers will probably not kill your woody plants but can weaken them, leaving them susceptible to attack by pests and diseases. A layer of mulch is a good way to suppress weeds.

MULCHING

Mulch is an important gardening tool. It helps soil retain moisture, it buffers soil temperatures and it prevents soil erosion during heavy rain or strong winds. Mulch prevents weed seeds from germinating by blocking out the light, and it can deter pests and help prevent diseases. It keeps lawn mowers and line trimmers away from plants, reducing the chance of damage. Mulch can also add aesthetic value to a planting.

Organic mulches can consist of compost, bark chips, shredded leaves and grass clippings. These mulches are desirable because they add nutrients to the soil as they break down. Because they break down, however, they must be replenished on a regular basis. Inorganic mulches consist of materials such as stones, gravel or plastic, which do not break down and so do not have to be topped up regularly.

For good weed suppression, the mulch layer should be 3" (8 cm) or more thick and be placed on top of a layer of newspaper. Avoid piling mulch up around the trunk or stems at the base of the plant because this can encourage fungal decay and rot. Try to maintain a mulch-free zone immediately around the trunk or lower stems.

WATERING

The weather, type of plant, type of soil and time of year all influence the amount of watering that will be required. If your region is naturally dry or if there has been a stretch of hot, dry weather, you will need to water more often than if you live in a naturally wet region or if your area has received a lot of rain. Pay attention to the wind, because it can dry out soil and plants quickly. Different plants require different amounts of water; some, such as birches, will grow in water-logged soil while others, such as pines, prefer a dry, gravelly soil. Heavy, clay soils retain water for a longer period than light, sandy soils. Plants will need more water when they are on slopes, when they are flowering and when they are producing fruit.

Plants are good at letting us know when they are thirsty. Look for wilted, flagging leaves and twigs as a sign of water deprivation. Make sure your trees and shrubs are well watered in fall, especially before the ground freezes. In regions where the ground does not freeze, continue with your regular watering regime, if it is needed.

Once trees and shrubs are established, they will likely need watering only during periods of excessive drought. To keep water use to a minimum, avoid watering in the heat of the day because much will be lost to evaporation. Also, add organic matter to the soil to help the soil absorb and retain water. Mulch also helps prevent water loss. Finally, collect and use rainwater whenever possible.

FERTILIZING

Most garden soils provide all the nutrients plants need, particularly if you mix compost or other organic fertilizers into the soil each year. Not all plants have the same nutritional requirements, however. Some plants are heavy feeders while others thrive in poor soils. Be sure to use the recommended quantity of fertilizer (if any), because too much does more harm than good. Roots can easily be burned by fertilizer applied in too high a concentration. Chemical fertilizers are more concentrated and therefore may cause more problems than organic fertilizers.

Granular fertilizers consist of small, dry particles that can be spread with a fertilizer spreader or by hand. Slow-release types are available. These reduce the risk of overapplication because the nutrients are released gradually over the growing season. One application per year is normally sufficient; applying the fertilizer in early spring will provide nutrients for spring growth. In garden beds they can be mixed into the soil.

Tree spikes are slow-release fertilizers that are quick and easy to use. Pound the spikes into the ground around the dripline of the tree or shrub, avoiding any roots. These spikes work very well for fertilizing trees in lawns, because the grass tends to consume most of the nutrients released from surface applications.

If you do not wish to encourage fast growth, do not fertilize. Remember that most trees and shrubs do not need fertilizer. In particular, fall fertilizing is not recommended because it may encourage tender growth that is easily damaged in winter.

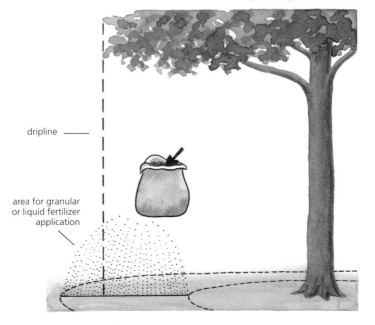

dripline ———

area for granular or liquid fertilizer application

PRUNING

*P*runing can maintain the health of a plant and its attractive shape; increase the quality and yield of fruit; control and direct growth; and create interesting plant forms and shapes such as espalier, topiary and bonsai. Pruning is possibly the most important maintenance task when growing trees and shrubs—and the easiest to mess up. Fortunately for new gardeners, it is not difficult to learn and is quite enjoyable if done correctly from the beginning and continued on a regular basis.

Proper pruning combines knowledge and skill. General knowledge about how woody plants grow and specific knowledge about the growth habits of your particular plant can help you avoid pruning mistakes that can ruin a plant's shape or make it susceptible to disease and insect damage.

If you are unsure about pruning, take a pruning course or hire a professional, such as a certified member of the International Society of Arborists (ISA). Pruning courses may be offered by a local garden center, botanical

Professional tree service

should develop the structure of the plant. For a strong framework, leave branches with a wide angle at the crotch (where the branch meets the trunk or another branch), because these branches are the strongest. Prune out branches with narrower crotches, while ensuring an even distribution of the main (scaffold) branches. These branches will support all future top growth.

Trees and shrubs vary greatly in their pruning needs. Some plants, such as boxwoods, can handle heavy pruning and shearing, while other plants, such as flowering cherries, may be killed if given the same treatment. The amount of pruning also depends on your reasons for doing it; much less work is involved in simply tidying the growth, for example, than in creating an elaborate bonsai specimen. Most pruning can be done once a year; at minimum you should inspect trees and shrubs annually to see if pruning is needed.

garden, post-secondary institution or master gardener. Certified professionals understand the plants and have all the specialty pruning equipment to do a proper job. They might even be willing to show you some pruning basics. You should **always** call a professional to prune a tree growing near a power line or other hazardous area.

Plants are genetically programmed to grow to a certain size, and they will always try to reach that potential. If you are spending a lot of time pruning to keep a tree or shrub in check, the plant is probably wrong for that location. It cannot be emphasized enough how important it is to consider the mature size of a plant before you put it into the ground.

When to Prune

Aside from removing damaged growth, do not prune for the first year after planting a tree or shrub. After that time, the first pruning

Many gardeners are unsure about what time of year they should prune. Knowing when a plant flowers is the easiest way to know when to prune. Trees and shrubs that flower in the early part of the year, before about July, such as rhododendrons and forsythias, should be pruned after they are finished flowering. These plants form flower buds for the following year over summer and fall. Pruning just after the current year's flowers fade allows a full season for the next year's flowers to develop. Trees and shrubs that flower in about July or later, such as Pee Gee Hydrangea and Rose-of-Sharon, can be pruned early in the year. These plants form flower buds as the season progresses, and pruning in spring just before or as the new growth begins developing will encourage the best growth and flowering.

Plants with a heavy flow of sap in spring, such as maples, should not be pruned in spring. To avoid excessive bleeding of the sap, wait until these species have started their summer growth before pruning.

Pruning trees in fall is not recommended because a number of wood-rotting fungal species release spores at that time.

Always remove dead, diseased, damaged, rubbing and crossing branches as soon as you discover them, at any time of year.

THE KINDEST CUT

Trees and shrubs have a remarkable ability to heal themselves. Making pruning cuts properly allows the tree or shrub to heal as quickly as possible, preventing disease and insect attacks.

Using the right tools makes pruning easier and more effective. The size of the branch being cut determines the type of tool to use. *Secateurs,* or hand pruners, should be used for cutting branches up to ³/₄" (2 cm) in diameter. Using secateurs for cutting larger stems increases the risk of damage, and it can be physically strenuous. *Loppers* are long-handled pruners used for branches up to 1¹/₂" (4 cm) in diameter. Loppers are good for removing old stems. Secateurs and

loppers must be properly oriented when making a cut. The blade of the secateurs or loppers should be to the plant side of the cut and the hook to the side being removed. If the cut is made with the hook toward the plant, the cut will be ragged and slow to heal.

Pruning saws have teeth specially designed to cut through green wood. They can be used to cut branches up to 6" (15 cm) in diameter and sometimes larger. Pruning saws are easier to use and much safer than chainsaws. *Hedge clippers* or *shears* are good for shearing and shaping hedges.

Make sure your tools are sharp and clean before you begin any pruning task. If the branch you are cutting is diseased, you will need to sterilize the tool before using it again. A solution of bleach and water (1 part bleach to 10 parts water) is effective for cleaning and sterilizing.

Proper secateur orientation

Heading back cuts

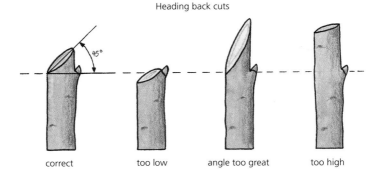

| correct | too low | angle too great | too high |

You should have a basic familiarity with the following types of pruning cuts.

Heading back cuts are used for shortening a branch, redirecting growth or maintaining the size of a tree or shrub. The cut should be made slightly less than ¼" (0.5 cm) above a bud. If the cut is too far away from or too close to the bud, the wound will not heal properly. Make sure to cut back to buds that are pointing in the direction you want the new growth to grow in.

Cutting to a lateral branch is used to shorten limbs and redirect growth. This cut is similar to the heading back cut. The diameter of the branch to which you are cutting back must be at least one-third of the diameter of the branch you are cutting. The cut should be made slightly less than ¼" (0.5 cm) above the lateral branch and should line up with the angle of the branch. Make cuts at an angle whenever possible so that rain won't sit on the open wound.

Removing limbs can be a complicated operation for large branches. Because of the large size of the wound, it is critical to cut in the correct place—at the branch collar—to ensure quick healing. The cut must be done in steps to avoid damaging the bark. The first cut is on the

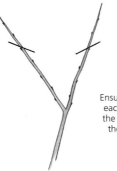

Ensure the bud beneath each cut is pointing in the direction you want the branch to grow.

Heading back cuts

Cutting to a lateral branch

bottom of the branch a short distance from the trunk of the tree. The purpose of this cut is to prevent bark from peeling down the tree when the second cut causes the main part of the branch to fall. The first cut should be 12–18" (30–45 cm) up from the crotch and should extend one-third of the way through the branch. The second cut is made a bit farther along the branch from the first cut and is made from the top of the branch. This cut removes the majority of the branch. The final cut should be made just above the branch collar. The plant tissues at the branch collar quickly create a barrier to disease and insects. Some sources suggest that using a sharp knife to bevel the edges of the cut promotes quicker healing.

Heading back cuts

The use of pruning paint or paste has been much debated. These substances may do more harm than good. Trees and shrubs have a natural ability to compartmentalize dead and decaying sections, and an unpainted cut will eventually heal over. A cut that has been treated may never heal properly.

To prune or cut down large trees, it is best to hire a certified arborist. These professionals are trained for the task and have the necessary equipment. Many fences, cars and even houses have been damaged by people who simply didn't have the equipment or the know-how when they tried to remove a large branch or tree.

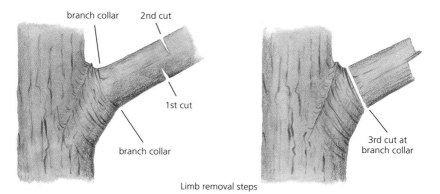

Limb removal steps

branch collar · 2nd cut · 1st cut · branch collar · 3rd cut at branch collar

Shearing a rhododendron

Shearing is used to trim and shape hedges. Only plants that can handle heavy pruning should be sheared because some of the normal pruning rules (such as being careful where you cut in relation to buds) are disregarded here. Informal hedges take advantage of the natural shape of the plant and require only minimal trimming. These hedges generally take up more room than formal hedges, which are trimmed more severely to assume a neat, even appearance. Formal hedges are generally sheared a minimum of twice per growing season. Make sure all sides of the hedge are trimmed to encourage even growth. The base of the hedge should always be wider than the top to allow light to reach the entire hedge and to prevent it from thinning out at the base. Remember that a hedge will gradually increase in size despite shearing, so allow room for this expansion when planting your hedge.

Thinning is a rejuvenation process that maintains the shape, health and productivity of trees and shrubs. It opens up space for air and light to penetrate and provides room for younger, healthier branches and selected suckers to grow. Thinning often combines the first three cuts discussed above, and it is the most frequently performed pruning practice.

A plant that is thinned annually should have one-quarter to one-third of the growth removed. Cutting the oldest stems encourages new growth without causing excess stress from loss of top growth. Although some plants can be cut back completely to the ground and seem to suffer no ill effects, it is generally better to remove only up to one-third of the growth.

incorrect   correct

Hedge shape

The following steps can be followed to thin most multi-stemmed shrubs.

1) Remove all dead, diseased, damaged, rubbing and crossing branches to branch junctions, buds or ground level.

2) Remove about one-third of the growth each year, leaving a mix of old and new growth, and cutting unwanted stems at or close to the ground. Avoid cutting stems below ground level because many disease organisms are present in soil.

3) Thin the top of the shrub to allow air and light penetration and to balance the growth. This step is not always necessary because removing one-third of the stems generally thins out the top as well.

4) Repeat the process each year on established, mature shrubs. Regular pruning of shrubs will keep them healthy and productive for many years.

Thinning cuts

Topping disfigures and stresses trees.

Pom-pom topiary

TREE TOPPING

One pruning practice that should **never** be used is tree topping. Trees have been topped to control their height or size, to prevent them from growing into overhead power lines, to allow more light onto a property or to prevent a tall tree from toppling onto a building.

Topped trees are weak and can create a hazard. A tree may be killed by the stress of losing half its live growth, or by the gaping, slow-to-heal wounds that make the tree vulnerable to insects and wood-rotting fungi. The heartwood of topped trees rots out quickly, resulting in a weak trunk. The crotches on new growth also tend to be weak. Topped trees, therefore, are very susceptible to storm damage and blowdown. Hazards aside, topped trees can ruin the aesthetic value of a landscape.

It is much better to completely remove a tree, and start again with one that will grow to a more appropriate size, than to attempt to control the growth of a mature specimen that is too large.

SPECIALTY PRUNING

Custom pruning methods such as topiary, espalier and bonsai are used to create interesting plant shapes.

Topiary is the shaping of plants into animal, abstract or geometric forms. True topiary uses species of hedge plants sheared into their desired shape. Species that can handle heavy pruning, such as boxwoods, are chosen. A simpler form of topiary involves growing vines or other trailing plants over a wire frame to achieve the desired form. Small-leaved ivy types often work well for this kind of topiary.

Wire-frame topiary (above), espalier (center)

Espalier involves training a tree or shrub to grow in two dimensions instead of three, with the aid of a solid wire framework. The plant is often trained against a wall or fence, but it can also be free standing. This method is popularly applied to fruit trees, such as apples, when space is at a premium. Many gardeners consider the forms attractive and unusual, and you may wish to try your hand at it even if you have lots of space.

Bonsai (below)

Bonsai is the art of creating miniature versions of large trees and landscapes. A gardener prunes the top growth and roots and uses wire to train the plant to the desired form. The severe pruning creates a dwarfed form of the species.

PROPAGATION

S ome gardeners are daunted by the often hefty expense of purchasing trees and shrubs. These plants cost more than perennials and annuals because nurseries must spend much more time and effort raising woody plants to a marketable size. Though many gardeners are willing to try starting annuals from seeds and perennials from seeds, cuttings or divisions, they may be unsure how to go about propagating their own trees and shrubs. Yet many woody plants can be propagated with ease, allowing the gardener to buy a single specimen and then clone it, rather than buying several expensive plants.

Do-it-yourself propagating is more than a way to cut costs. It can become an enjoyable part of gardening and an interesting hobby in itself. As well, it allows gardeners to add species to their gardens that may be hard to find at nurseries.

A number of methods can be used to propagate trees and shrubs. Many species can be started from seed; this can be a long, slow process, but some gardeners enjoy the variable and sometimes unusual results. Simpler techniques include cuttings, ground layering and mound layering.

CUTTINGS

Cut segments of stems can be encouraged to develop their own roots and form new plants. Taking cuttings is a more difficult method for starting your own plants than layering, but the basic principles are useful to know nonetheless.

Cuttings are treated differently depending on the maturity of the growth. Those taken in spring or early summer from new growth are called *greenwood* or *softwood* cuttings. These can actually be the most difficult cuttings to start because they require warm, humid conditions that are as likely to cause the cuttings to rot as to root.

Dipping in rooting powder

Cuttings taken in fall from mature, woody growth are called *hardwood* or *ripe* cuttings. In order to root, these cuttings require a coarse, gritty, moist soil mix and cold, but not freezing, temperatures. They may take all winter to root. These special conditions make it difficult to start hardwood cuttings unless you have a cold frame, heated greenhouse or propagator.

The easiest cuttings to start are taken in late summer or early fall. They are taken from new, but mature, growth that has not become completely woody yet. These are called *semi-ripe, semi-mature* or *semi-hardwood* cuttings.

Follow these basic steps when taking and planting semi-ripe cuttings.
• Make cuttings about 2–4" (5–10 cm) long from the tip of a stem, cutting just below a leaf node (the node is the place where the leaf meets the stem). There should be at least four nodes on the cutting. Each cutting's tip will be soft, but the base will be starting to harden.
• Remove the leaves from the lower half of the cutting. Moisten the stripped end and dust it lightly with rooting hormone powder. Consult your local garden center to find an appropriate rooting hormone for your cutting.
• Plant cuttings directly in the garden, in a cold frame or in pots. The soil mix should be well drained but moist. Firm the cuttings into the soil to ensure there are no air spaces that will dry out roots as they emerge.
• Keep the cuttings out of direct sunlight and keep the soil moist.
• Plants should root by the time winter begins. Make sure roots are well established before transplanting.
• Protect the new plants from extreme cold for the first winter. Plants in pots should be kept in a cold but frost-free location.

PLANTS FOR SEMI-RIPE CUTTINGS

Butterfly Bush	Firethorn
Cotoneaster	Forsythia
Dawn Redwood	Hydrangea
Dove Tree	Incense-Cedar
Euonymus	Jasmine
False Cypress	Potentilla

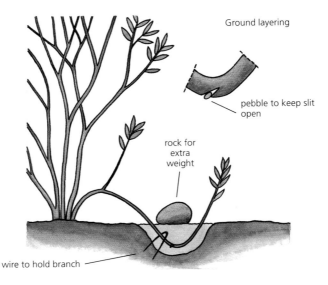

Ground layering

pebble to keep slit open

rock for extra weight

wire to hold branch

GROUND LAYERING

Layering, and particularly ground layering, is the easiest method and the one most likely to produce successful results. Layering allows future cuttings to form their own roots before they are removed from the parent plant. In ground layering, a section of a flexible branch is buried until it produces roots, at which time it is removed from the parent plant. The method is quite simple.

• Choose a branch or shoot growing low enough on the plant to reach the ground. Remove the leaves from the section that will be underground. At least four nodes should be buried, and at least another four should protrude above ground.
• Twist this section of the branch or make a small cut on the underside near a leaf node. This damage will stimulate root growth. A toothpick or small pebble can be used to hold the cut open.
• Bend the branch down to see where it will touch the ground, and dig a shallow trench about 4" (10 cm) deep in this position. The end of the trench nearest the shrub can slope gradually upwards, but the end where the branch tip will be should be vertical to force the tip upwards.
• Use a peg or bent wire to hold the branch in place. Fill the soil back into the trench, and water well. A rock or brick on top of the soil will help keep the branch in place.
• Keep the soil moist, but not soggy. Roots may take a year or more to develop. Once roots are well established, the new plant can be severed from the parent and planted in a permanent location.

The best shrubs for layering have low, flexible branches. The time of year that you start the layer is also important. Spring and fall are the best times to start, and many species respond better in one season or the other. Some plants, such as rhododendrons, respond equally well in spring and fall.

PLANTS TO LAYER IN SPRING

Daphne	Magnolia
Dogwood	Russian Olive
English Ivy	Smoketree
Enkianthus	Virginia Creeper
Grape	Wisteria
Lilac	Witch-Hazel

PLANTS TO LAYER IN FALL

Arborvitae	Jasmine
Euonymus	Kalmia
Forsythia	Katsura-Tree
Fothergilla	Kiwi
Hazel	Pieris
Huckleberry	Viburnum

PLANTS TO MOUND LAYER

Cotoneaster	Forsythia
Daphne	Heather
Dogwood	Lilac
Euonymus	Potentilla

MOUND LAYERING

Mound layering is a simple way to propagate low, shrubby plants. With this technique, the shrub is partially buried in a mound of well-drained soil mix. The buried stems will then sprout roots along their lengths. This method can provide quite a few new plants with little effort.

Mound layering should be initiated in spring, once new shoots begin to grow. Make a mound from a mixture of sand, peat moss and soil over half or more of the plant. Leave the tips of the branches exposed. More soil can be mounded up over the course of the summer. Keep the mound moist, but not soggy. At the end of the summer, gently wash the mound away and detach the rooted branches. You can plant them directly where you want them or in a protected, temporary spot if you want to shelter them for the first winter.

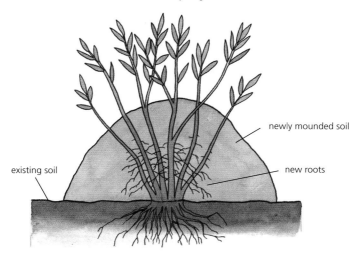

Mound layering

existing soil

newly mounded soil

new roots

PESTS & DISEASES

*T*ree and shrub plantings can be both assets and liabilities when it comes to pests and diseases. Many insects and diseases attack only one plant species. Mixed plantings can make it difficult for pests and diseases to find their preferred hosts and establish a population. At the same time, because woody plants are in the same spot for many years, the problems can become permanent. The advantage is that beneficial insects, birds and other pest-devouring organisms can also develop permanent populations.

For many years pest control meant spraying or dusting, with the goal to eliminate every pest in the landscape. A more moderate approach advocated by many authorities today is known as IPM (Integrated Pest Management or Integrated Plant Management). The goal of IPM is to reduce pest problems to levels at which only negligible damage is done. Of course, you, the gardener, must determine what degree of damage is acceptable to you. Consider whether a pest's damage is localized or covers the entire plant. Will the damage being done kill the plant or is it affecting only the outward appearance? Are there methods of controlling the pest without chemicals?

Chemicals are the last resort, because they may do more harm than good. They can endanger the gardener and his or her family and pets, and they kill as many good as bad organisms, leaving the whole garden vulnerable to even worse attacks. A good IPM program includes learning about your plants and the conditions they need for healthy growth; what pests might affect your plants; where and when to look for those pests; and how to control them. Keep records of pest damage because your observations can reveal patterns useful in spotting recurring problems and in planning your maintenance regime.

Sticky trap

There are four steps in effective and responsible pest management. Cultural controls are the most important. Physical controls should be attempted next, followed by biological controls. Resort to chemical controls only when the first three possibilities have been exhausted.

Cultural controls are the gardening techniques you use in the day-to-day care of your garden. Keeping your plants as healthy as possible is the best defense against pests. Growing trees and shrubs in the conditions they prefer and keeping your soil healthy, with plenty of organic matter, are just two of the cultural controls you can use to keep pests manageable. Choose resistant varieties of trees and shrubs that are not prone to problems. Space the plants so that they have good air circulation around them and are not stressed from competing for light, nutrients and space. Remove diseased foliage and branches and either burn the material or take it to a permitted dump site. Prevent the spread of disease by keeping your gardening tools

Leaf galls

clean and by tidying up fallen leaves and dead plant matter at the end of every growing season. Remove plants from the landscape if they are decimated by the same pests every year.

Physical controls are generally used to combat problems with insects. An example of such a control is picking insects off shrubs by hand, which is not as daunting as it may seem if you catch the problem when it is just beginning. Other physical controls include barriers that stop insects

Adelgid gall (above), ladybird beetle (below)

insects are probably already living in your landscape, and you can encourage them to stay by planting appropriate food sources. Many beneficial insects eat nectar from flowers such as the perennial yarrow.

Chemical controls should rarely be necessary, but if you must use them there are some 'organic' options available. Organic sprays are no less dangerous than chemical ones, but they will break down into harmless compounds. The main drawback to using any chemicals is that they may also kill the beneficial insects you have been trying to attract to your garden. Organic chemicals are available at most garden centers and you should follow the manufacturer's instructions very carefully. A large amount of insecticide is not going to be any more effective in controlling insect pests than the recommended amount. Note that if a particular pest is not listed on the package, it will not be controlled by that product. Proper and early identification of pests is vital to finding a quick solution.

from getting to the plant, and traps that catch or confuse insects. Physical control of diseases often necessitates removing the infected plant part or parts to prevent the spread of the problem.

Biological controls make use of populations of predators that prey on pests. Animals such as birds, snakes, frogs, spiders, ladybird beetles and certain bacteria can play an important role in keeping pest populations at a manageable level. Encourage these creatures to take up permanent residence in your garden. A birdbath and birdfeeder will encourage birds to enjoy your yard and feed on a wide variety of insect pests. Beneficial

Whereas cultural, physical, biological and chemical controls are all possible defenses against insects, diseases can only be controlled culturally. It is most often weakened plants that succumb to diseases. Healthy plants can often fight off illness, although some diseases can infect plants regardless of their level of health. Prevention is often the only hope: once a plant has been infected, it should probably be destroyed in order to prevent the disease from spreading.

GLOSSARY OF PESTS & DISEASES

ANTHRACNOSE
Fungus. Yellow or brown spots on leaves; sunken lesions and blisters on stems; can kill plant.

What to Do. Choose resistant varieties and cultivars; keep soil well drained; thin out stems to improve air circulation; avoid handling wet foliage. Remove and destroy infected plant parts; clean up and destroy debris from infected plants at end of growing season.

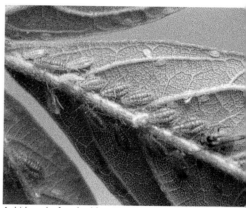
Aphids on leaf underside

APHIDS
Tiny, pear-shaped insects, winged or wingless; green, black, brown, red or gray. Cluster along stems, on buds and on leaves. Example: woolly adelgids. Suck sap from plants; cause distorted or stunted growth. Sticky honeydew forms on surfaces and encourages sooty mold growth.

What to Do. Squish small colonies by hand; brisk water spray dislodges them; many predatory insects and birds feed on them; spray serious infestations with insecticidal soap.

BEETLES
Many types and sizes; usually rounded in shape with hard, shell-like outer wings covering membranous inner wings. Some types are beneficial, e.g., ladybird beetles ('ladybugs'); others are not, e.g., June beetles, leaf skeletonizers and weevils. Larvae: see Borers, Grubs. Leave wide range of chewing damage: make small or large holes in or around margins of leaves; consume entire leaves or areas between leaf veins ('skeletonize'); may also chew holes in flowers. Some bark beetle species carry deadly plant diseases.

What to Do. On shrubs, pick beetles off at night and drop them into an old coffee can half filled with soapy water (soap prevents them from floating); spread an old sheet under small trees and shrubs and shake off beetles to collect and dispose of them; use a broom to reach tall branches.

BLIGHT
Fungal diseases, many types; e.g., leaf blight, needle blight, snow blight. Leaves, stems and flowers blacken, rot and die.

What to Do. Thin stems to improve air circulation; keep mulch away from base of plant; remove debris from garden at end of growing season. Remove and destroy infected plant parts.

Leaf skeletonizer damage

BORERS

Larvae of some moths, wasps, and beetles; among the most damaging plant pests. Burrow into plant stems, leaves and/or roots; destroy vascular tissue (plant veins and arteries) and structural strength. Worm-like; vary in size and get bigger as they bore under bark and sometimes into heartwood. Tunnels left by borers create sites for infection and decomposition to begin.

What to Do. Keeping tree or shrub as healthy as possible with proper fertilizing and watering prevents some borer damage; may be able to squish borers within leaves. Remove and destroy bored parts; may need to remove entire plant.

BUGS (TRUE BUGS)

Small insects, up to ½" (1 cm) long; green, brown, black or brightly colored and patterned. Many beneficial; a few pests, such as lace bugs, pierce plants to suck out sap. Toxins may be injected that deform plants; sunken areas left where tissue pierced; leaves rip as they grow; leaves, buds and new growth may be dwarfed and deformed.

What to Do. Remove debris and weeds from around plants in fall to destroy overwintering sites. Spray plants with insecticidal soap.

CANKER

Swollen or sunken lesion on stem or branch, surrounded by living tissue. Caused by many different bacterial and fungal diseases. Most canker-causing diseases enter through wounded wood. Woodpeckers may unwittingly infect plants when they drill for insects.

What to Do. Maintain plant vigor; avoid wounds on trees; control borers and other bark-dwelling insects. Prune out and destroy infected material. Sterilize pruning tools before and after use on infected plants.

CASE BEARERS
see Caterpillars

CATERPILLARS

Larvae of butterflies, moths, sawflies. Include bagworms, budworms, case bearers, cutworms, leaf rollers, leaf tiers, loopers. Chew foliage and buds. Can completely defoliate a plant if infestation severe.

What to Do. Removal from plant is best control. Use high-pressure water and soap or pick caterpillars off by hand if plant is small enough. Cut off and burn large tents or webs of larvae. Control biologically using the naturally occurring soil bacterium *Bacillus thuringiensis* var. *kurstaki*, or *B.t.* for short (commercially available), which breaks down gut lining of caterpillars. Dormant oil can be applied in spring. Tree trunks can be wrapped or banded to prevent caterpillars from climbing tree to access leaves.

FIRE BLIGHT

Highly destructive bacterial disease of the rose family, whose members include the apples, cotoneasters, hawthorns, cherries and Firethorn. Infected areas appear to have been burned. Look for bent-over twigs, branches that retain leaves over winter and cankers forming on lower parts of plant.

What to Do. Choose resistant plant varieties. Remove and burn infected material, making cuts a minimum of 24" (60 cm) below infected area. Sterilize tools after each cut on infected plant. Reinfection is possible because fire blight is often carried by pollinating birds and insects and enters plant through flowers. If whole plant is infected it must be removed and burned.

GALLS

Unusual swellings of plant tissues. Can affect leaves, buds, stems, flowers, fruit or trunks. May be caused by insects or diseases. Often a specific gall affects a single genus or species.

Caterpillar on fir

What to Do. Cut galls out of plant and destroy them. Galls caused by insects usually contain the insect's eggs and juvenile forms. Prevent these galls by controlling insect before it lays eggs; otherwise try to remove and destroy infected tissue before young insects emerge. Generally insect galls more unsightly than damaging to plant. Galls caused by diseases often require destruction of plant. Avoid placing other plants susceptible to same disease in that location.

GRUBS

Larvae of different beetles, commonly found below soil level; usually curled in C-shape. Body white or gray; head may be white, gray, brown or reddish. Problematic in lawns; may feed on roots of shallow-rooted trees and shrubs. Plant wilts despite regular watering; may pull easily out of ground in severe cases.

What to Do. Toss any grubs found while digging onto a stone path or patio for birds to devour; apply parasitic nematodes or milky disease spore to infested soil (ask at your local garden center).

Fuzzy oak galls

LEAFHOPPERS & TREEHOPPERS

Small, wedge-shaped insects; can be green, brown, gray or multi-colored. Jump around frantically when disturbed. Suck juice from plant leaves. Cause distorted growth. Carry diseases such as aster yellows. Treehoppers also damage tree bark when they slit it to lay eggs.

What to Do. Encourage predators by planting nectar-producing species like yarrow. Wash insects off with strong spray of water; spray with insecticidal soap.

LEAF MINERS

Tiny, stubby larvae of some butterflies and moths; may be yellow or green. Tunnel within leaves leaving winding trails; tunneled areas lighter in color than rest of leaf. Unsightly rather than health risk to plant.

What to Do. Remove debris from area in fall to destroy overwintering sites; attract parasitic wasps with nectar

plants such as yarrow. Remove and destroy infected foliage; can sometimes squish by hand within leaf.

LEAF ROLLERS
see Caterpillars

LEAF SKELETONIZERS
see Beetles

LEAF SPOT

Two common types. *Bacterial:* small speckled spots grow to encompass entire leaves; brown or purple in color; leaves may drop. *Fungal:* black, brown or yellow spots; leaves wither; e.g., scab, tar spot.

What to Do. Bacterial infection more severe; must remove entire plant. For fungal infection, remove and destroy infected plant parts. Sterilize removal tools; avoid wetting foliage or touching wet foliage; remove and destroy debris at end of growing season.

MEALYBUGS

Tiny crawling insects related to aphids; appear to be covered with white fuzz or flour. Sucking damage stunts and stresses plant. Mealybugs excrete honeydew that promotes growth of sooty mold.

What to Do. Remove by hand on smaller plants; wash plant off with soap and water; wipe off with alcohol-soaked swabs; remove leaves with heavy infestations; encourage or introduce natural predators such as mealybug destroyer beetle and parasitic wasps; spray with insecticidal soap. Keep in mind larvae of the mealybug destroyer beetles look like very large mealybugs.

MILDEW

Two types, both caused by fungus, but with slightly different symptoms. *Downy mildew:* yellow spots on the upper sides of leaves and downy fuzz on undersides; fuzz may be yellow, white or gray. *Powdery mildew:* white or gray powdery coating on leaf surfaces that doesn't brush off.

What to Do. Choose resistant cultivars; space plants well; thin stems to encourage air circulation; tidy any debris in fall. Remove and destroy infected leaves or other parts.

MITES

Tiny, eight-legged relatives of spiders; do not eat insects, but may spin webs. Almost invisible to naked eye; red, yellow or green; usually found on undersides of plant leaves. Examples: bud mites, spider mites, spruce mites. Suck juice out of leaves. May see fine webbing on leaves and stems; may see mites moving on leaf undersides. Leaves become discolored, speckled; then turn brown and shrivel up.

What to Do. Wash off with strong spray of water daily until all signs of infestation are gone; predatory mites available through garden centers; spray plants with insecticidal soap.

MOSAIC

see Viruses

NEMATODES

Tiny worms that give plants disease symptoms. One type infects foliage and stems; the other infects roots. *Foliar:* yellow spots that turn brown on leaves; leaves shrivel and wither;

Leaf miner damage

problem starts on lowest leaves and works up plant. *Root-knot:* plant is stunted; may wilt; yellow spots on leaves; roots have tiny bumps or knots.

What to Do. Mulch soil, add organic matter, clean up debris in fall. Don't touch wet foliage of infected plants. Can add parasitic nematodes to soil. Remove infected plants in extreme cases.

ROT

Several different fungi that affect different parts of the plant and can kill plant. *Crown rot:* affects base of plant, causing stems to blacken and fall over and leaves to yellow and wilt. *Root rot:* leaves yellow and plant wilts; digging up plant will show roots rotted away.

What to Do. Keep soil well drained; don't damage plant if you are digging around it; keep mulches away from plant base. Destroy infected plant if whole plant affected.

Snail eating leaf

RUST

Fungi. Pale spots on upper leaf surfaces; orange, fuzzy or dusty spots on leaf undersides. Examples: blister rust, cedar-apple rust.

What to Do. Choose varieties and cultivars resistant to rust; avoid handling wet leaves; provide plant with good air circulation; clear up garden debris at end of season. Remove and destroy infected plant parts.

SAWFLIES

see Caterpillars

SCAB

see Leaf Spot

SCALE INSECTS

Tiny, shelled insects that suck sap, weakening and possibly killing plant or making it vulnerable to other problems. Once female scale insect has pierced plant with mouthpart it is there for life. Juvenile scale insects are called crawlers.

What to Do. Wipe off with alcohol-soaked swabs; spray with water to dislodge crawlers; prune out heavily infested branches; encourage natural predators and parasites; spray dormant oil in spring before bud break.

SLUGS & SNAILS

Common pests in Northwestern gardens. Both are mollusks; slugs lack shells whereas snails have spiral shells. Slimy, smooth skin; can be up to 8" (20 cm) long, many are smaller; gray, green, black, beige, yellow or spotted. Leave large, ragged holes in leaves and silvery slime trails on and around plants.

What to Do. Attach strips of copper to wood around raised beds or to smaller boards inserted around susceptible groups of plants; slugs and snails will get shocked if they touch copper surfaces. Pick off by hand in the evening and squish with boot or drop in can of soapy water. Spread wood ash or diatomaceous earth (available in garden centers) on the ground around plants; it will pierce their soft bodies and cause them to dehydrate.

SOOTY MOLD

Fungus. Thin black film forms on leaf surfaces and reduces amount of light getting to leaf surfaces.

What to Do. Wipe mold off leaf surfaces; control insects like aphids, mealybugs, whiteflies (honeydew left on leaves encourages mold).

TAR SPOT

see Leaf Spot

THRIPS

Difficult to see; may be visible if you disturb them by blowing gently on an infested flower. Yellow, black or brown; tiny, slender; narrow, fringed wings. Suck juice out of plant cells, particularly in flowers and buds, resulting in mottled petals and leaves, dying buds and distorted and stunted growth.

What to Do. Remove and destroy infected plant parts; encourage native predatory insects with nectar plants like yarrow; spray severe infestations with insecticidal soap.

VIRUSES

Plant may be stunted and leaves and flowers distorted, streaked or discolored. Viral diseases in plants cannot be treated. Examples: mosaic virus, ringspot virus.

What to Do. Control insects like aphids, leafhoppers and whiteflies that spread disease. Destroy infected plants.

WEEVILS

see Beetles

WHITEFLIES

Tiny flying insects that flutter up into the air when plant is disturbed. Tiny, moth-like, white; live on undersides of plant leaves. Suck juice out of leaves, causing yellowed leaves and weakened plants; leave behind sticky honeydew on leaves, encouraging sooty mold growth.

What to Do. Destroy weeds where insects may live. Attract native predatory beetles and parasitic wasps with nectar plants like yarrow; spray severe cases with insecticidal soap. Can make a sticky flypaper-like trap by mounting tin can on stake; wrap

Wood-rotting fungi and other decay organisms

can with yellow paper and cover with clear plastic bag smeared with petroleum jelly; replace bag when full of flies.

WILT

If watering hasn't helped a wilted plant, one of two wilt fungi may be at fault. *Fusarium wilt:* plant wilts, leaves turn yellow then die; symptoms generally appear first on one part of plant before spreading elsewhere on plant. *Verticillium wilt:* plant wilts; leaves curl up at edges; leaves turn yellow then drop off; plant may die.

What to Do. Both wilts difficult to control. Choose resistant plant varieties and cultivars; clean up debris at end of growing season. Destroy infected plants; solarize (sterilize) soil before replanting (this may help if you've lost an entire bed of plants to these fungi)—contact local garden center for assistance.

WOOLLY ADELGIDS

see Aphids

WORMS

see Caterpillars, Nematodes

ABOUT THIS GUIDE

*T*he trees and shrubs in this book are organized alphabetically by common name. Alternative common names and scientific names are given beneath the main headings and in the index. The illustrated **Trees & Shrubs at a Glance** will help you find a plant if you aren't sure what it's called.

Clearly displayed at the beginning of each entry are the special features of the plant or group of plants; height and spread ranges; preferred planting forms (container, B & B or bare-root) and planting seasons; and hardiness zones (see map, p. 17).

The **Quick Reference Chart** at the back of the book is a handy guide to planning a diversity of features, forms, foliage types and blooming times in your garden.

Our favorite species, hybrids and cultivars are listed in each entry's 'Recommended' section. Sizes and zones are given only if these differ from the information at the beginning of the entry. Keep in mind there are often many more types available; check with your local garden center.

Common pests and problems, if any, are noted for each entry. Consult the 'Pests & Diseases' section of the Introduction for information on how to solve these problems.

Because our region is so climatically diverse, we can refer to seasons only in a general sense. Keep in mind the timing and duration of seasons in your area when planning your garden. Hardiness zones, too, can vary within a region; consult a local horticulturalist or garden center.

The *Trees*
&Shrubs

Abelia

Abelia

Features: flowers, foliage, stems **Habit:** large, rounded, evergreen or semi-evergreen shrubs
Height: 3.5–8' (1–2.5 m)
Spread: 3.5–10' (1–3 m)
Planting: B & B, container; spring, fall
Zones: 5–9

*A*belias' delightful, bell-shaped blooms ring joy into any garden, and the graceful form and delicate foliage of these shrubs give them a gentle, feminine look that harmonizes well with Victorian or traditional-style homes. When abelias begin blooming, you know you have reached the summit of spring, so surround them with tulips and primroses to really celebrate the season.

GROWING

Abelias prefer **full sun,** but tolerate partial shade. The soil should be **fertile, moist, acidic** and **well drained**. Plant abelias in a **sheltered** part of the garden; a location protected from wind, particularly during the winter, will help prevent desiccation of the leaves.

Pruning is best done in late winter or early spring. At the very least, remove winter-damaged growth and trim stems that are growing in undesired directions. Trimming or shearing the ends off the branches will create distorted growth, so branches to be removed should be cut right back to the ground. An old abelia can be rejuvenated by cutting the entire plant back to within a few inches (8 cm) of the ground.

TIPS

Abelias are valued for their glossy, dark green leaves and attractive, funnel-shaped, white or pink flowers that are produced sporadically all summer. They are good plants for both formal and informal gardens and hedges, and are attractive individually or in groups. They can be used in shrub and mixed borders combined with rhododendrons and other evergreens.

In the mildest areas these plants are evergreen; in cooler areas they are semi-evergreen. The roots are more cold hardy than the leaves, and stems and plants that are severely damaged in cold winters will grow back from root level.

RECOMMENDED

A. x *grandiflora* (Glossy Abelia) has white or pale pink flowers. The foliage turns red or bronze in fall and this color will persist through the winter in mild areas. The shrub grows up to 8' (2.5 m) tall and spreads 5–10' (1.5–3 m). In colder areas the leaves will drop, revealing the attractive exfoliating stems. The cultivar **'Sherwood'** ('Nana') is more compact, growing 3–4' (0.9–1.2 m) tall, and spreading up to 5' (1.5 m). It makes a useful groundcover on banks too steep to mow. (Zones 6–9; plants will survive, but may suffer damage, in Zone 5.)

A. x *grandiflora* (this page)

A. **'Edward Goucher'** has larger, showier, dark pink flowers, and it is a smaller plant, growing to about 5' (1.5 m) tall. This hybrid is not quite as hardy as *A.* x *grandiflora* and is likely to drop its leaves in winter. (Zones 7–9.)

PESTS & PROBLEMS

Infrequent problems with fungal leaf spot, root rot or mildew are possible.

Aralia
Hercules' Club, Devil's Walking Stick
Aralia

Features: foliage, flowers, fruit, stems **Habit:** deciduous small trees or large shrubs
Height: 10–30' (3–9 m) **Spread:** 10–20' (3–6 m)
Planting: early spring to early winter **Zones:** 4–9

*A*n aralia is sure to start
a conversation in the garden.
The thorns alone are enough to pique
the imagination—it is easy to see why certain species are also called
Hercules' Club or Devil's Walking Stick. These robust shrubs produce large,
fluffy flowerheads in mid- to late summer. The purple berries that follow in
fall are much loved by birds and don't last long on the bush.

GROWING

Aralias prefer **full sun** or **light shade.** They grow best in **fertile, moist, well-drained** soil, but will tolerate dry soils, clay soils and rocky soils. Provide
shelter from strong winds, which can dry out the foliage.

Pruning of this shrub is rarely required, which is fortunate, considering its
plentiful prickles. You will have to spend some time controlling the spread of
this plant. Suckers grow up from the roots and the plant can spread widely.
Barriers such as buildings and driveways can help prevent it from spreading
too far, but you may still want to pull some or all of the suckers as they grow.

If you get them while they are small, they are easier to remove and the prickles are a bit softer to handle. Tough gloves are an absolute requirement when handling this shrub. I have found thick rubber gloves good for pulling up suckers. They allow a good grip and will stretch rather than puncture when prickles are encountered.

TIPS
These shrubs are best suited to an informal garden. They can be included in a border at the edge of a wooded area and should be used where their spread can be controlled and where you won't inadvertently brush against the thorny stems.

The **berries** should not be eaten; they are thought to be **poisonous.**

RECOMMENDED
A. elata (Japanese Angelica Tree) is the larger of the two recommended species, potentially growing to 30' (9 m). This species doesn't sucker quite as vigorously as *A. spinosa*. The cultivar **'Variegata'** has creamy margins on the leaves, but its suckers may produce solid green foliage.

A. spinosa (Hercules' Club) usually grows 10–20' (3–6 m) tall. What it lacks in height, compared to *A. elata*, it makes up for by spreading vigorously with suckers. Unless you can provide this plant with lots of room to grow, be prepared to wade in with thick gloves at least once a year to pull up suckers.

PESTS & PROBLEMS
Problems are rare, limited to occasional trouble with fungal leaf spot, aphids or mealybugs.

Aralias make an excellent burglar deterrent along the foundation of a house.

A. elata (this page)

Arborvitae
Cedar
Thuja

Features: foliage, bark, form **Habit:** small to large, evergreen trees
Height: 3–75' (1–23 m) **Spread:** 3–25' (1–7.5 m)
Planting: B & B, container; spring, fall **Zones:** 2–9

These shrubs could be considered the bread and butter of the nursery industry, so popular and useful have they become as a hedging material. Gardeners need not live by bread alone, however, and I've planted clematis at the base of arborvitae hedges and enjoyed how the vine scampers across the green wall, weaving in and out of the evergreen branches. I married a large, purple-blooming clematis to an arborvitae hedge and now the two are inseparable, drawing attention to themselves each summer. More than one visitor has asked me where I found an arborvitae that blooms with purple flowers.

GROWING

Arborvitae prefer **full sun.** The soil should be of **average fertility, moist** and **well drained.** These plants enjoy humidity and in the wild are often found growing near marshy areas. Arborvitae will look best in a location with some **shelter** from the wind, especially in winter, when the foliage can easily dry out and give the entire plant a rather brown, drab appearance.

These plants take very well to pruning and are often grown as hedges. Though they may be kept formally shaped, they are also attractive if just clipped to maintain a loose but compact shape and size.

TIPS

Large varieties of arborvitae make excellent specimen trees, and smaller cultivars can be used in foundation plantings, shrub borders and formal or informal hedges.

Arborvitae foliage makes a great deer snack. If deer or other ungulates are a problem in your area, you may wish to avoid using this plant. Alternatively, mechanical protection, such as a fence or chicken wire, can help reduce damage.

T. occidentalis cultivar, pruned by deer

T. occidentalis dwarf cultivar

RECOMMENDED

T. occidentalis (American Arborvitae, Eastern Arborvitae) is native to east-central North America. In the wild this tree can grow to about 60' (18 m) in height. In cultivation it grows about half this size or smaller. **'Emerald'** ('Smaragd') can grow 10–15' (3–4.5 m) tall, spreading about 4' (1.2 m). This cultivar is small and very cold hardy; the foliage does not lose color in winter. **'Hetz Midget'** is a dwarf, rounded cultivar. It grows to 4' (1.2 m) tall and wide, but can be kept smaller with pruning. **'Little Gem'** is a globe-shaped dwarf with dark green foliage. It grows 3' (1 m) tall and 4–6' (1.2–1.8 m) wide. **'Rheingold'** has bright golden yellow foliage that turns coppery gold in winter. It grows to about 6' (1.8 m) tall and is popular for hedges. (Zones 2–7; cultivars may be less cold hardy.)

T. orientalis (*Platycladus orientalis*) (Oriental Arborvitae) can grow as high as 50' (15 m), but usually grows 15–25' (4.5–7.5 m) high in the garden. Many cultivars are available, including **'Aurea Nana'** (Berkman's Golden Arborvitae), a popular dwarf cultivar. It grows up to 5' (1.5 m) tall. New foliage emerges a golden color that fades to yellow-green as it matures. (Zones 5–9.)

T. plicata (Western Redcedar, Western Arborvitae) is native to the Pacific Northwest. It can grow to 200' (60 m) tall in the wild, but restricted growing space in the garden often keeps it to about half this size—still a very large tree. This tree is popular in Europe, where many cultivars have been developed; some are available here. **'Pygmaea'** is a dwarf cultivar with

Crush some foliage between your fingers to enjoy the wonderful aroma. Be cautious, though, if you have sensitive skin; the pungent oils may irritate.

T. occidentalis 'Little Gem' (below & right)

dark, blue-tinged foliage. It grows about 24–36"
(60–90 cm) tall and spreads 12–24" (30–60 cm).
'Stoneham Gold' is another dwarf cultivar. New
growth emerges a bright yellow that matures to
dark green. This cultivar grows about 6' (1.8 m)
tall and spreads half that much. (Zones 5–7.)

PESTS & PROBLEMS
Bagworm, heart rot and red spider mites are possible, though not frequent, problems. The most
likely problem is winter browning, which usually
occurs in cold, windy, exposed areas.

*T. occidentalis was grown in Europe as
early as 1536. It was named 'arborvitae'
(Latin for 'tree of life') because a Vitamin
C–rich tea made from its foliage and bark
saved Jacques Cartier's crew from scurvy.*

T. plicata

Arbutus
Strawberry Tree, Madrone
Arbutus

Features: flowers, fruit, bark, form
Habit: spreading or shrubby, broad-leaved, evergreen trees
Height: 5–70' (1.5–21 m) **Spread:** 5–70' (1.5–21 m)
Planting: B & B, container; spring, fall **Zones:** 7–9

*A*rbutus trees grow wild on the island where I grew up, and the papery skin we peeled from the bark revealed a smoothness so startling we thought we were exposing the bare-naked skin of the trees. Growing in clumps with twisted forms, these trees were perfect for building tree forts. The berries attracted plenty of birds, adding to our sense of adventure. The much smaller but closely related Mediterranean Strawberry Tree has similar shedding bark, but the bumpy, barely edible fruit is quite a disappointment to a child thinking of shortcakes.

GROWING

Arbutus prefer a **sheltered** spot in the **full sun.** The soil should be **fertile, humus rich** and **well drained.** Avoid overwatering these trees, which are drought and salt tolerant. Pruning is not usually required.

Arbutus do not like having their roots disturbed. Plant young stock and make sure the location is a permanent one.

TIPS

Use arbutus in a woodland garden or as specimen trees. Include the smaller cultivars in a shrub or mixed border.

RECOMMENDED

A. 'Marina' has large green leaves, rosy pink flowers and red and yellow fruit. It grows 20–30' (6–9 m) tall.

A. menziesii (Arbutus, Pacific Madrone) is a spreading or shrubby tree that is native to western North America. It grows 50–70' (15–21 m) tall, with an equal spread. White flowers appear in erect clusters in early summer, followed by the warty red fruits, borne in equally striking clusters. The fruits may stay on the tree until December. A particularly attractive feature is the distinctive reddish bark that continuously peels off to reveal the perfectly smooth, greenish young bark underneath.

A. unedo (Mediterranean Strawberry Tree) is a spreading, shrubby tree with shredding, exfoliating red-brown bark. It grows 15–30' (4.5–9 m) tall and wide. White flowers appear in fall, followed by warty red fruits. **'Compacta'** is a slow-growing tree with slightly contorted branches. It grows to about 15' (4.5 m) tall. **'Elfin King'** is a compact, bushy form that flowers and fruits profusely. It grows 5–10' (1.5–3 m) in height and width.

PESTS & PROBLEMS

Fungal leaf spot, tent caterpillars and scale insects can cause some trouble.

Both arbutus *(Latin) and* madroño *(Spanish) mean 'strawberry tree,' in reference to the bright red fruits of these magnificent evergreen trees.*

A. menziesii bark

Birds love arbutus fruits, but people can suffer stomachaches if they eat too many.

A. menziesii

Barberry
Berberis

Features: foliage, flowers, fruit
Habit: small, medium or large, evergreen or semi-evergreen shrubs
Height: 1–6' (0.3–1.8 m) **Spread:** equal to or greater than height
Planting: spring, fall **Zones:** 6–9

Barberries have come a long way since my schoolyard days, when they were used under windows to keep kids from sneaking in or out. Now there are barberries that glow lime green or golden yellow, barberries with burgundy or pink leaves and dwarf barberries that stay neat and tidy. The good news is that these new varieties still keep the dependable, easy-growing personality of the barberry, making this multi-barbed shrub one to get stuck on.

GROWING

Barberries develop the best fall color and the most fruit when grown in **full sun,** but the plants tolerate partial shade. As long as the soil is **well drained,** barberries will tolerate almost any conditions.

Barberries are very flexible when it comes to pruning. They can take heavy pruning well and are grown as hedges for this reason. A plant in an informal border can be left unpruned or can be only lightly pruned. Removing old or dead wood as well as unwanted suckers is always a good idea in order to keep the plant looking its best and to control its growth.

Extracts from the rhizomes of Berberis *have been used for rheumatic and other inflammatory disorders, as well as the common cold.*

B. darwinii

B. thunbergii var. *atropurpurea*

TIPS

The larger barberries make excellent hedges with formidable prickles. Barberries can also be included in shrub and mixed borders. Small cultivars can be grown in rock gardens, in raised beds and along rock walls.

B. darwinii (above)

RECOMMENDED

B. darwinii (Darwin's Barberry) is an evergreen species from South America. In early spring and sometimes again in fall it produces many small yellow flowers, which are followed by small, dark blue berries. This species is not as spiny as some others. It grows 6–10' (1.8–3 m) tall, with an equal spread. (Zones 7–9.)

B. x mentorensis (Mentor Barberry) is a large, generally deciduous shrub. It is considered one of the best hedging plants because of its even, dense growth and impassable prickles. It also forms an attractive mound if left unpruned. Mentor Barberry grows 5–7' (1.5–2 m) tall, with an equal or greater spread. The spring flowers are yellow, and the fall color is very attractive. (Zones 5–8.)

B. thunbergii (Japanese Barberry) is one of the most widely grown barberries. This species has many attractive cultivars and is not susceptible to the rust fungi that afflict other barberries. Smaller than some other species, it grows 3–6' (1–1.8 m) tall and can spread up to 7' (2 m). Some of the

many cultivars are even smaller. **'Aurea'** (Golden Barberry) grows up to 5' (1.5 m) tall and wide and has bright yellow new growth. **Var. *atropurpurea*** (Burgundy Barberry) is the parent of many purple-leaved cultivars. In size and habit it is like the species, and its fall color is bright red. **Var. *atropurpurea***'Crimson Pygmy' is popular because of its attractive purple foliage as well as its neat, mounded, compact habit. It grows 18–30" (45–75 cm) tall, with a spread of up to 36" (90 cm). **Var. *atropurpurea* 'Rose Glow'** has purple leaves splotched with pink on new shoots. The foliage matures to a reddish purple and turns red in fall. It grows 5–6' (1.5–1.8 m) tall, with an equal spread. (Zones 5–8.)

PESTS & PROBLEMS

Though healthy barberries rarely suffer from any problems, possible afflictions include leaf spot, mites, aphids, weevils, root rot, rust, wilt, mosaic, scale insects, webworm, canker and root-knot nematodes.

Because some barberry species harbor the overwintering phase of the devastating wheat rust fungus, some regions have banned all barberries. Many of these regions are now lifting the ban on those species that have never been proven to harbor the fungus.

B. thunbergii var. atropurpurea

Beautyberry

Callicarpa

Features: fruit **Habit:** bushy, deciduous shrubs with arching stems
Height: 3–10' (1–3 m) **Spread:** 3–8' (1–2.5 m)
Planting: spring, fall **Zones:** 6–10

*B*eautyberries are among the rare shrubs with truly appropriate names. The late summer and fall berries really are beautiful, in shades of lavender, purple and even white, depending on the variety. Enjoy these casually sprawling shrubs by removing a couple of branches in winter and placing them in a tall glass vase with water. Extend the gardening season and your enjoyment of the garden with beautyberries.

GROWING

Beautyberries grow well in **full sun** or **light shade.** The soil should be **well drained** and of **average fertility.**

Pruning can be done in spring. Flowers and fruit are formed on the current year's growth. Cut the plant back to within 12" (30 cm) of the ground once the buds start to swell in spring. This will encourage new growth and lots of fruit later in summer. This annual trimming will also keep the plants looking neat.

In colder areas the branches may be damaged over winter. Cut off any damaged growth in spring. Even plants that are completely killed back in winter will revive with new growth in spring.

If the growth is getting out of hand or if you have missed pruning for a couple of years, you can cut a beautyberry back hard to within 4" (10 cm) of the ground in spring.

TIPS

Beautyberries can be used in naturalistic gardens and in shrub and mixed borders. These shrubs can be treated as herbaceous perennials, if the plants regularly die back in winter, because the flowers are produced on new wood.

RECOMMENDED

C. bodinieri (Bodinier Beautyberry) grows up to 10' (3 m) tall and up to 8' (2.5 m) wide. This species produces many pinkish-purple berries and has a loose, relaxed habit.

C. dichotoma (Purple Beautyberry) grows about 3–4' (1–1.2 m) tall, with an equal or slightly greater spread. The purple fruits are borne in dense clusters at the base of each leaf, surrounding the arching branches.

C. japonica (Japanese Beautyberry) can grow 10' (3 m) tall and spread 4–6' (1.2–1.8 m). It is a large open shrub

with arching branches and purple fruit. The foliage turns reddish purple in fall. **'Leucocarpa'** is a white-fruited cultivar.

PESTS & PROBLEMS

Scale insects, leaf spot, mildew and dieback are possible problems, but these are not serious and do not occur frequently.

To encourage vigorous new growth, fertilize plants that suffer winter dieback.

C. bodinieri (this page)

Beech

Fagus

Features: foliage, bark, habit, fall color, fruit
Habit: large, oval, deciduous shade trees
Height: 50–80' (15–24 m)
Spread: 35–70' (10–21 m)
Planting: B & B, container; spring
Zones: 4–9

Beautiful, smooth gray bark highlights any garden lucky enough to have a beech, and in large gardens a group of these trees makes a stunning display. Small gardens can enjoy dwarf weeping beeches and the rich mahogany foliage of a purple-leaved variety. Add some gray-leaved perennials such as lamb's ears or artemisia near your purple beech for a striking contrast in color and foliage.

GROWING

Beeches grow equally well in **full sun** or **partial shade.** The soil should be of **average fertility, acidic, loamy** and **well drained,** though almost all well-drained soils are tolerated.

Young lovers' initials carved into a beech will remain visible for the life of the tree—an effect that outlasts most relationships.

Very little pruning is required. Remove dead or damaged branches in spring or after the damage occurs. European Beech is a popular hedging plant that responds well to the severe pruning hedges need.

TIPS

Beeches make excellent specimen trees. They are also used as street trees and shade trees, or in woodland gardens. These trees need a lot of space. The European Beech's adaptability to pruning makes it a better choice in a small garden.

The nuts are edible if roasted.

RECOMMENDED

F. grandifolia (American Beech) is a broad-canopied tree. It can grow 50–80' (15–25 m) tall and often grows almost as wide. This species is native to most of eastern North America. It doesn't like having its roots disturbed and should be transplanted when very young.

F. sylvatica (European Beech) is a spectacular tree that can grow 60' (18 m) tall and wide or even larger.

F. sylvatica

Beeches retain their very smooth and elastic bark long into maturity.

F. grandifolia

Too massive for most settings, the species is best used for hedges in smaller gardens. It transplants easily and is more tolerant of varied soil conditions than American Beech. You can find a number of interesting cultivars of this tree, and several are small enough to use in the home garden. **'Fastigiata'** ('Dawyck') is a narrow, upright tree. It can grow to 80' (25 m), but spreads only about 10' (3 m). Yellow- or purple-leaved forms are available. **'Pendula'** (Weeping Beech) is a dramatic tree whose pendulous branches reach down to the ground. It varies in form; some spread widely, resulting in a cascade effect, while other specimens may be rather upright with branches drooping from the central trunk. This cultivar can grow as tall as the species, but a specimen with the branches drooping from the central trunk may be narrow enough for a home garden. **'Purpurea'** is a purple-leaved form with the same habit as the species. Purple-leaved weeping forms are also available. **'Tricolor'** has striking foliage with pink-and-white variegation that develops best in partial shade. This slow-growing tree matures to about 30' (9 m). It can be grown as a smaller tree in a large planter.

F. sylvatica 'Purpurea'

PESTS & PROBLEMS
Canker, powdery mildew, leaf spot, bark disease, borers, scale insects and aphids can afflict beech trees. None of these pests causes serious problems.

Beech nuts provide food for a wide variety of forest creatures, including squirrels and birds. They were a favorite food of the passenger pigeon, now extinct.

F. sylvatica 'Purpurea' (above), 'Pendula' (below)

Birch
Betula

Features: foliage, fall color, habit, bark, winter and early-spring catkins **Habit:** open, deciduous trees **Height:** 30–70' (9–21 m) **Spread:** 20–60' (6–18 m) **Planting:** B & B, container; spring, fall **Zones:** 2–9

Graceful birch trees add elegance and winter color to a landscape. They can be used individually or in groups for a casual look or as a focal point. Much loved for their attractive white bark, winter catkins and delicate foliage, birches are great trees for creating contrast with Northwest evergreens.

GROWING

Birches grow well in **full sun, partial shade** or **light shade.** The soil should be of **average to rich fertility, moist** and fairly **well drained.** Many birch species naturally grow in wet areas, such as along streams. They don't, however, like to grow in permanently soggy conditions.

Minimal pruning is required. Remove any dead or damaged branches, as well as those that are growing awkwardly.

Any pruning of live wood should be done in late summer or fall to prevent the excessive bleeding of sap that occurs if branches are cut in spring.

TIPS

Birch trees are generally grown for their attractive, often white and striped bark that contrasts nicely with the glossy red or chestnut younger branches and twigs. Often used as specimen trees, birches' small leaves and open canopy provide light shade that allows perennials, annuals or lawns to flourish beneath. Birch trees are also attractive when grown in groups near natural or artificial water features. They do need quite a bit of room to grow and are not the best choice in gardens with limited space.

RECOMMENDED

B. jacquemontii (*B. utilis* var. *jacquemontii*) (Whitebarked Himalayan Birch) has striking, pure white bark. It grows 40–60' (12–18 m) tall and spreads about half as wide. This tree is very effective in winter against a dark green background. (Zones 5–7.)

B. nigra (River Birch, Black Birch) has shaggy, cinnamon brown bark that flakes off in sheets when it is young, but thickens and becomes ridged as it matures. This fast-growing tree attains a height of 60–90' (18–27 m). The bright green leaves are silvery white on the undersides. River Birch is one of the most disease-resistant species. (Zones 4–9.)

Some people make birch syrup from the heavy flow of sap in spring, in the same way maple syrup is made.

B. papyrifera (this page)

B. nigra

B. papyrifera (Paper Birch, Canoe Birch) has creamy white bark that peels off in layers, exposing cinnamon-colored bark beneath. It grows about 70' (21 m) tall and spreads about 30' (9 m). Yellowish catkins dangle from the branches in early spring. This tree prefers moist soil. Native to most cool climates in North America, the Paper Birch dislikes hot summer weather. (Zones 2–7.)

The bark of B. papyrifera *has been used to make canoes, shelters, utensils and—as both the Latin and common names imply—paper.*

PESTS & PROBLEMS

Aphids are fond of birch trees, and the sticky honeydew these insects secrete may drip off the leaves. Avoid planting birch where drips can fall onto parked cars, patios or decks. Leaf miners and tent caterpillars can be a problem in Northwest gardens. The Bronze Birch borer can be a fatal problem, though mostly on trees in the eastern part of our region. River Birch and Paper Birch are resistant to this borer.

B. papyrifera (above), *B. jacquemontii* (below)

Bluebeard

Bluebird, Blue Spirea

Caryopteris x *clandonensis*

Features: flowers, foliage, scent **Habit:** rounded, spreading, deciduous shrub
Height: 24–36" (60–90 cm) **Spread:** 2–6' (0.5–1.8 m)
Planting: spring, fall **Zones:** 5–9

L ate summer may be considered a time of fading glory in the border, but it won't be if you add the cheerful Bluebeard to your garden. Its true-blue blooms will wake up the August border, and its fancy golden foliage will stand out brilliantly against a white fence or purple-leaved plants. I grow a bushy Bluebeard under a 'Royal Purple' Smoketree, and neither seems to mind the dry, rocky soil.

GROWING

Bluebeard prefers **full sun,** but tolerates light shade. It does best in soil of **average fertility** that is **light** and **well drained**.

Pruning this shrub is a snap. It flowers in late summer, so each spring cut the plant back to within 2–6" (5–15 cm) of the ground. Flowers will form on the new growth that emerges. Deadheading or light shearing in fall once the flowers begin to fade will encourage more flowering. This plant can be treated as a herbaceous perennial in areas where it is killed back each winter.

TIPS

Include Bluebeard in your shrub or mixed border. The bright blue, late-season flowers are welcome when many other plants are looking bedraggled and are past their flowering best.

RECOMMENDED

'Blue Mist' has fragrant, light blue flowers. It is a low-growing, mounding plant, rarely exceeding 24" (60 cm) in height.

'Worcester Gold' has bright, yellow-green foliage that contrasts vividly with the violet-blue, late-summer flowers. It grows about 36" (90 cm) tall, with an equal spread. This cultivar is often treated like a herbaceous perennial because the growth may be killed back over winter. New growth will emerge from the base in spring if this occurs.

Bluebeard is cultivated for its aromatic stems, foliage and flowers.

'Worcester Gold'

Bog Rosemary
Marsh Rosemary
Andromeda polifolia

Features: foliage, flowers **Habit:** low-growing, evergreen shrub
Height: 6–24" (15–60 cm) **Spread:** 8–36" (20–90 cm)
Planting: container; spring, fall **Zones:** 2–8

*I*f you've ever worried about an evergreen shrub growing too tall and blocking the light from your windows, Bog Rosemary is the compact dwarf that won't be misbehaving. The "Rosemary" in the name refers to the fact that the tiny gray leaves resemble that culinary herb, but this shrub should be used to flavor landscapes, not main dishes. Use it in groups of three to five around large boulders and enjoy the globular repetition of form that these mounding shrubs provide.

GROWING

Bog Rosemary can grow well in **light shade** or **full sun.** The soil should be **moist, well drained** and **acidic** with lots of **organic** matter worked in.

It is not the cold of winter but the heat and humidity of summer that bear the greatest influence on how well this plant will do. In warmer climates plant Bog Rosemary in a cool part of the garden in light shade to protect it from the summer heat.

TIPS

Include this pink- or white-flowered plant in a rock garden or woodland garden, by a water feature or as a groundcover underneath other acid-loving shrubs.

Do not make a tea with or otherwise ingest Bog Rosemary—it contains **andromedotoxin,** which can lower blood pressure, disrupt breathing and cause cramps and vomiting.

RECOMMENDED

A. polifolia is an attractive plant, with light pink flowers in late spring and early summer. It grows 12–24" (30–60 cm) tall and spreads up to 36" (90 cm). There are also several cultivars. **'Alba'** is a dwarf cultivar that bears white flowers. It grows about 6" (15 cm) tall and spreads about 8" (20 cm). **'Compacta'** is a dwarf cultivar with pink flowers. It grows about 12" (30 cm) tall and spreads about 8" (20 cm). (Zones 2–6; can do well to Zone 8 if protected from excess heat in summer.)

In Greek mythology, Andromeda was the daughter of Cassiopeia. She angered Poseidon and was chained to a rock in the ocean— as isolated as wild Bog Rosemary, which grows on moss hummocks in a boggy sea.

Boxwood
Box
Buxus

Features: foliage **Habit:** dense, rounded, evergreen shrubs
Height: 3–15' (1–4.5 m) **Spread:** equal to height
Planting: B & B, container; spring **Zones:** 4–9

Nothing says 'formal garden' like a boxwood hedge, and whether trimmed into geometric or animal shapes or allowed to grow loose and natural, boxwoods are versatile evergreens. I think they are most beautiful in winter, after a snowfall, when the small leaves and the strong, short stems trap snow to form white castles in the dormant garden.

GROWING

Boxwoods prefer to grow in **partial shade,** but they tolerate full sun if kept well watered. The soil should be **fertile, moist** and **well drained.**

Many formal gardens include boxwoods because they can be pruned to form neat hedges, geometric shapes or fanciful creatures. The dense growth and small leaves form an even green surface, which, along with the slow rate of growth, makes this plant one of the most popular for creating topiary. When left unpruned, a boxwood shrub forms an attractive rounded mound.

Boxwoods will sprout new growth from old wood. A plant that has been neglected or is growing in a lopsided manner can be cut back hard in spring. By the end of summer the exposed areas will have filled in with new green growth.

A good mulch will benefit these shrubs because their roots grow very close to the surface. For this same reason it is best not to disturb the earth around a boxwood once it is established.

TIPS

These shrubs make excellent background plants in a mixed border. Brightly colored flowers show up

B. microphylla var. *koreana*

Boxwoods are steeped in legend and lore. The foliage was a main ingredient in an old mad-dog bite remedy, and boxwood hedges were traditionally planted around graves to keep the spirits from wandering.

B. microphylla

well against the even, dark green surface of the boxwood. Dwarf cultivars can be trimmed into small hedges for edging garden beds or walkways. An interesting topiary piece can create a formal or whimsical focal point in any garden. Larger species and cultivars are often used to form dense evergreen hedges.

Boxwood foliage contains **toxic** compounds that, when ingested, can cause severe digestive upset and possibly even death.

RECOMMENDED

B. microphylla (Littleleaf Boxwood) grows about 4' (1.2 m) in height and spread. This species is quite pest resistant. It is hardy in Zones 6–9. The foliage tends to lose its green in winter, turning shades of bronze, yellow or brown. **Var. *koreana*** is far more cold resistant than the species; it is hardy to Zone 4.

B. sempervirens (Common Boxwood) is a much larger species. If left unpruned it can grow to 20' (6 m) in height and width. It has lower tolerance to extremes of heat and cold, but in a mild climate like that of the Pacific Northwest it does well. The foliage stays green in winter. Many cultivars are available with interesting features such as compact or dwarf growth, variegated foliage and pendulous branches. (Zones 5–8.)

Several cultivars have been developed from crosses between *B. m. var. koreana* and *B. sempervirens*. Some of these have inherited the

B. sempervirens

best attributes of each parent—hardiness and pest resistance on the one hand and attractive foliage year-round on the other. **'Green Gem'** forms a rounded 24" (60 cm) mound. The deep green foliage stays green all winter. **'Green Mountain'** forms a large upright shrub 5' (1.5 m) tall with dark green foliage. (Zones 4–8.)

PESTS & PROBLEMS
Leaf miners, psyllids, scale insects, mites, powdery mildew, root rot and leaf spot are all possible problems affecting boxwoods.

The wood of Buxus, *particularly the wood of the root, is very dense and fine-grained, making it valuable for carving. It has been used to make ornate boxes, hence the common name.*

Broom
Woadwaxen, Greenwood
Genista

Features: late-spring flowers
Habit: low, deciduous shrubs or groundcovers
Height: 18–36" (45–90 cm)
Spread: 24–36" (60–90 cm)
Planting: spring, fall **Zones:** 3–9

*I*n late spring and early summer these plants are completely covered in blooms. The low-growing spreaders, when planted at the tops of rock walls, will cascade down and create the effect of a golden yellow waterfall. Brooms will grow well in poor, dry soil on the sunny side of a stand of evergreens.

GROWING

Broom plants grow best in a **warm, sunny** location. Soil that is fairly **infertile, dry** and **sandy or gravelly** is best. These plants tolerate soil of any acidity, but prefer **alkaline** soil. **Excellent drainage** is essential.

Brooms rarely need pruning but can be cut back after flowering, if desired, to control spread and possibly encourage more flowers.

These shrubs resent being transplanted and should not be moved once they are established in the garden.

TIPS

The taller species of broom can be used in a shrub border. The ground-cover species can be used in rock gardens and along the tops of rock walls. All species can be used to prevent erosion on exposed, gravelly slopes.

Genista is closely related to Scotch Broom (*Cytisus scoparius*), which is seriously invasive in wild areas on the west coast. If you live on the coast, plant *Genista* cultivars, which are not thought to be invasive.

RECOMMENDED

G. lydia is a mounding groundcover plant that generally grows to about 24" (60 cm) tall and 36" (90 cm) wide. It may suffer frost damage in areas colder than Zone 6.

G. pilosa (Silkleaf Woadwaxen) is a groundcover plant. This fast-growing species grows 12–18"

(30–45 cm) tall and spreads 3–7' (1–2 m). **'Vancouver Gold'** has a more mounding habit and flowers more profusely than the species. It may suffer frost damage in areas colder than Zone 6.

G. tinctoria (Dyer's Greenwood) is an upright shrub. It grows 3–6' (1–1.8 m) tall, with an equal spread. It is more cold hardy than the other species; with adequate protection it can survive temperatures as low as those found in Zone 3.

G. lydia (this page)

Butterfly Bush
Summer Lilac
Buddleia (Buddleja)

Features: flowers, habit, foliage
Habit: deciduous large shrubs or small trees with arching branches
Height: 4–20' (1.2–6 m) **Spread:** 4–20' (1.2–6 m)
Planting: container; spring, fall **Zones:** 4–9

*A*theme garden can be built around a butterfly bush, using one of these fountain-shaped shrubs in the center of a butterfly garden with nectar-rich rudbeckia, coreopsis and Sweet William filling in around the perimeter. The bottle-shaped purple, pink, white or blue blooms look like shooting fireworks of color arching from the plant, and butterflies will flit happily from flower to flower.

GROWING

Butterfly bushes prefer to grow in **full sun,** and plants grown in shady conditions will produce few, if any, flowers. The soil should be **fertile** and **well drained,** though most average to rich soils that are well drained can be tolerated.

Pruning is different for each of the species mentioned below. *B. alternifolia* and *B. globosa* form flowers on the previous year's growth. Each year, once the flowers have faded, cut the flowering shoots back to within a couple of buds of the main plant framework. *B. alternifolia* will also benefit from some formative pruning. It can be trained as a shrub or into a tree form.

B. davidii forms flowers on the current year's growth. Early each spring cut the shrub back to within 6–12" (15–30 cm) of the ground to encourage new growth and plenty of flowers. Removing spent flowerheads will encourage new shoots and extend the blooming period.

B. davidii 'Black Knight' (above), *B. davidii* (below)

TIPS

These species make beautiful additions to shrub and mixed borders. The graceful, arching branches make a butterfly bush an excellent specimen plant. *Buddleia alternifolia* is a particularly beautiful specimen when trained to form a small weeping tree. The dwarf forms that stay under 5' (1.5 m) are suitable for small gardens.

RECOMMENDED

B. alternifolia (Alternate-Leaved Butterfly Bush) grows 10–20' (3–6 m) tall, with a spread that is equal to or slightly narrower than the height. It can be trained to form a tree, leaving the branches lots of room to arch down around the trunk. In late spring or early summer, panicles of light purple flowers form at the ends of the branches, flopping around in a wonderful state of disarray. The cultivar **'Argentea'** has silvery gray leaves.

B. davidii (Orange-Eye Butterfly Bush, Summer Lilac) is a more commonly grown species. It grows 4–10' (1.2–3 m) tall, with an equal spread. This plant has a long blooming period, bearing flowers in bright and pastel shades of purple, white, pink or blue from mid-summer to fall. A few popular cultivars of the many available: **'Black Knight,'** with dark

Butterfly bushes self-seed, and you may find tiny bushes popping up in unlikely places in the garden.

B. globosa

purple flowers; **'Charming,'** with
pink flowers; **'Dubonnet,'** with
large spikes of pinky-purple flowers;
'White Bouquet,' with white
flowers. (Zones 5–9.)

B. globosa (Orange Butterfly Bush,
Orange Ball Tree) is a tall, deciduous or sometimes semi-evergreen
shrub that reaches 8–15' (2.5–4.5 m)
in height and spread. In spring, it
bears distinctive small balls of
fragrant, yellow to deep orange
flowers. The dark green, strikingly
veined leaves may be up to 8" (20 cm)
long. (Zones 6–9.)

PESTS & PROBLEMS

Many insects are attracted to butterfly bushes, but most just come for
the pollen and any others aren't
likely to be a big problem. Good air
circulation will help prevent fungal
problems that might otherwise
afflict these plants.

*Butterfly bushes are among the
best shrubs for attracting
butterflies and bees to your
garden. Don't spray your bush
for pests—you will harm the
beautiful and beneficial insects
that make their homes there.*

B. davidii (this page)

California Lilac

Ceanothus

Features: flowers, form, foliage
Habit: bushy, low-growing or mounding, deciduous or evergreen shrubs
Height: 1–20' (0.3–6 m) **Spread:** 5–20' (1.5–6 m)
Planting: container; spring **Zones:** 7–9

*A*dd fragrance to your summer garden and a touch of blue heaven with these heat-loving shrubs. You won't need to worry about pampering them. Drought resistant and undemanding, California lilacs are welcome imports to Northwestern gardens. They are among the few shrubs that can bloom a true blue, and they can also bloom purple, pink or white. Pair them with bright yellow daylilies or golden broom for a sunny yellow and blue color scheme that will return year after year.

GROWING

California lilacs prefer a **sheltered** site in **full sun.** The soil should be **fertile, well drained** and somewhat **acidic.**

Pruning should take place in early spring on deciduous species and cultivars, which can be cut back to within 6–12" (15–30 cm) of the ground at that time. Flowers will form on the new growth. Evergreen species and cultivars flower on the previous year's growth and need very little pruning. The flowering shoots can be cut back after they are finished flowering. Remove any growth that is damaged over winter.

TIPS

California lilacs can be included in a shrub or mixed border. The low-growing cultivars can be used as groundcovers or trained to grow up walls or over rocks.

Though these plants are best adapted to warmer areas of our region, they can tolerate some frost and will often recover from winter damage. Coastal gardeners will have the best luck with California lilacs, but gardeners in cooler areas may wish to give them a try in a sheltered setting.

RECOMMENDED

Ceanothus species are attractive, dense, bushy shrubs. Look for *C.* **'Gloire de Versailles,'** a rounded, deciduous shrub that flowers in late summer; *C. gloriosus,* a low, evergreen spreader that flowers in early summer; and *C.* **'Ray Hartman,'** a large, evergreen shrub or small tree that flowers in early spring. All bear clusters of light purple or blue flowers.

PESTS & PROBLEMS

Fungal leaf spot, powdery mildew, root rot, scale insects, mealybugs and caterpillars may occasionally afflict these plants.

These shrubs are considered short-lived, lasting about 5 to 10 years in the garden. Full sun and a protected site will prolong their lives.

Cedar
Cedrus

Features: habit, foliage, cones, bark
Habit: large, upright, spreading or pendulous, evergreen trees
Height: 3–130' (1–40 m) **Spread:** 15–40' (4.5–12 m)
Planting: container; spring **Zones:** 5–9

A mature cedar tree is truly a magnificent sight to behold, a towering form with elegant, layered, sweeping branches. The bundles of short needles remind me much more of larch than of the native arborvitae we in the Pacific Northwest commonly refer to as 'cedar.' These trees are steeped in history. *Cedrus libani*, native to the Middle East, was one of the only sources of lumber in that region in ancient times.

GROWING

Cedars grow well in **full sun** or **partial shade.** The soil can be of any type as long as it is **well drained.** A **moist, loamy** soil of **average to high fertility** is preferable. Very little pruning is required. Remove damaged or dead branches.

These trees are best grown in the warmer coastal regions of the Pacific Northwest. They are likely to suffer some damage in colder areas. Daring gardeners who wish to try these species in colder gardens should choose a sheltered location and be prepared to remove any cold-damaged growth.

An image of Cedrus libani *graces the national flag of Lebanon.*

TIPS

The cedar species are very large trees—much too large for the average home garden, and best suited to large properties and parks. Several cultivars are much smaller and can be used as impressive specimen trees in all but the smallest home gardens.

RECOMMENDED

C. atlantica (Atlas Cedar, Blue Atlas Cedar) generally grows 40–60' (12–18 m) high, but it can grow to 100' (30 m) in good conditions, with adequate space. The branches sweep the ground, spreading to 40' (12 m). Though this species is a bit too large for the average garden, the cultivar **'Glauca Pendula'** is interesting and not as tall. The branches of this cultivar are long and trailing, however, and it can spread just as far as the species. Train it to grow over an arbor, where the branches can trail down. (Zones 6–9.)

C. deodara (Deodar Cedar) grows up to 130' (40 m) high, with a spread of 30' (9 m). This species is the fastest-growing cedar, but it is not very cold hardy. Some cultivars are more reasonable in size and more tolerant of winter cold. **'Aurea'** is hardy in Zones 7–9, but is slow growing, reaching a mature height of about 15' (4.5 m). The foliage is bright yellow and deepens to green as it matures.

C. libani (Cedar of Lebanon) is another species that is too big for the home garden, but that has suitable cultivars available for space-restricted settings. **'Pendula'** is a weeping cultivar that is often grafted to create a small weeping tree, ideal for use as a specimen. **'Sargentii'** is a slow-growing, dwarf cultivar that reaches heights of only 3–5' (1–1.5 m).

PESTS & PROBLEMS

The biggest problem is top dieback, which can be caused by cold, weevils or canker. Root rot can occur in poorly drained soils.

These trees are the 'true cedars'—that is, Cedrus *species. Confusingly, some 70 different types of trees have been called 'cedar.'*

C. deodara

Clethra
Summersweet Clethra
Sweet Pepperbush
Clethra alnifolia

Features: mid- to late-summer flowers, foliage
Habit: dense, rounded, suckering, deciduous shrub
Height: 3–8' (1–2.5 m) **Spread:** 3–8' (1–2.5 m)
Planting: B & B, container; spring **Zones:** 3–9

*I*n the late summer, Clethra's pointed white blooms perfume the air with spicy sweetness. Its dark green leaves resist slugs and bugs and add a golden autumn color before the foliage drops to the ground. This is a princess of a plant in wet or shady gardens. Keep in mind, though, that while you may find Clethra growing wild in a swamp, you'll have to acclimate nursery-grown plants to standing water gradually.

GROWING

Clethra grows best in **light or partial shade**, but it can grow in full shade. The soil should be **fertile, acidic, moist** and rich in **organic** matter. This shrub is tolerant of seashore conditions.

This sweet-scented shrub is attractive to bees and butterflies.

A light pruning can be done in early spring. Simply trim off any wayward shoots that may be spoiling the symmetry of the plant.

This shrub spreads by sending up suckers from the roots, and though it generally doesn't become invasive in the garden, you may wish to prevent it from spreading beyond the space you intended. Pathways and other hard surfaces in the garden can stop its spread. Alternatively, insert a metal or plastic barrier several feet into the soil to demarcate the desired area.

TIPS

Clethra is a useful plant for shrub or mixed borders. It grows naturally in shaded, wet areas, and it can be included in a pondside planting or a bog garden. This shrub makes a good companion for rhododendrons.

RECOMMENDED

'Hummingbird' is a small cultivar with white flowers. It grows about 3' (1 m) tall and spreads 3–5' (1–1.5 m).

'Paniculata' has white flowers. It grows up to 5' (1.5 m) tall, with an equal spread.

'Pink Spires' has bright pink buds that open to light pink. It grows up to 8' (2.5 m) tall and wide.

PESTS & PROBLEMS

Root rot can be a problem if the soil remains very wet around the roots for extended periods. The foliage is resistant to pests.

'Paniculata' (this page)

Cotoneaster

Cotoneaster

Features: foliage, early-summer flowers, persistent fruit, variety of forms
Habit: evergreen groundcovers, shrubs or small trees
Height: 1–15' (0.3–4.5 m) **Spread:** 3–15' (1–4.5 m)
Planting: container; spring, fall
Zones: 4–9

I think of cotoneasters—tough, handsome and dependable—as heroes of the landscape. They save me from all kinds of maintenance nightmares, including the hassle of weeding on steep slopes and amending poor soil. Tiny white blooms in spring and bright red berries in winter give these shrubs star appeal. The forgiving cotoneasters will quickly recover from even the hardest pruning.

The name is pronounced cuh-tone-ee-aster *rather than* coton-easter.

GROWING

Cotoneasters prefer **full sun** or **partial shade.** The soil should be of **average fertility** and **well drained.**

Though pruning is rarely required, these plants tolerate even a hard pruning. Pruning cotoneaster hedges in mid- to late summer will let you see how much you can trim off while still leaving some of the ornamental fruit in place. Hard pruning will encourage new growth and can rejuvenate plants that are looking worn out.

TIPS

Cotoneasters can be included in shrub or mixed borders. Low spreaders work well as groundcovers and shrubby species can be used to form hedges. Larger species are grown as small specimen trees and some low growers are grafted onto standards and grown as small weeping trees.

Although cotoneaster berries are not poisonous, they can cause stomach upset if eaten in large quantities. The **foliage** may be **toxic.**

C. dammeri (this page)

RECOMMENDED

C. adpressus (Creeping Cotoneaster) is a low-growing species that is used as a groundcover plant. It grows only 12" (30 cm) high, but spreads up to 6' (1.8 m). The foliage turns reddish purple in fall. (Zones 4–6.)

C. apiculatus (Cranberry Cotoneaster) grows about 36" (90 cm) high and spreads up to 6' (1.8 m). The bright red fruits persist into winter. (Zones 4–7.)

C. dammeri (Bearberry Cotoneaster) has low-growing, arching stems that gradually stack up on top of one another as the plant matures. It grows to 18" (45 cm) high and spreads to 6' (1.8 m). Small white flowers blanket the stems in early summer and are followed by bright red fruit in fall. One attractive cultivar is **'Coral Beauty,'** a groundcover that grows up to 36" (90 cm) in height and spreads 6' (1.8 m). The abundant fruits are bright orange to red. (Zones 5–8.)

C. horizontalis (Rockspray Cotoneaster) is a low-growing species that has a distinct, attractive herringbone branching pattern. It grows 24–36" (60–90 cm) tall and spreads 5–8' (1.5–2.5 m). The leaves turn bright red in fall. Light pink, early-summer flowers are followed by red fall fruit. (Zones 5–9.)

Try a mix of low-growing cotoneasters as a bank planting or use a shrubby type as a foundation plant.

ALTERNATE SPECIES

C. salicifolius* var. *floccosus (*C. floccosus*) (Willowleaf Cotoneaster) is a large shrub that can be trained to form a small tree. It grows 10–15' (3–4.5 m) tall, with an equal or lesser spread. White flowers in early summer are followed by red fruits that persist through winter. The leaves turn an attractive red color in fall. Several cultivars are much smaller than the species, growing about 12–30" (30–75 cm) high. (Zones 6–8.)

C. horizontalis

PESTS & PROBLEMS

These plants are generally problem free, but occasional attacks of rust, canker, powdery mildew, fire blight, scale insects, lace bugs, slugs, snails and spider mites are possible.

C. apiculatus

Daphne
Daphne

Features: foliage, fragrant spring flowers
Habit: upright, rounded or low-growing, evergreen or semi-evergreen shrubs
Height: 0.5–5' (0.2–1.5 m) **Spread:** 3–5' (1–1.5 m)
Planting: container; early spring, early fall **Zones:** 4–8

T hink of a daphne as delicate royalty in the garden, a beautiful princess of a bloomer with a sweet, refined fragrance and an elegant crown of pink blooms. Tragically, this princess is prone to a mysterious early death, even when it seems she is doing well. I've tried adding gravel to the drainage furrow in her planting hole to keep root rot away, but a few years of good health is all she ever seems to enjoy. The possible premature demise of this fragrant shrub should not put you off; just be prepared to replace her.

GROWING

Daphnes prefer **full sun** or **partial shade.** The soil should be **moist, well drained** and of **average to high fertility.** A layer of mulch will keep the shallow roots cool.

These plants have neat, dense growth that needs very little pruning. Remove damaged or diseased branches. Flowerheads can be removed once flowering is finished. Cut flowering stems back to where they join main branches in order to preserve the natural growth habit of the shrub.

TIPS

Rose Daphne makes an attractive groundcover in a rock garden or woodland garden. Burkwood and Winter daphnes can be included in shrub or mixed borders; plant them near paths, doors, windows or other places where the wonderful scent can be enjoyed. Note that *Daphne laureola* (Spurge Laurel) is an invasive species in wild areas on the west coast and should be avoided.

All parts of daphne plants are **toxic** if eaten, and the sap may cause skin irritations. Avoid planting these species where children may be tempted to sample the berries.

RECOMMENDED

D.* x *burkwoodii (Burkwood Daphne) is an upright, semi-evergreen shrub. It bears fragrant white or light pink flowers in late spring and sometimes again in fall. It grows 3–5' (1–1.5 m) in height and spread. **'Carol Mackie'** is a common cultivar; its dark green

D. x *burkwoodii* 'Somerset'

leaves have creamy edges. **'Somerset'** has darker pink flowers than the hybrid species.

D. cneorum (Rose Daphne, Garland Flower) is a low-growing evergreen shrub. It grows 6–12" (15–30 cm) tall and can spread to 4' (1.2 m). The fragrant, pale to deep pink or white flowers are borne in late spring. **'Alba'** has white flowers, and **'Ruby Glow'** has reddish-pink flowers. **'Variegata'** has leaves edged with creamy yellow; its flowers are like those of the species.

In late winter cut a few stems and arrange them in a vase indoors—they should come into bloom in a warm, bright room. Enjoy both the sweet scent and the delicate flowers.

D. odora (Winter Daphne or Fragrant Daphne) is a round, mounding evergreen. It grows 3–4' (1–1.2 m) in height and spread. The pink, long-lasting, sweetly fragrant flowers are borne in mid-winter. This species is more shade tolerant than the other species. It is also the easiest to transplant. **'Aureo-marginata'** has narrow yellow margins around the leaves. The flowers are a lighter pink than those of the species. **Var. *leucantha*** (var. *alba*) has white or creamy flowers.

D. x burkwoodii 'Somerset'

PESTS & PROBLEMS

Viruses, leaf spot, crown or root rot, aphids, scale insects and twig blight affect daphnes. Poor growing conditions can result in greater susceptibility to these problems. A plant may wilt and die suddenly if diseased.

Daphnes have fragrant flowers and attractive, often evergreen, foliage, making these shrubs appealing all year round.

D. odora var. *leucantha* (this page)

Dawn Redwood

Metasequoia glyptostroboides

Features: foliage, bark, cones, buttressed trunk
Habit: narrow, conical, deciduous conifer
Height: 70–125' (21–38 m)
Spread: 15–25' (4.5–7.5 m)
Planting: spring, fall **Zones:** 5–9

My first experience with the golden fall color of a Dawn Redwood was startling. Because it looked so similar to the evergreen hemlock, I thought it was dying. The foliage of the Dawn Redwood, however, is deciduous, taking on a warm golden glow in the fall before dropping.

This magnificent tree, with its cinnamon red, flaking bark and its ridged trunk, is a welcome addition to the Northwest winter garden. Keep in mind, though, the size implications of the name 'redwood,' and give this 'golden giant,' as it is nicknamed, plenty of room.

This tree is often called a 'living fossil' because it was described from fossils before it was observed growing in China in the 1940s.

GROWING

Dawn Redwood grows well in **full sun** or **light shade.** The soil should be **humus rich,** slightly **acidic, moist** and **well drained.** Wet or dry soils are tolerated, though the rate of growth will be reduced in dry conditions. This tree likes humidity and should be mulched and watered regularly until it is established.

Pruning is not necessary. The lower branches must be left in place in order for the buttressing to develop. (Buttressed trunks are flared and deeply grooved, and the branches appear to be growing from right inside the grooves.)

TIPS

These large trees need plenty of room to grow. Larger gardens and parks can best accommodate them. As single specimen plants or in groups, these trees are attractive and impressive.

RECOMMENDED

The cultivars do not differ significantly from *M. glyptostroboides.* Both **'National'** and **'Sheridan Spire'** are narrower than the species. They have not been in cultivation long enough to have reached their mature heights, but they are expected to be as tall as the species.

PESTS & PROBLEMS

Dawn Redwood is not generally prone to pest problems, though it can be killed by canker infections.

Don't worry when this ancient tree drops its needles each fall; it's deciduous.

Deutzia
Deutzia

Features: early-summer flowers **Habit:** bushy, deciduous shrubs
Height: 2–7' (0.5–2 m) **Spread:** 2–7' (0.5–2 m)
Planting: preferably spring **Zones:** 5–9

An old-fashioned frilly lady, a deutzia earns only a brief spell in the spotlight when she puts on a fantastic show in May, covered with a lacy veil of white blossoms. These shrubs quickly fade into the background once the flowers are gone, so use them as a backdrop in a mixed planting with shrubs and perennials that flower later in the season.

GROWING

Deutzias grow best in **full sun.** They will tolerate light shade, but will not bear as many flowers. The soil should be of **average to high fertility, moist** and **well drained.** These shrubs bloom on the previous year's growth.

After flowering, cut flowering stems back to strong buds, main stems or basal growth as required to shape the plant. Remove one-third of the old growth on established plants at ground level to encourage new growth.

TIPS

Include deutzias in shrub or mixed borders or in rock gardens. As specimens, they are beautiful in flower but not too interesting afterwards.

Deutzias are quite frost hardy. If you live in a colder area than is generally recommended for these plants, try growing them in a sheltered spot where they will be protected from the worst extremes of weather.

RECOMMENDED

D. gracilis (Slender Deutzia) is a low-growing, mounding species. It grows 2–4' (0.5–1.2 m) high, with a spread of 3–6' (1–1.8 m). In late spring the plant is completely covered with white flowers. (Zones 5–8.)

D. x *lemoinei* is a dense, rounded, upright hybrid. It grows 5–7' (1.5–2 m) high, with an equal spread. The early summer blooms are white. **'Avalanche'** grows 4' (1.2 m) in height and width and bears white flowers on arching branches. **'Compacta'** ('Boule de Neige') has denser, more compact growth than the hybrid species. It has large clusters of white flowers.

D. x *magnifica* 'Erecta' (this page)

D. x *magnifica* (Showy Deutzia) is a vigorous, multi-stemmed shrub that can reach 6' (1.8 m) or more in height. It may become leggy at the base. **'Erecta'** has very showy, single white flowers in erect clusters.

D. x *rosea* is a bushy, mounding shrub. It grows 24–36" (60–90 cm) high, with an equal spread. The late-spring flowers are light pink. **'Carminea'** has deep pink flowers.

PESTS & PROBLEMS

Problems are rare, though these plants can have trouble with fungal leaf spot, aphids or leaf miners.

The name 'deutzia' comes from Dutchman Johan van der Deutz, an 18th-century patron of botany who supported expeditions of the famous botanist Carl Peter Thunberg.

Dogwood
Cornus

Features: late-spring to early-summer flowers, fall foliage, fruit, habit
Habit: deciduous large shrubs or small trees
Height: 5–40' (1.5–12 m) **Spread:** 5–30' (1.5–9 m)
Planting: B & B, container; spring **Zones:** 2–9

A dogwood in bloom is top dog of any garden, and the foliage and fruit add mid- to late season interest. Sadly, fungal wilts and other pests have blighted the reputation—as well as the foliage—of both our native and many exotic flowering dogwoods. Despite the disease concerns, dogwoods are much-loved companions for rhodies, azaleas and camellias in the Northwest. Their delicate branch patterns and spreading crowns make these trees classic beauties in any style of landscape design.

GROWING

Most dogwoods prefer **full sun,** but tolerate light or partial shade. Native dogwoods prefer **light shade.** The soil should be of **average to high fertility,** high in **organic** matter, **neutral or slightly acidic** and **well drained.**

Most dogwoods require very little pruning. Simply removing damaged, dead or awkward branches in early spring is sufficient for most species. *Cornus alba* and *C. stolonifera*, which are grown for the colorful stems that are so striking in winter, require a little more effort because the color is best on young growth.

There are two ways to encourage new growth. A drastic, but effective, method is to cut back all stems to within a couple of buds of the ground, in early spring. Feed the plant once growth starts to make up for the loss of all top growth. The second, less drastic, method is to cut back about one-third of the old growth to within a couple of buds of the ground, in early spring. This leaves most of the growth in place, and branches can be removed as they age and lose their color.

C. stolonifera (above), *C. kousa* (below)

TIPS
Shrub dogwoods can be included in a shrub or mixed border. They look best in groups rather than as single specimens. The tree species make wonderful specimen plants and are small enough to include in most gardens. Use them along the edge of a woodland, in a shrub or mixed border, alongside a house, or near a pond, water feature or patio.

RECOMMENDED
C. alba (Red Twig Dogwood, Tartarian Dogwood) is grown for the bright red stems that provide winter interest. The stems are green all summer, only turning red as winter approaches. This species can grow 5–10' (1.5–3 m) tall, with an equal spread. It prefers cool climates and can develop leaf scorch and canker problems if the weather gets very hot. **'Aureo-marginata'** ('Elegantissima') has gray-green leaves with creamy margins. **'Sibirica'** has bright red winter stems. (Zones 2–8.)

C. kousa var. chinensis

C. kousa

*The strong wood of
C. nuttallii is in
demand for making
such items as piano
keys. The trees are
safe from this fate in
British Columbia,
where the species is
protected, and where
its showy blossom is
the provincial floral
emblem.*

C. alternifolia (Pagoda Dogwood) can be grown as a large, multi-stemmed shrub or a small, single-stemmed tree. It grows 15–25' (4.5–7.5 m) tall and spreads 10–25' (3–7.5 m). This species prefers light shade. The branches have an attractive layered appearance. Clusters of small white flowers appear in early summer. (Zones 3–8.)

C. 'Eddie's White Wonder' is a hybrid of *C. florida* and *C. nuttallii*. It grows about 20' (6 m) tall, with a spread of about 15' (4.5 m). In spring this small tree develops inconspicuous purple flowers surrounded by showy white bracts. The leaves turn shades of orange, red and purple in fall. (Zones 5–8.)

C. florida (Eastern Flowering Dogwood) is usually grown as a small tree. It has horizontally layered branches and grows 20–30' (6–9 m) tall, with an equal or greater spread. This species and its cultivars are susceptible to blight. The inconspicuous flowers with their showy pink or white bracts appear in late spring. **'Apple Blossom'** has light pink bracts with white at the bases. **'Cherokee Chief'** has dark pink bracts. **'Cloud Nine'** has large white bracts. **'Spring Song'** has rose pink bracts. (Zones 5–9.)

C. kousa (Kousa Dogwood) is grown for its flowers, fruit, fall color and interesting bark. It grows 20–30' (6–9 m) tall and spreads 15–30' (4.5–9 m). This species is more resistant to leaf blight and the other problems that plague *C. florida*. The white-bracted, early-summer flowers are followed by bright red fruit. The foliage turns red and purple in fall. *C. kousa* var. *chinensis* (Chinese Dogwood) grows more vigorously and has larger flowers. (Zones 5–9.)

C. mas (Cornelian Cherry Dogwood) can be grown as a small tree or large shrub. It reaches 15–25' (4.5–7.5 m) in height and spreads 15–20' (4.5–6 m). Clusters of small yellow flowers appear in late winter, and the edible fruits ripen in late summer. The foliage turns shades of red and purple in fall. (Zones 4–9.)

C. nuttallii (Pacific Dogwood, Western Flowering Dogwood) is a native tree that grows 25–40' (7.5–12 m) tall and spreads 20–25' (6–7.5 m). White- or pink-bracted flowers develop in late spring. (Zones 7–9.)

C. stolonifera *(C. sericea)* (Red-Osier Dogwood) is a widespread, vigorous native shrub with bright red stems. It grows about 6' (1.8 m) tall and spreads up to 12' (3.5 m). It bears clusters of small white flowers in early summer. The fall color is red or orange. This species tolerates wet soil. **'Flaviramea'** has bright yellow-green stems. (Zones 2–8.)

PESTS & PROBLEMS

The many possible problems include blight, canker, leaf spot, powdery mildew, root rot, borers, aphids, leafhoppers, scale insects, weevils, nematodes and thrips.

C. florida (above), *C. kousa* (below)

C. kousa is more dependable and disease resistant than many other dogwood species.

Douglas-Fir

Pseudotsuga menziesii

Features: foliage, cones, habit
Habit: conical evergreen, becoming columnar with age
Height: 6–200' (1.8–60 m) **Spread:** 6–25' (1.8–7.5 m)
Planting: B & B; spring, fall **Zones:** 4–9

Nothing says 'Northwest' like the majestic Douglas-fir, whose evergreen boughs spread holiday cheer year-round. These trees can be planted as seedlings in the smallest of gardens, then cut to be used as Christmas trees in the future. Their soft needles tend to persist longer on cut trees than needles of spruce and fir. Plant a Douglas-fir every year for a continuous supply of home-grown trees. Taking the time each spring to pinch the new growth will encourage fat, bushy trees, their chubby forms as attractive in the outdoor landscape as in the holiday decor.

GROWING

Douglas-fir prefers **full sun.** The soil should be of **average fertility, moist, acidic** and **well drained.** Pruning is generally not required.

TIPS

The species can be grown as a single large specimen tree or in groups of several trees. The smaller cultivars can be grown in space-limited gardens as specimens or as part of shrub or mixed borders.

RECOMMENDED

P. menziesii is native to the Pacific Northwest and south as far as Mexico. It grows 70–200' (20–60 m) tall and spreads 20–25' (6–7.5 m). For those with small gardens, several cultivars of Douglas-fir are not quite as imposing. **'Fletcheri'** is a dwarf cultivar that grows about 6' (1.8 m) tall and can spread 6–8' (1.8–2.5 m). **'Fretsii'** is a slow-growing cultivar that matures to a height of about 20' (6 m).

PESTS & PROBLEMS

Canker, leaf cast (needle version of leaf spot), spruce budworm, scale insects and aphids can cause occasional problems.

The cones have unique three-pronged bracts that look like the hind feet and tails of tiny mice hiding in the cones.

Dove Tree
Handkerchief Tree, Ghost Tree
Davidia involucrata

Features: mid- to late-spring flowers, scaly bark
Habit: rounded, pyramidal, deciduous tree
Height: 20–50' (6–15 m) **Spread:** about 30' (9 m)
Planting: B & B; spring **Zones:** 6–8

*T*his small to medium-sized tree is gaining popularity. Its neat growth, attractive form and reasonable size recommend it to almost any garden. The scaly, exfoliating bark and striking, unique blossoms are other appealing features. Pairs of large, white, wing-like bracts curve down around the inconspicuous flowers. Once you see a tree in full flower you'll understand the origin of the various common names, and you may be inspired to come up with a few of your own.

GROWING

Dove Tree grows well in **partial shade** or **full sun.** The soil should be **rich, moist, well drained** and have plenty of **organic** matter worked in. Plant in a location that is **sheltered** from strong winds.

Very little pruning is required. Remove any branches that are dead or damaged. While the tree is young, encourage a strong main leader and remove any awkward branches.

TIPS

This species makes an excellent medium-sized specimen tree. Don't panic if your young tree doesn't flower after you first plant it. Dove Tree rarely flowers before it is ten years old.

RECOMMENDED

D. involucrata is commonly grown. The more cold-hardy **var.** *vilmoriniana* has yellow-green leaves but is otherwise similar.

The orange-brown, scaly bark of the Dove Tree adds interesting texture to the winter landscape.

Elder
Elderberry
Sambucus

Features: early-summer flowers, fruit, foliage
Habit: large, bushy, deciduous shrubs
Height: 7–30' (2–9 m) **Spread:** 7–30' (2–9 m) **Planting:** spring, fall **Zones:** 3–9

*I*f you love birds, plant an elder—you'll be offering a buffet of colorful berries. The attractive compound leaves and enthusiastic growth will add a graceful touch as well as bird chatter to the garden. Elderberry wine is the main claim to fame of these fruiting shrubs or small trees, but for less trouble you can buy the wine and enjoy the plants for their good looks alone.

GROWING

Elders grow well in **full sun** or **partial shade.** Types grown for leaf color develop the best color in light or partial shade. The soil should be of **average fertility, moist** and **well drained.** These plants tolerate dry soil once established.

Though elders do not require pruning, they can become scraggly if ignored. These shrubs will tolerate severe pruning. Plants can be cut back to within a couple of buds of the ground in early spring to control the spread and encourage the best foliage color on specimens grown for this purpose.

Plants cut right back this way will not flower or produce fruit. If you desire flowers and fruit, remove only one-third or one-half of the growth in early spring. Fertilize or apply compost after pruning to encourage strong new growth.

TIPS

Elders can be used in a shrub or mixed border, in a natural woodland garden or next to a pond or other water feature. Types with interesting or colorful foliage can be used as specimen plants.

Both the flowers and the fruit can be used to make wine. The berries are popular for pies and jelly. The raw berries are marginally edible but not palatable and can cause stomach upset, particularly in children. All other parts of elders are **toxic**.

RECOMMENDED

S. canadensis (American Elder/Elderberry) is a shrub about 12' (3.5 m) tall, with an equal spread. White flowers in mid-summer are followed by dark purple berries. Native to eastern North America, this species is generally found growing in damp areas. **'Aurea'** has yellow foliage and red fruit. (Zones 4–9.)

S. cerulea (*S. mexicana*) (Blue Elder/Elderberry) is a large shrub that grows 7–30' (2–9 m) tall, with about the same spread. Creamy white flowers in flat-topped clusters appear in summer, followed by light blue berries—actually blue-black with a waxy white coating. (Zones 5–9.)

S. nigra (European Elder/Elderberry, Black Elder/Elderberry) is a large shrub that can grow 20' (6 m) tall, with an equal spread. The early-summer flowers give way to purple-black fruit. **'Guinicho Purple'** has dark bronze-green leaves that darken to purple over the summer and turn

S. racemosa

red in fall. The flowers are pinkish white. **'Laciniata'** has deeply dissected leaves that give the shrub a feathery appearance. (Zones 6–8.)

S. racemosa var. *arborescens* (*S. callicarpa*) (Red Elder/Elderberry) is native to our region. It grows 8–12' (2.5–3.5 m) tall, with an equal spread. Red Elder bears pyramidal clusters of white flowers in spring, followed by bright red fruit. (Zones 3–7.)

PESTS & PROBLEMS

Powdery mildew, borers, dieback, canker and leaf spot may occasionally affect elders.

Elder berries will attract birds to your garden.

English Ivy
Hedera helix

Features: foliage, habit
Habit: evergreen or semi-evergreen, climbing or trailing vine
Height: indefinite **Spread:** indefinite
Planting: spring, fall **Zones:** 5–10

L ove it or hate it, English Ivy grows and grows and grows. Draped on brick buildings it gives a refined estate appearance, and blanketing slopes it covers all your mowing and weeding problems. Ivy provides a green cover for topiary forms, and it adds quiet elegance to hanging baskets, urn plantings and container gardens when a few strands are allowed to spill from the sides.

GROWING

English Ivy prefers **light or partial shade** but will adapt to any light conditions from full shade to full sun. The foliage can become damaged or dried out in winter if the plant is growing in a sunny, exposed site. The soil should be of **average to rich fertility, moist** and **well drained.** The richer the soil, the better this vine will grow. Gardeners in the mildest climates may wish to plant English Ivy in poorer soil to help limit its spread.

Once established, English Ivy can be pruned as much as necessary, at any time, to keep this strong grower where you want it.

TIPS

English Ivy is grown as a trailing groundcover or as a climbing vine. It clings tenaciously to house walls, tree trunks and many other rough-textured surfaces. Keep in mind that this vigorous vine will harm its host tree if allowed to grow uncontrolled, and it will make the tree more susceptible to blowdown. Ivy rootlets can also damage walls and fences.

Ivy has become seriously invasive on the coast. There it can flower and set fruit, and it seems to do so more frequently if allowed to grow upward. Birds eat the berries and spread the plant into natural areas, where the vines choke out native vegetation. Limit your ivy's vertical reach, and remove the flowers to prevent fruiting. You'll be doing the neighborhood children a favor, too, because the **berries** are **poisonous.**

RECOMMENDED

H. helix is a vigorous vine that can grow as high as 100' (30 m), though it is usually pruned to keep it well below its potential size. As a groundcover, it may spread indefinitely but grows about 12" (30 cm) high. Many cultivars have been developed. Some, like **'Thorndale,'** are popular for their increased cold hardiness. In a sheltered spot this cultivar is hardy to Zone 4. Others, like the yellow-variegated **'Gold Heart,'** have interesting foliage.

PESTS & PROBLEMS

English Ivy has very few serious problems. Keep an eye open for infestations of spider mites or leaf spot. Plants exposed to winter wind may suffer desiccation of the foliage. When grown as a groundcover, English Ivy creates a popular habitat for rats.

Enkianthus
Enkianthus

Features: mid-spring to early-summer flowers, fall foliage
Habit: bushy, deciduous shrubs or small trees
Height: 5–15' (1.5–4.5 m) **Spread:** 5–15' (1.5–4.5 m)
Planting: spring, fall **Zones:** 4–8

*E*nkianthus are simply lovely shrubs or small trees with a horrible-sounding name. When pronounced quickly it sounds a bit like 'icky ants on us,' but the graceful foliage and delicate, bell-shaped blooms highlight more refined specimen plants than their name implies. You'll love the spring and summer color these well-behaved shrubs contribute. It is when fall comes, however, that you'll really fall in love with enkianthus. Their glorious warm color looks especially fetching set off by yellow Vine Maple in a casual woodland garden.

GROWING

Enkianthus species grow equally well in **full sun, partial shade** or **light shade**. The soil should be **fertile, humus rich, moist, acidic** and **well drained.**

Very little pruning is required. Remove awkward branches in late winter or early spring and any dead or damaged branches later in spring.

TIPS

These shrubs are often grown with rhododendrons and other acid-loving plants. They work well in a natural woodland garden, and they can also be used as specimen plants or in shrub or mixed borders.

RECOMMENDED

E. campanulatus (Redvein Enkianthus) is a large shrub or small tree. It grows 12–15' (3.5–4.5 m) tall, with an equal spread. The late spring to early summer flowers are white with red veins. The foliage turns shades of yellow, orange and red in fall.

E. perulatus (White Enkianthus) is a compact shrub that grows 5–6' (1.5–1.8 m) tall, with an equal spread. White flowers appear in mid-spring. The leaves turn bright red in fall. (Zones 5–8.)

E. campanulatus (this page)

The layered branching and tufted foliage of an enkianthus will add a unique touch to your garden.

Euonymus

Euonymus

Features: foliage, corky stems (*E. alatus*), habit
Habit: deciduous and evergreen shrubs, small trees, groundcovers, climbers
Height: 2–20' (0.5–6 m) **Spread:** 2–20' (0.5–6 m)
Planting: B & B, container; spring, fall **Zones:** 4–9

*L*ike enkianthus, euonymus are great plants with a somewhat homely name. They are versatile and often evergreen, and among the first shrubs I ever propagated—by accident. I pruned off some wayward stems of the Wintercreeper Euonymus and the pruning crumbs promptly rooted into the soil. This led me to plant an entire hedge as a substitute for the more costly boxwood, and 15 years later it still stands under one foot tall, with an annual trimming using a string trimmer.
Euonymus alatus, appropriately named Burning Bush, has fall leaves so bright red you can almost feel the heat. Team it up with the golden fall foliage of a Ginkgo tree or underplant with a red-berried cotoneaster for a traffic-stopping fall display.

The name Euonymus *translates as 'of good name'—rather ironically, given that all parts of these plants are poisonous and violently purgative.*

E. fortunei cultivars

GROWING

Euonymus species prefer **full sun** and tolerate light or partial shade. Soil of **average to rich fertility** is preferable, but any **moist, well-drained** soil will do.

Pruning requirements vary from species to species. *E. alatus* requires very little pruning except to remove dead, damaged or awkward growth. It tolerates severe pruning and can be used to form hedges. *E. fortunei* is a vigorous, spreading plant and can be trimmed as required; it too tolerates severe pruning. It is also easy to propagate. Bend a branch to the ground and hold it down with a rock. Cut this branch off once roots have formed and plant it where you wish.

E. alatus (above), *E. fortunei* 'Vegetus' (below)

TIPS

E. alatus can be grown in a shrub or mixed border, as a specimen, in a naturalistic garden or as a hedge. Dwarf cultivars can be used to create informal hedges. *E. fortunei* can be grown as a shrub in borders or as a hedge. It is an excellent substitute for the more demanding boxwood. The trailing habit also lends it to use as a groundcover or climber.

E. fortunei 'Gold Prince'

E. fortunei 'Vegetus' (above), *E. alatus* (below)

RECOMMENDED

E. alatus (Burning Bush, Winged Euonymus) is an attractive, open, mounding, deciduous shrub. It grows 15–20' (4.5–6 m) tall, with an equal or greater spread. The foliage turns a vivid red in fall. The small, red fall berries are somewhat obscured by the bright foliage. Winter interest is provided by the corky ridges, or wings, that grow on the stems and branches. This plant is often pruned to form a neat, rounded shrub, but if left to grow naturally it becomes an attractive, wide-spreading, open shrub. 'Compactus' (Dwarf Burning Bush) is a popular cultivar. It has more dense, compact growth—reaching up to 10' (3 m) tall and wide—and it lacks the corky ridges on the branches. It is commonly used as a hedge plant and in shrub and mixed borders.

E. fortunei (Wintercreeper Euonymus) as a species is rarely grown in the garden owing to the wide and attractive variety of cultivars. These can be prostrate, climbing or mounding evergreens, often with attractive, variegated foliage. 'Coloratus' (Purple Leaf Wintercreeper) is a popular cultivar, usually grown as a groundcover. The foliage turns red or purple over winter. 'Emerald Gaiety' is a vigorous, shrubby cultivar that grows about 5' (1.5 m) tall, with an equal or greater spread. It sends out long shoots that will attempt to scale any nearby wall. This rambling habit can be encouraged or the long shoots can be trimmed back to maintain the plant as a shrub. The foliage is bright green with irregular, creamy margins that turn pink in winter. **'Gold Prince'** ('Gold Tip') is a compact, mounded form that grows about 2' (60 cm) in height and spread. The leaves are deep green and edged with gold. **'Gold Spot'** grows about 3' (90 cm) tall, with an equal or greater spread. It has dark green leaves, each with a yellow spot in the center. The habit is fairly upright, making this cultivar a good choice for a hedge. **'Vegetus'** grows up to 5' (1.5 m) in height and width. This cultivar has large, dark green leaves, and it can be trained up a trellis as a climber or trimmed back to form a shrub.

PESTS & PROBLEMS

The two worst problems are crown gall and scale insects, both of which can prove fatal to the infected plant. Other possible problems include leaf spot, aphids, powdery mildew and leaf miners.

E. alatus achieves the best fall color when grown in full sun.

E. alatus (this page)

False Cypress

Chamaecyparis

Features: foliage, habit, cones
Habit: narrow, pyramidal,
evergreen trees
Height: 1–150' (0.5–45 m)
Spread: 1–65' (0.5–20 m)
Planting: B & B, container;
spring, fall **Zones:** 4–9

*F*alse cypresses are real workhorses in Northwest gardens, providing evergreen screens, walls or compact shrubs. The evergreen foliage means this group of plants provides winter color as well as solid structure for the landscape. The fast-growing varieties will give impatient gardeners a quick screen to block views of the neighbors as soon as possible.

GROWING

False cypresses prefer **full sun.** The soil should be **fertile, moist, neutral to acidic** and **well drained.** Alkaline soils are tolerated. No pruning is required on tree specimens. Plants grown as hedges can be trimmed at any time during the growing season. Avoid severe pruning as new growth will not sprout from old wood. In shaded areas growth may be sparse or thin. Dry, brown, old leaves can be pulled from the base by hand to tidy shrubs up.

TIPS

Tree varieties are used as specimen plants and for hedging. The dwarf and slow-growing cultivars are used in borders and rock gardens and as bonsai. False cypress shrubs can be grown near the house or as evergreen specimens in large containers.

As with the related arborvitae and False Arborvitae, oils in the foliage of false cypresses may be irritating to sensitive skin.

C. nootkatensis (this page)

RECOMMENDED

C. lawsoniana (Lawson False Cypress) is native to the western United States. It grows 50–130' (15–40 m) tall and spreads 6–15' (1.8–4.5 m). Over 250 cultivars are available. **'Gnome'** is a loosely rounded cultivar about 36" (90 cm) tall. **'Pembury Blue'** grows to 50' (15 m) tall, with pendulous, gray-green sprays of foliage.

C. nootkatensis (Yellow-cedar, Nootka False Cypress) is a west coast native. It grows 30–100' (9–30 m) tall with a spread of about 25' (7.5 m). The growth of this species is quite pendulous. **'Pendula'** has a very open habit and even more pendulous foliage than the species. (Zones 4–8.)

C. obtusa (Hinoki False Cypress), a native of Japan, has foliage arranged in fan-like sprays. It grows about 70' (21 m) tall with a spread of 20' (6 m). **'Minima'** is a very dwarf, mounding culti-var. It grows about 10" (25 cm) tall and spreads 16" (40 cm). **'Nana'** is a slow-growing cultivar that reaches 24–36" (60–90 cm) in height, with a slightly greater spread.

C. lawsoniana (above & below)

C. pisifera (Japanese False Cypress, Swara Cypress) is another Japanese native. It grows 70–150' (21–45 m) tall and spreads 15–25' (4.5–7.5 m). The cultivars are more commonly grown than the species. **'Filifera Aurea'** (Golden Thread-Leaf False Cypress) is a slow-growing cultivar with golden yellow, thread-like foliage. It grows about 40' (12 m) tall. **'Nana'** (Dwarf False Cypress) is a dwarf cultivar with feathery foliage similar to that of the species. It grows into a mound about 12" (30 cm) in height and width. **'Plumosa'** (Plume False Cypress) has very feathery foliage. It grows about 20–25' (6–7.5 m) tall with an equal or greater spread. **'Squarrosa'** (Moss False Cypress) has less pendulous foliage than the other cultivars. Young plants grow very densely, looking like fuzzy stuffed animals. The growth becomes more relaxed and open with maturity. This cultivar grows about 65' (20 m) tall, with a spread that may be equal or a little narrower.

PESTS & PROBLEMS
False cypresses are not prone to problems, but can occasionally be affected by spruce mites, root rot, gall or blight.

In the wild, C. nootkatensis trees can grow as tall as 165' (50 m) and as old as 1800 years.

C. nootkatensis

Fir

Abies

Features: foliage, cones
Habit: narrow, pyramidal or columnar, evergreen trees
Height: 2–100' (0.5–30 m) **Spread:** 3–30' (1–9 m)
Planting: B & B, container; spring **Zones:** 3–7

Firs are the aristocrats of the evergreen trees. Their straight spines and evenly spaced branches create a pyramidal form just begging to be decorated. Plant a fir tree in the front yard if you have plenty of room and string it with tiny white lights each December. All firs look great planted on mounds or berms of soil and paired with large boulders, to imitate the montane environments from which many originated.

GROWING

Firs usually prefer **full sun,** but tolerate partial shade. The soil should be **rich, moist, neutral to acidic** and **well drained.** These trees prefer a **sheltered** site, out of the wind, and are generally not tolerant of polluted city conditions.

No pruning is required. Dead or damaged growth can be removed as needed.

TIPS

Firs make impressive specimen trees in large areas. The species tend to be too large for the average home garden. Several compact or dwarf cultivars can be included in shrub borders or used as specimens, depending on their size.

A. concolor is far more tolerant of pollution, heat and drought than other *Abies* species, thus is better adapted for city conditions.

RECOMMENDED

A. balsamea (Balsam Fir) is quite pyramidal when young but narrows as it ages. This slow-growing tree can reach 45–75' (14–23 m) in height, with a spread of 15–25' (4.5–7.5 m). Though Balsam Fir prefers a well-drained soil, it will tolerate wet soil. This species is native to northcentral and northeastern North America and does better in interior than coastal regions. **'Hudsonia'** grows only 24" (60 cm) tall, with a spread of 36" (90 cm). It is a natural form of the species, but it is usually sold as a cultivar. It is also sometimes called **'Nana,'** although this cultivar is sometimes sold as a different plant. The two are very similar in size and habit. These dwarf cultivars are more suitable to a small garden than the much larger parent species.

A. concolor (White Fir) is an impressive native of the western United States. The needles have a whitish coating, which gives the tree a hazy blue appearance. It grows 40–70' (12–21 m) tall in garden

A. balsamea

'I spent three weeks in a forest composed of this tree, and day by day could not cease to admire it.'—David Douglas, 1830 (of A. procera)

conditions, but can grow up to 130' (40 m) in unrestricted natural conditions. It spreads 15–25' (4.5–7.5 m). **'Compacta'** is a dwarf cultivar. It has whiter needles than the species and grows to 10' (3 m) in height and spread. This cultivar makes an attractive specimen tree. **'Violacea'** has silvery needles and is very attractive; it grows as large as the species.

A. procera (Noble Fir) is a native of the Pacific Northwest, where trees in natural stands can reach lofty heights of 180–270' (55–80 m). In gardens it grows 50–100' (15–30 m) tall and spreads 20–30' (6–9 m). The cultivar **'Glauca'** has blue-gray needles and can grow as tall as the species, but specimens that don't form leaders will develop into spreading shrubs. Attempts to discourage leaders by pruning young trees may give similar results. (Zones 5–6.)

Firs and spruces resemble each other, but fir needles are flat and spruce needles are sharply pointed. Also, fir cones sit on top of the branches, while spruce cones hang downwards.

A. balsamea 'Hudsonia' (above), *A. concolor* 'Violacea' (right)

PESTS & PROBLEMS

Firs are susceptible to quite a few problems, including aphids, bark beetles, spruce budworm, bagworm, rust, root rot and needle blight.

Firs make nice Christmas trees, but the needles drop quickly in a dry house.

A. balsamea 'Hudsonia'

A. concolor

Firethorn

Pyracantha coccinea

Features: foliage, early-summer flowers, late-summer and fall fruit
Habit: dense, thorny, evergreen or semi-evergreen shrub
Height: 6–18' (1.8–5.5 m) **Spread:** equal to or greater than height
Planting: container; spring **Zones:** 5–9

The name says it all with this shrub. *Pyr* means 'fire,' an apt description of the berries, and *acantha* means 'thorn,' of which this bush has plenty. The fall berries are a hot, blazing red that can't be ignored, and the thorns quickly make themselves known as soon as you get close enough to do any pruning damage. Grow Firethorn up a brick chimney and you'll be heating up the house with color. Grow it under a window and it will put on a great show—and deter all but the most determined of burglars.

GROWING

Firethorn prefers **full sun** and tolerates partial shade, but does not fruit
as heavily in partial shade. The soil
should be **rich, moist** and **well
drained.** Well-established plants
will tolerate dry soil. Shelter plants
from strong winds. Firethorn
resents being moved once established.

Some pruning is required in order
to keep this plant looking neat and
attractive. In a naturalized setting,
this shrub can be left much to its
own devices. Remove any damaged
growth or wayward branches, and
trim back new growth to better
show off the fruit.

If you are using Firethorn in a shrub
or mixed border, you will have to
prune more severely to prevent it
from overgrowing its neighbors.
Hedges can be trimmed in early
summer to mid-summer. Espalier

*Firethorn obeys the version of
Murphy's Law that states that
the more prickly a plant is, the
more pruning it will need.*

and other wall-trained specimens can be trimmed in mid-summer. Growth to be used to extend the framework of the specimen can be tied in place as needed.

TIPS

Despite its potential for rampant growth, Firethorn has a wide variety of uses. It is often used for formal or informal hedges and barriers because the prickles make this plant unappealing to walk through. It can be grown as a large informal shrub in naturalized gardens and borders. It can also be used as a climber if tied to a trellis or other supportive framework. Firethorn's responsiveness to pruning and its dense growth habit make it an ideal espalier specimen.

RECOMMENDED

P. coccinea is a large, spiny shrub that grows 6–18' (1.8–5.5 m) tall and wide. White flowers cover the

The showy fruits of Firethorn resemble tiny apples and are attractive to birds.

plant in early summer, followed by bright scarlet fruit in fall and winter. **'Aurea'** is remarkable for its distinctive yellow fruit. It is hardy in Zones 6–9. **'Chadwick'** is a compact, spreading plant. It bears a prolific amount of red-orange fruit. This is one of the most hardy cultivars, to Zone 5. **'Fiery Cascade'** is an upright cultivar hardy in Zones 6–9. It grows about 10' (3 m) tall and spreads 8' (2.5 m), making it ideal for use in a border or as a hedge. The fruit ripens from orange to bright red.

PESTS & PROBLEMS

Unfortunately, Firethorn is susceptible to a few problems, the worst of which are fire blight and scab. Fire blight can kill the plant, and scab disfigures the fruit, turning it a sooty brown. A few less serious or less frequent problems are root rot, aphids, spider mites, scale insects and lace bugs.

Flowering Cherry, Plum & Almond

Prunus

Features: late-spring to early-summer flowers, fruit, bark, fall foliage **Habit:** upright, rounded, spreading or weeping, deciduous trees or shrubs
Height: 4–75' (1.2–23 m)
Spread: 4–50' (1.2–15 m)
Planting: bare-root, B & B, container; spring
Zones: 2–9

*I*t just wouldn't be spring without these beautiful flowering trees, covered with blossoms and gently dusting the ground with their pastel petals. Plants of the *Prunus* group form small garden trees, just right for growing tulips and daffodils beneath. As a winter bonus I always cut a few whip-like branches from early-flowering plums and cherries and arrange them in a vase, then await their blooms for a week or two. January is a much more tolerable month when an indoor display of flowering plum, cherry or almond provides a tantalizing glimpse of garden delights to come.

GROWING

These flowering fruit trees prefer **full sun.** The soil should be of **average fertility, moist** and **well drained.**

Pruning should be done after flowering. See below for specific pruning requirements for each species.

Plant on mounds when possible to encourage drainage. Shallow roots will emerge up out of the lawn if the tree is not getting sufficient water.

TIPS

Prunus species are beautiful as specimen plants and are small enough to be included in almost any garden. Small species and cultivars can also be included in borders or grouped to form informal hedges or barriers. Pissard Plum and Purpleleaf Sand Cherry can be trained to form formal hedges.

Because of the pest problems that afflict many of the cherries, they can be rather short-lived. Choose resistant species like Sargent Cherry or Higan Cherry. If you plant a more susceptible species, like the Japanese Flowering Cherry, enjoy it while it thrives but be prepared to replace it.

P. serrulata

Pissard Plum was one of the first purple-leaved cultivars, introduced into cultivation in 1880.

The fruits, but not the pits, of *Prunus* species are edible. Too much of the often sour fruit can cause stomachaches.

RECOMMENDED

P. x *blireiana* (Flowering Plum, Blireiana Plum) is a spreading shrub or small tree that grows 12–25' (3.5–7.5 m) tall, with an equal spread. The foliage opens a reddish-purple color then fades to dark green as it matures. Fragrant double flowers appear as early as February, before the leaves emerge. The small, inconspicuous fruits rarely set in our climate. Pruning off the flowering shoots once the flowers are finished will keep the plant looking neat but is not required. (Zones 5–8.)

P. cerasifera 'Atropurpurea' (Pissard Plum) is a shrubby tree that grows 20–30' (6–9 m) tall, with an equal spread. Light pink flowers that fade to white emerge before the deep purple foliage. The leaves turn dark green as they mature. Pissard Plum can be pruned to form a hedge, but plants grown as shrubs or trees need very little pruning. After flowering is finished, remove damaged growth and awkward branches as required. (Zones 5–8.)

P. x *cistena* (Purpleleaf Sand Cherry, Purpleleaf Dwarf Plum) is a dainty, upright shrub that grows 5–10' (1.5–3 m) high, with an equal or lesser spread. The deep purple leaves keep their color all season. The fragrant white or slightly pink flowers open in mid- to late spring after the leaves have developed. The fruits ripen to purple-black in July. This hybrid needs very little pruning if

grown as a shrub. It can be trained to form a small tree in space-restricted gardens. Hedges can be trimmed back after flowering is complete. (Zones 4–8.)

P. glandulosa (Dwarf Flowering Almond) is a scruffy-looking shrub that grows 4–6' (1.2–1.8 m) in height and width. The beautiful pink double flowers completely cover the stems in early spring, before the leaves emerge. Though very attractive when in flower, this species loses much of its appeal once flowering is done. Companion planting with other trees and shrubs will allow it to fade into the background as the season wears on. This shrub may spread by suckers; keep an eye open for plants that may turn up in unexpected and unwanted places. Prune one-third of the old wood to the ground each year, after flowering is complete. (Zones 4–8.)

P. maackii (Amur Chokecherry) is a rounded tree that grows 30–45' (9–14 m) tall and spreads 25–45' (7.5–14 m). Fragrant, white mid-spring

P. padus

The flowering of 'Autumnalis' is a most welcome sight in the winter garden.

P. serrulata 'Shirofugan' (opposite)
P. subhirtella 'Pendula' (below)

flowers are followed by red fruits that ripen to black. The glossy, peeling bark is a reddish or golden brown and provides interest in the garden all year. Amur Chokecherry needs little or no pruning. Remove damaged growth and wayward branches as required. (Zones 2–7.)

P. padus (European Bird Cherry) is a rounded, spreading tree that grows 30–50' (9–15 m) tall and 30–40' (9–12 m) wide. The new leaves are bright to bronzy green, maturing to dark green and turning red or yellow in fall. Fragrant white flowers appear in tubular, slightly drooping clusters in spring, after the leaves have matured, followed by round, glossy black fruits. (Zones 4–8.)

P. sargentii (Sargent Cherry) is a rounded or spreading tree that grows 20–70' (6–21 m) tall, with a spread of 20–50' (6–15 m). Fragrant light pink or white flowers appear in mid- to late spring, and the fruits ripen to a deep red by mid-summer. The orange fall color and glossy, red-brown bark are very attractive. This tree needs little pruning; remove damaged growth and wayward branches as needed. **'Columnaris'** is a narrow, upright cultivar that is suitable for tight spots and small gardens. (Zones 4–9.)

P. serrulata (Japanese Flowering Cherry) is a large tree that grows up to 75' (23 m) tall, with a spread of up to 50' (15 m). It bears white or pink flowers in mid- to late spring. The species is rarely grown in favor of the cultivars. **'Kwanzan'** (Kwanzan Cherry) is a popular cultivar with droopy clusters of pink double flowers. It is sometimes grafted onto a single trunk, creating a small, vase-shaped tree. Grown on its own roots it becomes a large spreading tree

P. padus

30–40' (9–12 m) tall, with an equal spread. Because this cultivar has been planted in such large numbers, it has become susceptible to many problems. These problems may shorten the life of the tree, but for 20 to 25 years it can be a beautiful addition to the garden. **'Mount Fuji'** ('Shirotae') bears pink buds that open to fragrant white flowers in early spring. It has a spreading habit and grows 15–30' (4.5–9 m) tall, with an equal spread. **'Shirofugan'** is a spreading, vigorous tree that grows 25' (7.5 m) tall and 30' (9 m) wide. The leaves are bronze when young and mature to dark green, turning orange-red in fall. Pink flower buds appear in mid-spring and open to fragrant white flowers. These cultivars need little pruning; remove damaged and wayward branches as needed. (Zones 5–8.)

P. subhirtella (Higan Cherry) is a rounded or spreading tree that grows 20–40' (6–12 m) tall and spreads 15–25' (4.5–7.5 m). The light pink or white flowers appear in early to mid-spring. The cultivars are grown more frequently than the species. **'Autumnalis'** (Autumn Flowering Cherry) bears light pink flowers in early to mid-winter in coastal gardens. In colder areas it will flower sporadically in fall and prolifically in early to mid-spring. It grows up to 25' (7.5 m) tall, with an equal spread. **'Pendula'** (Weeping Higan Cherry) has flowers in many shades of pink, appearing in early to mid-spring, before the leaves. The weeping branches make this tree a cascade of pink when in flower. It rarely needs pruning; remove damaged and wayward branches as needed. It is sometimes grafted onto a standard, creating a small weeping tree under 6' (1.8 m). (Zones 4–8.)

PESTS & PROBLEMS
The many possible problems include aphids, borers, caterpillars, leafhoppers, mites, nematodes, scale insects, canker, crown gall, fire blight, powdery mildew and viruses. Root rot can occur in poorly drained soils.

P. serrulata 'Kwanzan' (above)

Flowering Crabapple

Malus

Features: spring flowers, late-summer and fall fruit, fall foliage, habit, bark
Habit: rounded, mounded or spreading, small to medium, deciduous trees
Height: 5–30' (1.5–9 m) **Spread:** 8–30' (2.5–9 m)
Planting: B & B, container; spring, fall **Zones:** 4–8

*B*irds chattering happily above as you walk along any sidewalk lined with crabapple trees is reason enough to invest in a crabapple for your own garden. The spring flowers, autumn color and winter fruit make these trees to enjoy all year long, and their small size makes them perfect for street and front-yard plantings.

GROWING

Crabapples prefer **full sun** but tolerate partial shade. The soil should be of **average to rich fertility, moist** and **well drained.** These trees are tolerant of damp soil.

One of the best ways to prevent the spread of crabapple pests and diseases is to clear up all the leaves and fruit that fall off the tree. Many pests overwinter in the fruit, leaves or soil at the base of the tree. Clearing up their winter shelter helps keeps populations under control.

Crabapples require very little pruning but tolerate even hard pruning. Remove damaged or wayward branches and suckers when necessary. The next year's flower buds form in early summer, so any pruning done to form the shape of the tree should be done by late spring.

TIPS
Crabapples make excellent specimen plants. As many varieties are quite small, there is one to suit almost any size of garden. Some forms are even small enough to grow in large containers.

RECOMMENDED
The following are just a few suggestions among the hundreds of crabapples available. When choosing a species, variety or cultivar, the most important attribute to look for is disease resistance. Even the most beautiful flowers, fruit or habit will never look good if the plant is susceptible to any of the numerous possible crabapple diseases and pests. Many new cultivars have been

Though crabapples are usually grown as trees, their excellent response to training makes them good candidates for use as bonsai and espalier.

An espalier specimen

developed that have increased disease resistance.

M. 'Centurion' is highly resistant to all diseases. It is an upright tree that becomes rounded as it matures. It grows to 25' (7.5 m) in height, with a spread of 20' (6 m). Dark pink flowers appear in late spring. The bright red fruits persist for a long time on the tree. (Zones 5–8.)

M. 'Donald Wyman' is resistant to all diseases except powdery mildew, which can be prevented by pruning out enough growth to allow good air circulation. This cultivar has an open, rounded habit and grows to 20' (6 m) tall and 25' (7.5 m) in spread. Dark pink buds open to white flowers in mid-spring; flowering tends to be heavier in alternating years. The persistent fruits are bright red. (Zones 5–8.)

M. floribunda (Japanese Flowering Crabapple, Showy Crabapple) is a medium-sized, densely crowned, spreading tree. It can reach 30' (9 m) in both height and width. This species is fairly resistant to crabapple problems. Pink buds open to pale pink flowers in mid- to late spring. The fruits are small and yellow.

M. sargentii (Sargent Crabapple) is a small, mounding tree that is also fairly resistant to disease. It grows 6–10' (1.8–3 m) tall and spreads 8–15' (2.5–4.5 m). In late spring, red buds open to white flowers. The dark red fruits are long lasting. **'Tina'** is almost identical to the species, except that it grows only 5' (1.5 m) tall and spreads up to 10' (3 m). With a bit of pruning to control the spread, this cultivar makes an interesting specimen for a large container on a balcony or patio.

M. **'Snowdrift'** is a dense, quick-growing, rounded tree that is somewhat susceptible to diseases. It grows 15–20' (4.5–6 m) tall, with an equal spread. Red buds open to white flowers in late spring or early summer. The foliage is dark green and the fruits are bright orange. (Zones 5–8.)

PESTS & PROBLEMS

Aphids, beetles, borers, caterpillars, fruit worms, leaf rollers, leaf skeletonizers and scale insects are pests to look out for. Though the damage insect pests cause is largely cosmetic, the tree becomes weakened and more susceptible to diseases such as apple scab, cedar-apple rust, fire blight, heart rot, leaf spot, powdery mildew and root rot.

M. floribunda

Some adventurous gardeners use crabapple fruit to make preserves, cider or even wine.

Flowering Quince
Chaenomeles

Features: spring flowers, fruit, spines
Habit: spreading, deciduous shrubs with spiny branches
Height: 2–10' (0.5–3 m) **Spread:** 2–15' (0.5–4.5 m)
Planting: B & B, container; spring, fall **Zones:** 4–9

The most notably placed flowering quince I've seen was grown as an espalier against a bamboo fence. When a few of its large salmon blossoms opened, they were positioned as perfectly as any master designer could plan. I use one of these adaptable shrubs in the woodland part of my garden, paired with an early-blooming forsythia, and the two compete to see which will break first from winter dormancy.

GROWING

Flowering quinces grow equally well in **full sun** or **partial shade** but bear fewer flowers and fruit in shaded locations. The soil should be of **average fertility, moist** and **well drained,** and slightly **acidic** soil is preferred. These shrubs tolerate urban pollution.

Prune back about one-third of the old growth on established plants to the ground each year. Tidy plants by cutting back flowering shoots to a strong branch after flowering is finished.

TIPS

Flowering quinces can be included in a shrub or mixed border. They are very attractive grown against a wall. The spiny habit also makes them useful for barriers. Use them along the edge of a woodland or in a naturalistic garden. The dark bark stands out well in winter.

Leaf drop in summer is usually caused by leaf spot. Try hiding the plant with later-flowering perennials.

RECOMMENDED

C. japonica (Japanese Flowering Quince) is a spreading shrub that grows 24–36" (60–90 cm) tall and spreads up to 6' (1.8 m). Orange or red flowers appear in early to mid-spring, followed by small, fragrant, greenish-yellow fruit. This species is not as common as *C. speciosa* and its cultivars. (Zones 4–9.)

C. speciosa (Common Flowering Quince) is a large, tangled, spreading shrub. It grows 6–10' (1.8–3 m) tall and spreads 6–15' (1.8–4.5 m). Red flowers emerge in spring and are followed by fragrant, greenish-yellow fruit. Many cultivars are available. **'Cameo'** has large, peach-pink double flowers. **'Toyo-Nishiki'** has a more upright habit than the species, with a mixture of white, pink and red flowers that all appear on the same plant. (Zones 5–8.)

PESTS & PROBLEMS

In addition to leaf spot (see above), possible but not often serious problems include aphids, canker, fire blight, mites, rust and viruses.

C. speciosa (this page)

The fruits of flowering quinces are edible when cooked.

Forsythia
Forsythia

Features: early- to mid-spring flowers
Habit: spreading, deciduous shrubs with upright or arching branches
Height: 3–10' (1–3 m) **Spread:** 5–12' (1.5–3.5 m)
Planting: B & B, container in spring or fall; bare-root in spring **Zones:** 4–9

The first shrub I ever fell in love with was forsythia, which I mistakenly thought was called 'for Cynthia.' I imagined it to be named after a little girl with a February birthday. I have celebrated the blooming sunshine of these easy-growing shrubs ever since. I always trim off the longest shoots of my forsythia right after Christmas, anticipating spring and fooling Mother Nature by forcing the branches to flower indoors. Plant a few purple crocuses at the feet of your forsythia, or surprise a fellow gardener—sneak those bulbs into the ground and enjoy the vibrant splash of purple and yellow as this dynamic duo jump-starts the race to spring.

GROWING

Forsythias grow best in **full sun** but tolerate light shade. The soil should be of **average fertility, moist** and **well drained.**

Correct pruning is essential to keep forsythias attractive. Flowers emerge on growth that is two years old. Prune after flowering is finished. On mature plants, one-third of the oldest growth can be cut right back.

Some gardeners trim these shrubs into a formal hedge, but this practice often results in uneven flowering. An informal hedge allows the plants to grow more naturally. Size can be restricted by cutting shoots back to a strong junction.

TIPS

These shrubs are gorgeous while in flower, but they aren't very exciting the rest of the year. Include one in a shrub or mixed border where other flowering plants will take over once the forsythia's early-season glory has passed.

F. x *intermedia* (this page)

Forsythias can be used as hedging plants, but they look most attractive when grown informally.

The cold-hardiness designation for forsythias can be somewhat misleading. The plants themselves are very cold hardy, surviving in Zone 3 quite happily. The flowers, however, are not as tolerant because the buds form in summer and are then vulnerable to winter cold.

Gardeners in the warmest areas of our region will have no trouble getting this plant to flower consistently. In colder areas snow cover is often the deciding factor in flower bud survival. A tall shrub may flower only on the lower half—the part that was buried in, and protected by, snow. Don't despair, therefore, if your garden is outside the recommended region. If you have a good snowfall every year and choose a hardy cultivar, you should be able to get forsythia to flower.

RECOMMENDED

F. **'Arnold Dwarf'** is an attractive, low, mounding shrub with long, trailing branches. It is sometimes listed as a cultivar of *F.* x *intermedia*. It generally grows about 36" (90 cm) tall, but can reach 6' (1.8 m) tall, and it spreads up to 7' (2 m). The flowers are a slightly greenish yellow and are rather sparse on young plants, becoming more abundant on plants over six years old. This cultivar makes an interesting groundcover and can be used to prevent erosion on steep banks. (Zones 5–8.)

F. **x *intermedia*** is a large shrub with upright stems that arch as they mature. It grows 5–10' (1.5–3 m) tall and spreads 5–12' (1.5–3.5 m). Yellow flowers emerge in early to mid-spring before the leaves. Many cultivars have been developed from this hybrid. **'Lynwood'** ('Lynwood Gold') grows to 10' (3 m) in both height and width. The light yellow flowers open widely and are distributed evenly along the branches. **'Spectabilis'** grows to 10' (3 m) in height and width. It bears bright yellow flowers that are more cold tolerant than those of the hybrid. (Zones 6–9.)

F. **'Northern Sun'** is a hardy, upright shrub that develops a more arching habit as it matures. It grows 8–10' (2.5–3 m) tall and spreads up to 9' (2.7 m). The yellow flowers are very cold hardy. (Zones 4–8.)

Allow a clematis to twine through your forsythia for an ongoing display of flowers and color.

PESTS & PROBLEMS

Most problems are not serious but may include root-knot nematodes, stem gall and leaf spot.

F. x intermedia

Fothergilla

Fothergilla

Features: spring flowers, fall foliage
Habit: dense, rounded or bushy, deciduous shrubs
Height: 2–10' (0.5–3 m) **Spread:** 2–10' (0.5–3 m)
Planting: B & B, container; spring, fall **Zones:** 4–9

*F*oliage is a key element in a well-planned garden. These shrubs have not only fragrant flowers but lovely gray-green leaves that stand out against evergreens in a woodland garden. As if that's not enough, there's also the bonus of fiery fall foliage, which gives an autumn jolt to evergreen plantings of rhododendrons and azaleas.

The name is in honor of British physician John Fothergill (1712–80), who studied the cultivation of American plants.

GROWING

Fothergillas grow equally well in **full sun** or **partial shade.** In full sun these plants bear the most flowers and have the best fall color. The soil should be of **average fertility, acidic, humus rich, moist** and **well drained.**

These plants require little pruning. Remove wayward and dead branches as needed.

TIPS

Fothergillas are useful in shrub or mixed borders, in woodland gardens or combined with evergreen groundcovers.

RECOMMENDED

F. gardenii (Dwarf Fothergilla) is a bushy shrub that grows 24–36" (60–90 cm) tall, with an equal spread. In mid- to late spring it bears fragrant white flowers. The foliage turns yellow, orange and red in fall. '**Blue Mist**' is similar to the species, but the summer foliage is blue-green rather than dark green.

F. major (Large Fothergilla) is a rounded shrub that grows 6–10' (1.8–3 m) tall, with an equal spread. The fall colors are yellow, orange and scarlet. '**Mount Airy**' is a more compact cultivar, growing 5–6' (1.5–1.8 m) in height and width. It bears lots of flowers and has more consistent fall color than the species.

The bottlebrush-shaped flowers of fothergillas have a delicate honey scent. Use these plants with rhododendrons and azaleas.

F. major (this page)

Fringe Tree

Chionanthus

Features: early-summer flowers, bark, habit
Habit: rounded or spreading, deciduous large shrubs or small trees
Height: 10–25' (3–7.5 m) **Spread:** 10–25' (3–7.5 m)
Planting: B & B, container; spring **Zones:** 4–9

You will make the birds happy if you add a summer-blooming, autumn-fruiting fringe tree to your garden. The compact, rounded form looks most spectacular when displayed alongside a pond or when accenting a dry streambed. The flowers have long, narrow petals that somewhat resemble the fringe on the hem of Roaring Twenties' flapper dresses.

GROWING

Fringe trees prefer **full sun.** They do best in soil that is **fertile, acidic, moist** and **well drained** but will adapt to most soil conditions. In the wild they are often found growing alongside stream banks.

Little pruning is required for mature plants. The stems can be thinned out when the plant is young to encourage an attractive habit. Prune after flowering, or in spring for young plants that aren't yet flowering.

TIPS

Fringe trees work well as specimen plants, as part of a border or beside a water feature.

These trees may not produce fruit because not all trees of a given species bear both female and male flowers. Male flowers produce no fruit, and if only a female tree is present there may not be a male close enough to pollinate it. When fruit is produced it attracts birds.

RECOMMENDED

C. retusus (Chinese Fringe Tree) is a rounded, spreading shrub or small tree. It grows 15–25' (4.5–7.5 m) tall, with an equal spread. In early summer it bears erect, fragrant white flowers followed in late summer by dark blue fruit. The bark is deeply furrowed and peeling.

C. virginicus (White Fringe Tree) is a spreading small tree or large shrub. It grows 10–20' (3–6 m) tall and has an equal or greater spread. In early summer it bears drooping, fragrant white flowers, followed only occasionally by dark blue fruit.

PESTS & PROBLEMS

Fringe trees rarely have any serious problems but can be affected by borers, leaf spot, powdery mildew or canker.

C. virginicus (this page)

These pollution-tolerant trees are good choices for city gardens.

Ginkgo
Ginko, Maidenhair Tree
Ginkgo biloba

Features: summer and fall foliage, habit, bark
Habit: conical in youth, variable with age; deciduous tree
Height: 50–100' (15–30 m) **Spread:** 25–100' (7.5–30 m)
Planting: spring, fall **Zones:** 3–9

This unique tree has existed on earth for 150 million years. It has a neat form when it is young, but at maturity it may range from gently cascading to wildly erratic. Ginkgo is a slow starter, sometimes taking 10 or 12 years to get going, but it is well worth the wait. The foliage turns a warm golden yellow in fall. I remember seeing it in my first fall at college in eastern Washington—a beautiful scene of giant, exotic trees glowing golden in the afternoon sun.

GROWING

Ginkgo prefers **full sun.** The soil should be **fertile, sandy** and **well drained,** but this tree adapts to most conditions. It is also tolerant of urban conditions and cold weather. Little or no pruning is necessary.

TIPS

Though its growth is very slow, Ginkgo eventually becomes a large tree that is best suited as a specimen tree in parks and large gardens. It can be used as a street tree. If you buy an unnamed plant, be sure it has been propagated from cuttings. Seed-grown trees may prove to be female and the stinky fruit is not something you want dropping all over your lawn, driveway or sidewalk.

RECOMMENDED

G. biloba is variable in habit. It grows 50–100' (15–30 m) tall, with an equal or greater spread. The leaves can turn an attractive shade of yellow in fall, after a few cool nights. Female plants are generally avoided because the fruits have a very unpleasant odor. Several cultivars are available. **'Autumn Gold'** is a broadly conical male cultivar. It grows 50' (15 m) tall and spreads 30' (9 m). Fall color is bright yellow-gold. **'Princeton Sentry'** is a narrow, upright male cultivar. It grows 50–80' (15–25 m) tall and spreads 25' (7.5 m).

PESTS & PROBLEMS

This tree seems to have outlived most of the pests that might have afflicted it. A leaf spot may affect Ginkgo, but it doesn't cause any real trouble.

Ginkgo appears to have been saved from extinction by its long-time use in Asian temple gardens. Today this 'living fossil' grows almost entirely in horticultural settings.

The unique and beautiful leaves of Ginkgo are shaped like those of the Maidenhair Fern (inset).

Goldenchain Tree

Laburnum x *watereri*

Features: late-spring to early-summer flowers
Habit: spreading, deciduous tree
Height: 15–25' (4.5–7.5 m)
Spread: 15–25' (4.5–7.5 m)
Planting: B & B, container; spring
Zones: 5–8

My neighbor's Goldenchain Tree didn't look like much in winter, when its many trunks and sloppy posture made me wonder why he had added it to his front yard. Come spring, though, I knew I had to have one of my own. The bright yellow flowers drip in dramatic chains right at the height of the spring rhododendron season—and all that pink and red rhodie color means a tree of yellow is most welcome. For even more drama, underplant with giant purple orbs of flowering allium for a striking contrast in flower form as well as color.

GROWING

Goldenchain Tree prefers **full sun** or **light shade.** The soil should be of **average fertility** and **well drained.** This tree tolerates alkaline soils. Plant it in light or afternoon shade in hot areas, because Goldenchain Tree is not heat tolerant.

Goldenchain Tree can be trained to grow over an arbor, pergola or other such structure.

This tree needs very little pruning, but it responds well to training and can be encouraged to grow over structures and frames in the garden.

TIPS

Goldenchain Tree can be used as a specimen tree in small gardens.

All parts of this tree, but especially the seeds, contain a **poisonous** alkaloid. Children have been poisoned by eating the seeds, which resemble beans or peas.

RECOMMENDED

L. x *watereri* bears bright yellow flowers in pendulous clusters up to 10" (25 cm) long. This plant lives longest in climates with cool summers. **'Vossii'** has a denser growth habit and bears flower clusters up to 24" (60 cm) long. This cultivar can be trained to form an espalier.

PESTS & PROBLEMS

Goldenchain Tree may have occasional difficulties with aphids, canker, laburnum vein mosaic, leaf spot, mealybugs and twig blight.

Grape
Vitis

Features: summer and fall foliage, late-summer to fall fruit, habit
Habit: woody, climbing, deciduous vines
Height: 22–50' (7–15 m)
Spread: 22–50' (7–15 m)
Planting: bare-root, container; spring
Zones: 5–9

Nothing gives a garden Old-World, classic charm like a grape vine, whether it is sprawling over a pergola, clambering up a wall or shading an entryway. Ornamental grapes may not taste like much, but their bold foliage and colorful fruit give a certain amount of substance to a garden, a feel of permanence and weight that many new gardens need.

GROWING
Grapes prefer **full sun** or **partial shade.** The soil should be **moist, acidic** and **well drained.** These plants tolerate most well-drained soil conditions.

Trim grape plants to fit the space you have, in mid-winter and again in mid-summer. If you wish to train a grape more formally, cut the side shoots back to within two or three buds of the main stems. Such pruning encourages flowering and fruiting.

TIPS

Grape vines can be trained to grow up and over almost any sturdy structure. They may need to be tied in place until established.

The ripe fruit can attract wasps. You may wish to avoid planting this vine near the house if any family members are allergic to bee or wasp stings.

RECOMMENDED

V. cognetiae (Crimson Glory Vine) is a woody climber that can grow up to 50' (15 m) tall. It has attractive scarlet fall color and bears inedible, small, dark purple fruit.

V. rotundifolia (Muscadine Grape) can climb up to 30' (9 m). The purple or greenish-purple fruits are edible, but quite bitter. Fall color is yellow. (Zones 5–8.)

V. vinifera (Wine Grape) is a woody climber, best known for the wine grapes it produces. It also makes an attractive addition to the garden. It grows up to 22' (7 m) tall and bears edible fruit. **'Purpurea'** (Purple-leaf Grape) is an attractive cultivar. It has inedible fruit, but the leaves are the main attraction; greenish purple in summer, they turn dark purple in fall. (Zones 6–9.)

PESTS & PROBLEMS

Possible problems include downy mildew, powdery mildew, canker, dieback, gray mold, black rot, root rot, leaf spot, grape leaf skeletonizer, scale insects and mealybugs. None of these is likely to be serious in a garden with only one or two plants.

V. vinifera (this page)

Though the fruits of garden grapes are edible, they can be quite bitter. Use them to make jelly, juice and, if you're really adventurous, wine.

Hawthorn

Crataegus

Features: late-spring or early-summer flowers, fruit, foliage, thorny branches
Habit: rounded, deciduous trees, often with a zig-zag, layered branch pattern
Height: 15–30' (4.5–9 m)
Spread: 12–30' (3.5–9 m)
Planting: B & B, container; early spring
Zones: 3–8

These well-armed small trees are great plants to get stuck on, especially if you're making a point to attract more bees and birds to the garden. The bright red fruits make hawthorns good candidates for the winter garden, and their spring blooms make a lovely backdrop for early perennials. The small leaves have a scalloped edging that provides a delicate, feminine counterpoint to the nasty thorns.

Hawthorn fruits are edible, but dry and seedy. Some people use them to make jelly, or ferment them and mix them with brandy.

GROWING

Hawthorns grow equally well in **full sun** or **partial shade.** They adapt to any well-drained soil and tolerate urban conditions.

When grown as trees, hawthorns need little pruning. Those grown as hedges can be pruned after flowering or in fall. Remove any dead or diseased growth immediately, to prevent the spread of diseases like fire blight.

Hawthorns can become weedy, with seedlings and suckers popping up unexpectedly. Remove any that you find while they are young, because they become quite tenacious once they get bigger.

TIPS

Hawthorns can be grown as specimen plants or hedges in urban sites, coastal gardens and exposed locations. They are popular in areas where vandalism is a problem

C. laevigata 'Paul's Scarlet' (this page)

because very few people wish to grapple with plants bearing stiff two-inch (5 cm) thorns. As a hedge, hawthorns create an almost impenetrable barrier.

These trees are small enough to include in most gardens. With the long, sharp thorns, however, a hawthorn might not be a good selection if there are children about.

RECOMMENDED

C. laevigata (*C. oxyacantha*) (English Hawthorn) is a low-branching, rounded tree with zig-zag layers of thorny branches. It grows 15–25' (4.5–7.5 m) tall and spreads 12–25' (3.5–7.5 m). White or pink late-spring flowers are followed by bright red fruit in late summer. Many cultivars are available. **'Paul's Scarlet'** ('Paulii,' 'Coccinea Plena') has many showy, deep pink double flowers. (Zones 4–8.)

C. phaenopyrum (*C. cordata*) (Washington Hawthorn) is an oval to rounded, thorny tree. It grows 25–30' (7.5–9 m) tall, with a spread of 20–30' (6–9 m). It bears white flowers from early to mid-summer and has persistent shiny red fruit

The hawthorns are members of the rose family, and their fragrant flowers call to mind the scent of apple blossoms.

in fall. The glossy green foliage turns red and orange in fall. This species is least susceptible to fire blight.

PESTS & PROBLEMS
Borers, caterpillars, leaf miners, skeletonizers, scale insects, fire blight, canker, rust, powdery mildew, scab and fungal leaf spot are all possible problems. Healthy, stress-free plants will be less susceptible.

The genus name Crataegus *comes from the Greek* kratos, *'strength,' in reference to the hard, fine-grained wood.*

C. laevigata (all photos)

Hazel
European Hazel, European Filbert
Corylus avellana

Features: early-spring catkins, nuts, foliage, habit
Habit: large, dense, deciduous shrub or small tree
Height: 8–20' (2.5–6 m) **Spread:** 10–15' (3–4.5 m)
Planting: B & B, container; spring, fall **Zones:** 3–9

A contorted Hazel weaves its crooked spell right outside my front window. It grows more twisted each year, the shiny-barked branches changing directions as they grow—no wonder the wayward form has earned this plant the nickname 'Politician's Tree.' And the branches aren't its only charm. Winter catkins that bloom in early spring attract a host of cheery chickadees.

C. avellana is grown for commercial nut production, both for the delicious nuts themselves and for the extracted oil.

GROWING

Hazel grows equally well in **full sun** or **partial shade.** The soil should be **fertile** and **well drained.**

This plant requires very little pruning, but tolerates it well. Entire plants can be cut back to within 6" (15 cm) of the ground to encourage new growth in spring. On grafted specimens of Corkscrew Hazel, suckers that come up from the roots can be cut out because they will not have the twisted habit.

TIPS

These plants can be used as specimens or in shrub or mixed borders.

RECOMMENDED

C. avellana grows as a large shrub or small tree. It reaches 12–20' (3.5–6 m) in height and spreads up to 15' (4.5 m). Male plants bear long, dangling catkins in late winter and early spring and female plants develop edible nuts. Cultivars are more commonly grown than the species, and **'Contorta'** (Corkscrew Hazel, Harry Lauder's Walking Stick) is perhaps the best known. It grows 8–10' (2.5–3 m) tall. The stems and leaves are twisted and contorted. This is a particularly interesting feature in winter, when the bare stems are most visible. Cut out any growth that is not twisted.

PESTS & PROBLEMS

Powdery mildew, blight, canker, fungal leaf spot, rust, bud mites, tent caterpillars and webworm may cause occasional problems.

C. avellana 'Contorta' (this page)

Forked Hazel branches have been used as divining rods to find underground water or precious metals.

Heather
Spring Heath, Winter Heath
Erica

Features: late-winter to mid-spring flowers, foliage, habit
Habit: low, spreading, evergreen shrubs
Height: 6–12" (15–30 cm) **Spread:** 8–36" (20–90 cm)
Planting: container; spring **Zones:** 5–7

Reminiscent of the romantic, misty moors of Britain, these plants come in so many forms with such varied flowering times that you can enjoy a textural tapestry of flowering heather almost year-round. Plant an early-spring bloomer at the base of a flowering plum, a late-spring bloomer under a Korean Dogwood and a summer bloomer in rockeries or mixed borders to add late-season color.

GROWING

Heathers prefer **full sun,** but tolerate partial shade. The soil should be of **average fertility, acidic, moist** and **well drained.** Though they prefer acidic soils and enjoy having peat moss mixed in to the substrate, these plants will tolerate alkaline soil. Do not overfertilize.

To keep the plants compact and tidy, shear back new growth to within 1" (2.5 cm) of the previous year's growth once flowering is finished.

The center of each clump tends to mat down and dry out. Use a claw tool to fluff the soil in the middle of the mound in early spring.

TIPS

Heathers make excellent groundcovers or rock garden plants. They can be combined with other acid-loving plants in a shrub or mixed border.

RECOMMENDED

E. carnea bears pinkish-purple flowers in late winter. The species and its many cultivars, which are

E. carnea (this page)

more commonly available, grow up to 12" (30 cm) high and 24" (60 cm) wide. **'Ghost Hill'** has red flowers; **'Springwood Pink'** has light pink flowers; and **'Springwood White'** has white flowers.

E. x *darleyensis* **'Mediterranean Pink'** is a common mounding, groundcover heather. It bears rose-lavender flowers in early spring. It grows about 12" (30 cm) tall and spreads about 36" (90 cm).

PESTS & PROBLEMS

Rare problems with rust, verticillium wilt, root rot or powdery mildew are possible.

Hemlock
Tsuga

Features: foliage, habit, cones
Habit: pyramidal or columnar, evergreen trees
Height: 5–130' (1.5–40 m)
Spread: 6–35' (1.8–10 m)
Planting: B & B, container; spring, fall
Zones: 3–8

You know you have an authentic Northwest look to your garden when a Western Hemlock sprouts from a Western Redcedar stump. Graceful dancers of the garden evergreens, hemlocks' fine needles shimmy in the breeze, and their delicate textures make a great contrast to broad-leaved rhododendrons and camellias. These trees are perfect for creating cool, green-shade gardens.

GROWING

Hemlocks generally grow well in any light from **full sun** to **full shade.** The soil should be **humus rich, moist** and **well drained.** These trees are drought sensitive and grow best in a cool, damp climate. They are also sensitive to air pollution and suffer salt damage, so keep them away from roadways.

Hemlock trees need little pruning. The cultivars can be pruned to control their growth as required. Trim hemlock hedges in summer.

TIPS

These elegant trees, with their delicate needles, are among the nicest evergreens to use as specimen trees. They can also be trimmed to form a hedge. The smaller cultivars may be included in a shrub or mixed border.

These hemlocks are not poisonous, bearing no relation to the herb that killed Socrates.

RECOMMENDED

T. canadensis (Canadian Hemlock, Eastern Hemlock) is a graceful, narrowly pyramidal tree. It grows 40–80' (12–25 m) tall and spreads 25–35' (7.5–10 m). Many cultivars are available, including groundcovers and dwarf forms. **'Jeddeloh'** is a rounded, mound-forming, slow-growing cultivar. It grows 5' (1.5 m) tall and spreads 6' (1.8 m). **'Sargentii'** ('Pendula') is a spreading, mounding form with long, pendulous branches. It grows 10–15' (3–4.5 m) tall and spreads 20–30' (6–9 m). It can be trimmed back to restrict its growth.

The name Tsuga *is derived from a Japanese word meaning 'tree-mother.'*

T. canadensis (above), *T. heterophylla* (below)

T. heterophylla (Western Hemlock) is a Pacific Northwest native with a spire-like habit. It grows 70–130' (21–39 m) tall, with a spread of 20–30' (6–9 m). It prefers a sheltered site and is very shade tolerant. (Zones 6–8.)

T. mertensiana (Mountain Hemlock) is a columnar native of high elevations in the coastal mountain ranges. It grows up to 50' (15 m) tall and spreads up to 20' (6 m). It is very slow growing and doesn't tolerate polluted and urban conditions or the hot summers in parts of our region.

It is not as shade tolerant as Western Hemlock. **'Glauca'** is a dwarf cultivar with silvery green foliage. It grows up to 10' (3 m) tall and spreads 6' (1.8 m).

PESTS & PROBLEMS
Healthy, stress-free trees have few problems. Possible problems may be caused by gray mold, rust, needle blight, snow blight, weevils, mites, aphids, woolly adelgids or scale insects.

Don't cut the evergreen boughs for use as holiday decorations. The needles drop quickly once the branches are cut.

T. canadensis (left), *T. canadensis* 'Jeddeloh' (below)

T. heterophylla

Holly

Ilex

Features: spiny foliage, fruit, habit
Habit: erect or spreading, evergreen shrubs or trees
Height: 3–80' (1–25 m) **Spread:** 3–50' (1–15 m)
Planting: B & B, container; spring, fall **Zones:** 4–9

*A*s comforting as a holiday carol, a holly in the garden supplies winter color as well as winter berries for the birds. The first seedling I ever nurtured was a bird-sown holly plant that sprouted in the dry shade under a maple tree. In a few years it had grown to a sizable specimen, making a prickly point about how tough and invasive these evergreens can be.

GROWING

These plants prefer **full sun** but tolerate **partial shade.** The soil should be of **average to rich fertility, humus rich, moist** and **well drained. Shelter** from winter wind helps prevent the leaves from drying out. Apply a summer mulch to keep the roots cool and moist.

Grown as a shrub, a holly requires little pruning. Damaged growth can be removed in spring. Trim plants grown as hedges in summer. Dispose of all trimmings carefully to prevent the spiny leaves from puncturing bare feet and paws.

TIPS

Hollies can be used in groups, in woodland gardens and in shrub and mixed borders. They can also be used as hedge plants.

Male and female flowers occur on separate plants and both must be present for the females to set fruit. One male will adequately pollinate two to three females.

In coastal regions of the Pacific Northwest, English Holly is becoming invasive. The berries, enjoyed by birds, are sprouting in wild areas, and holly is successfully competing with native vegetation. This problem should make coastal gardeners think twice before planting female holly, at least until sterile cultivars become available. For a broad-leaved evergreen tree with colorful fruits, try Arbutus (p. 80) instead.

The showy, scarlet berries look tempting, especially to children, but are not edible.

I. aquifolium

I. opaca

'Deck the halls with boughs of holly…'
Ilex aquifolium *branches with bright red fruits have been used for centuries as a holiday decoration.*

I. aquifolium

RECOMMENDED

I. aquifolium (English Holly) is a dense, pyramidal shrub or tree. It grows 30–80' (9–25 m) tall and spreads 20–50' (6–15 m). The red berries persist into winter and look striking against the glossy, evergreen foliage. Many cultivars are available, with yellow berries, weeping or dwarf habits, variegated foliage and other features. **'Golden Milkmaid'** has scarlet berries and spiny leaves with irregular gold patches. (Zones 7–9.)

I. glabra (Inkberry) is a rounded shrub with glossy green foliage and dark purple fruit. It grows 6–10' (1.8–3 m) tall and spreads 8–10' (2.5–3 m). **'Nigra'** is a dwarf female cultivar that bears many fruits. The foliage develops a purple hue in winter. This shrub grows up to 3' (1 m) tall, with an equal spread.

I. x *meserveae* (Blue Holly) is an erect or spreading, dense shrub. It grows 10–15' (3–4.5 m) tall, with an equal spread. It bears glossy red fruits that persist into winter. Tolerant of pruning, it makes a formidable hedge or barrier. Many cultivars have been developed, often available in male and female pairs. The males and females can be mixed and matched. **'Blue Boy'** and **'Blue Girl'** grow about 10' (3 m) tall, with an equal spread. 'Blue Girl' bears abundant red berries. Both are quite cold hardy. **'Blue Prince'** and **'Blue Princess'** have larger leaves, and 'Blue Princess' bears even more fruit than 'Blue Girl.' These cultivars grow 10–12' (3–3.5 m) tall, with an equal spread. (Zones 5–8.)

I. opaca (American Holly) is an excellent tree holly that grows 40–50' (12–15 m) tall and spreads 20–40' (6–12 m). The form is often neatly pyramidal when young, becoming more open at maturity. Leaves and fruits vary among the many cultivars; ask at your local garden center for the types that grow best in your area. (Zones 5–9.)

I. pernyi (Perny Holly) is an upright shrub that grows 9–30' (2.7–9 m) tall and spreads 4–10' (1.2–3 m). The dark green, spiny leaves are borne in attractive flat sprays. Yellowish spring flowers give way to bright red fruits. (Zones 6–9.)

PESTS & PROBLEMS

Aphids may attack young shoots. Scale insects and leaf miners can present problems, as can root rot in poorly drained soils.

I. pernyi

I. aquifolium 'Golden Milkmaid'

Horsechestnut

Aesculus

Features: early-summer flowers, foliage, spiny fruit
Habit: rounded or spreading, deciduous trees
Height: 30–80' (9–25 m) **Spread:** 30–70' (9–21 m)
Planting: B & B, container; spring, fall **Zones:** 3–8

O ne fall our family moved to a big house in the country to find the huge leaves of horsechestnut trees smothering the lawn and clogging the gutters. We were ready to have the monsters severely pruned or removed altogether, until a hot summer day made us think again. The trees blocked the afternoon sun, keeping the large two-story house cool all summer. This benefit, along with the gorgeous spikes of spring flowers, more than compensated for the extra work the fallen leaves created.

GROWING

Horsechestnuts grow well in **full sun** or **partial shade.** The soil should be **fertile, moist** and **well drained.** These trees dislike excessive drought. Little pruning is required. Wayward branches can be removed in winter or early spring.

TIPS

Horsechestnuts are used as specimen and shade trees. They are best suited to large gardens. Note also that the roots of horsechestnuts can break up sidewalks and patios if planted too close, and the spiny fruits can be hazardous when they fall.

These trees give heavy shade, excellent for cooling buildings, but difficult to grow grass beneath. Consider a shade-loving groundcover as an alternative.

The entire tree and especially the **seeds** contain a **poisonous** compound that breaks down blood proteins. People are commonly poisoned when they confuse the nuts with edible sweet chestnuts (*Castanea* species).

A. hippocastanum (this page)

RECOMMENDED

A. x *carnea* (Red Horsechestnut) is a dense, rounded to spreading tree. It grows 30–70' (9–21 m) tall, with a spread of 30–50' (9–15 m). It is smaller than *A. hippocastanum*, but needs more regular water in summer. Spikes of dark pink flowers are borne in late spring and early summer. 'O'Neill' bears bright red flowers. This tree grows slowly to 35' (10 m) in height. (Zones 4–8.)

A. hippocastanum (Common Horsechestnut) is a large rounded tree that will branch right to the ground if grown in an open setting. It grows 50–80' (15–25 m) tall and spreads 40–70' (12–21 m). The flowers, borne in spikes up to 12" (30 cm) long, appear in late spring; they are white with yellow or pink marks. (Zones 3–7.)

PESTS & PROBLEMS

Horsechestnuts are most susceptible to disease when under stress. Canker, leaf scorch, leaf spot, scale insects, anthracnose, rust and powdery mildew can all cause problems.

Horsechestnut flowers attract hummingbirds to the garden. Squirrels eat the apparently safe embryos in the otherwise poisonous seeds.

Huckleberry
Blueberry, Cranberry
Vaccinium

Features: late-spring to early-summer flowers, fruit, foliage
Habit: bushy, deciduous or evergreen shrubs or groundcovers
Height: 0.5–12' (0.2–3.5 m) **Spread:** 5' (1.5 m) or more
Planting: container; spring, fall **Zones:** 2–9

Huckleberries belong with hemlocks and Western Redcedar in a native garden, or tucked into any cool corner where late-summer berries and delicate foliage will be appreciated. When we gathered the berries from the forest as children, it took lots of sugar to balance their tartness in pies and syrups. Today I grow the berries for the birds, and enjoy the natural beauty of these native plants for myself.

GROWING

Huckleberries grow equally well in **full sun** or **partial shade.** The soil should be **peaty, acidic, moist** and **well drained.** Very little pruning is required. Deadhead after flowering unless fruits are desired.

TIPS

Huckleberries can be used in a woodland garden or in a shrub or mixed border. Some people grow them just for the fruit and include them in the vegetable garden or with other fruit-bearing plants. Grow huckleberries on top of old cedar stumps for a natural look.

RECOMMENDED

V. ovatum (Evergreen Huckleberry) is a west coast native. It is a dense, compact, bushy, evergreen shrub. It grows 3–12' (1–3.5 m) tall and spreads 5–10' (1.5–3 m). Small red or pink flowers in late spring or early summer are followed by edible dark blue berries in early autumn. The berries can remain on the shrub until December, and some say they taste better after the first frost. (Zones 7–9.)

V. parvifolium (Red Huckleberry, Deciduous Huckleberry) is native to the Pacific Northwest. It is an upright, bushy, mainly deciduous shrub that grows up to 10' (3 m) tall and spreads up to 6' (1.8 m). Small white or pink flowers appear in late spring and early summer, followed by edible, bright red berries. (Zones 5–8.)

V. vitis-idaea (Bog Cranberry, Lingonberry) is native to the arctic and boreal regions of North America. It is a low-growing, spreading, evergreen shrub. It grows up to 10" (25 cm) tall and can spread indefinitely. This species is tolerant of wet soils. It bears white or pink flowers in late spring and early summer, followed by edible red berries. Although it tolerates extremely severe winters without difficulty, it is less tolerant of summer heat and is best reserved for those gardeners in the coldest areas. **Var. *minimus*** is a smaller and even hardier variety. It grows up to 8" (20 cm) tall. (Zones 2–6.)

PESTS & PROBLEMS

Occasional problems with caterpillars, scale insects, gray mold, leaf and bud galls, crown rot, root rot, powdery mildew and rust are possible.

V. parvifolium

The edible, deliciously tart berries of Vaccinium *species can be used to make pies, syrups and wines.*

V. vitis-idaea

Hydrangea
Hydrangea

Features: flowers, habit
Habit: deciduous; mounding shrubs, woody climbers, spreading shrubs or trees
Height: 3–80' (1–25 m) **Spread:** 2–20' (0.5–6 m)
Planting: container; spring, fall **Zones:** 3–9

*E*very summer the baby blue orbs of Bigleaf Hydrangea decorated the back yard of my grandmother's garden, making the perfect floral background for family photographs at the annual reunion. With proper pruning, you'll have gobs of globular blooms even in the shade. The best part about these old-fashioned shrubs is that you can change the color of the blossoms from sky blue, in our naturally acidic soil, to soft pink just by adding lime or wood ashes to make the soil more alkaline.

GROWING

Hydrangeas grow well in **full sun** or **partial shade,** and some species tolerate full shade. Shade or part shade will reduce leaf and flower scorch in the hotter regions. The soil should be of **average to high fertility, humus rich, moist** and **well drained.** These plants perform best in cool, moist conditions.

H. macrophylla (this page)

Hydrangeas have an unusual reaction to the pH level of the soil. In an acidic soil the flowers will tend to be blue, while the same plant grown in an alkaline soil will tend to have pink flowers. Cultivars develop their best color in one or the other soil type.

Pruning requirements vary from species to species. See the Recommended section for specific suggestions.

TIPS

Hydrangeas come in many forms and have many uses in the landscape. They can be included in shrub or mixed borders, used as specimens or informal barriers and planted in groups or containers. Climbing varieties can be trained up walls, pergolas and arbors.

Hydrangea flowerheads consist of inconspicuous fertile flowers and showy sterile flowers. Hortensia-type flowerheads consist almost entirely of showy sterile flowers clustered together to form a globe shape. Lacecap-type flowerheads consist of a combination of sterile and fertile flowers. The showy flowers form a loose ring around the fertile ones, giving the flowerhead a delicate, lacy appearance.

The leaves and buds of some hydrangeas, but apparently not those of *H. paniculata* 'Grandiflora,' can cause **cyanide poisoning** if eaten or if the smoke is inhaled. Avoid burning hydrangea clippings.

H. paniculata

Hortensia flower-heads can be used in dried or fresh flower arrangements. For the longest-lasting fresh flowers, water the soil deeply the evening before to help keep the petals from wilting when the flowers are cut.

RECOMMENDED

H. anomala subsp. ***petiolaris*** (Climbing Hydrangea) is considered by some gardeners to be the most elegant climbing plant available. It clings to any rough surface by means of little rootlets that sprout from the stems. It grows 50–80' (15–25 m) tall. Though this plant is shade tolerant, it will produce the best flowers when exposed to some direct sun each day. The leaves are a dark, glossy green and sometimes show yellow fall color. For over a month in summer the vine is covered with white lacecap flowers, and the entire plant appears to be veiled in a lacy mist. This hydrangea can be pruned after flowering, if required, to restrict its growth. It can be trained to grow up walls, trees and fences. It will also grow over rocks and can be used as a groundcover. With careful pruning and some support when young it can be trained to form a small tree or shrub. (Zones 4–9.)

H. arborescens (Smooth Hydrangea) forms a rounded shrub 3–5' (1–1.5 m) tall, with an equal

width. This plant is tolerant of shady conditions. It
can be grown as a perennial in very cold climates.
The plants flower on new growth each year and will
look most attractive if cut right back to the ground
in fall. The flowers of the species are not very showy,
but the cultivars have large, showy blossoms.
'Annabelle' bears large, ball-like clusters of white
hortensia flowers. A single flowerhead may be up to
12" (30 cm) in diameter. This cultivar is more compact than the species and is useful for brightening
up a shady wall or corner of the garden.

H. macrophylla (Bigleaf Hydrangea) is a rounded
or mounding shrub that flowers from mid- to late
summer. It grows 3–6' (1–1.8 m) tall and spreads
up to 8' (2.5 m). Prune flowering shoots back to
strong buds or a strong branch once flowering is
finished. On mature, established plants, one-third
of the oldest growth can also be removed to
encourage vigorous new growth. The many cultivars can have hortensia or lacecap flowers in pink,
purple or blue. **'All Summer Beauty'** grows 3–4'
(0.9–1.2 m) tall. The dark blue hortensia flowers

H. macrophylla (above)
H. paniculata 'Grandiflora' (below)

*Hydrangeas have
escaped cultivation
in some areas of the
Pacific Northwest
and can be found
growing in ditches.*

occur on new growth. **'Mariesii'** grows 4–5' (1.2–1.5 m) tall. The lacecap flowers are pale blue in acidic soils and pale pink in alkaline soils. (Zones 6–9.)

H. paniculata (Panicle Hydrangea) is a spreading to upright large shrub or small tree. It grows 10–22' (3–7 m) tall and spreads to 8' (2.5 m). It bears white flowers from late summer to early fall. This plant requires little pruning. When young it can be pruned to encourage a shrub-like or tree-like habit. The entire shrub can be cut to within 12" (30 cm) of the ground each fall to encourage vigorous new growth the following summer. **'Grandiflora'** (Pee Gee Hydrangea) is a spreading large shrub or small tree 15–25' (4.5–7.5 m) tall and 10–20' (3–6 m) in spread. The mostly sterile flowers are borne in hortensia clusters up to 18" (45 cm) long. (Zones 4–8.)

H. quercifolia (Oak-leaf Hydrangea) is a mound-forming shrub with attractive, cinnamon brown, exfoliating bark. It grows 4–8' (1.2–2.5 m) tall, with an equal spread. The large leaves are lobed like an oak's and often turn bronze or bright red

H. anomala subsp. *petiolaris*

H. paniculata

in fall. Conical clusters of sterile and fertile flowers last from mid-summer to fall. Pruning can be done after flowering. Remove spent flowers and cut out some of the older growth to encourage young replacement growth. **'Snowflake'** bears clusters of double flowers 12–15" (30–45 cm) long that open white and fade to pink as they age. The flowers are so heavy that they cause the stems to arch towards the ground. This cultivar prefers partial shade. (Zones 4–8.)

PESTS & PROBLEMS

Occasional problems for hydrangeas include gray mold, slugs, powdery mildew, rust, ringspot virus and leaf spot. Hot sun and excessive wind will dry out the petals and turn them brown.

H. macrophylla

Softwood cuttings of H. arborescens *are easy to root.*

Incense-Cedar

Calocedrus decurrens

Features: foliage, habit, cones **Habit:** columnar, evergreen tree
Height: 30–50' (9–15 m) **Spread:** 6–30' (1.8–9 m)
Planting: B & B, container; spring, fall **Zones:** 5–8

*T*he smell of Western Redcedar reminds many people of the winter holidays, but the less common Incense-cedar releases its pungent scent on hot summer days. The evergreen foliage makes a great screen, and this tree loves the country life—it grows tall and columnar without any special pruning at all, and it is able to survive the hot, dry summers of the southern and eastern parts of our region.

The foliage of this very arborvitae-like tree is aromatic when crushed.

GROWING

Incense-cedar will grow equally well in **full sun, partial shade** or **light shade.** Ideally the soil should be **fertile, moist** and **well drained,** but poor soils will be tolerated. This tree dislikes urban conditions and exposed sites. It is both drought and heat tolerant.

Pruning is rarely required. Damaged or dead branches can be removed as needed.

TIPS

Incense-cedar makes an excellent specimen tree, but only in large gardens and parks. It is too big for smaller gardens.

RECOMMENDED

C. decurrens is native to California and Oregon, and in the wild it may grow as tall as 170' (50 m). **'Aureo-variegata'** has green foliage splashed with yellow markings.

PESTS & PROBLEMS

Rare occurrences of rust or heart rot are possible.

Japanese Acuba
Japanese Aucuba, Spotted Laurel
Aucuba japonica

Features: foliage, fruit, adaptability **Habit:** bushy, rounded, evergreen shrub
Height: 3–10' (1–3 m) **Spread:** 3–9' (1–2.7 m)
Planting: container; spring, fall **Zones:** 6–9

This tough, tropical-looking evergreen grows beautifully in containers, under trees and near the ocean. Not only is it adaptable, it boasts colorful foliage and gorgeous red fall berries. A large Japanese Acuba in a protected corner provides a perfect play area or campsite under the branches, where kids can pretend they're in a jungle or on a pre-historic adventure.

GROWING

Japanese Acuba grows well in all light conditions from **full sun** to **full shade.** Plants with variegated foliage show the best leaf color in partial shade. The soil should be of **average fertility, humus rich, moist** and **well drained.** This drought-resistant plant adapts to most soil conditions as long as the soil is not waterlogged, and it tolerates urban pollution and salty, windy coastal conditions. In Zone 6 it will benefit from protection from sun in summer and wind in winter.

Shrubs require no pruning; hedges can be trimmed in spring.

TIPS

Japanese Acuba can be used in deeply shaded locations where no other plants will grow. It can also be used as a specimen, in a large planter and as a hedge or screen. Under the canopy of larger trees, this shrub will compete well for moisture and nutrients.

Generally, both a male and female plant must be present for the females to set fruit. The fruits are **not edible.**

RECOMMENDED

A. japonica has a neatly rounded habit and glossy green leaves. It grows 6–10' (1.8–3 m) tall and spreads 5–9' (1.5–2.7 m). Female plants develop red berries in fall. Many cultivars are available, usually developed for their variegated foliage. **'Crotonifolia'** has yellow-splotched leaves. **'Rozannie'** is a compact plant with dark green leaves. It grows 36" (90 cm) tall, with an equal spread. It has male and female parts in the same flower,

'Crotonifolia' (this page)

rather than on separate plants, so only one plant is needed in order to have fruit. **'Variegata'** (Gold Dust Plant) is female, with yellow-spotted leaves.

PESTS & PROBLEMS

Blight may kill off parts of the plant. These damaged parts should be removed. Root rot and leaf spot may also occur.

This tough plant is tolerant of frost, deep shade, pollution and neglect. The young leaves may blacken in very hot sun.

Japanese Kerria
Kerria japonica

Features: mid- to late-spring flowers, habit
Habit: suckering, mounding, deciduous shrub
Height: 3–10' (1–3 m) **Spread:** 4–10' (1.2–3 m)
Planting: B & B, container; spring, fall **Zones:** 4–9

The fluffy, round blossoms that appear each spring on Japanese Kerria look much like a cheerleader's golden pom-poms. When the spring breeze rustles through this spreading bush, the pom-poms seem to be cheering for an end to winter weather. Tuck a golden Japanese Kerria under tall evergreen trees, with rhododendrons planted as a backdrop and purple Ajuga blooming below.

GROWING

Japanese Kerria prefers **light shade, partial shade** or **full shade.** The soil should be of **average fertility** and **well drained.** Fewer flowers will appear on a plant grown in soil that is too fertile.

Prune after flowering. Cut the flowering shoots back to young side shoots or strong buds, or right to the ground. The entire plant can be cut back to the ground after flowering if it becomes overgrown and needs rejuvenating.

TIPS

Japanese Kerria is useful in group plantings, woodland gardens and shrub or mixed borders.

Most flowers emerge in spring, but some may appear sporadically in summer.

RECOMMENDED

K. japonica grows 3–6' (0.9–1.8 m) tall and spreads 4–8' (1.2–2.5 m). It has single yellow flowers. **'Aurea-variegata'** has yellow leaf margins. **'Pleniflora'** has double flowers; it grows 10' (3 m) tall, with an equal spread. Its habit is more upright than that of the species.

PESTS & PROBLEMS

Leaf spot, leaf blight, twig blight, canker and root rot may occur but are not serious.

The distinct yellow-green to bright green, arching stems of Japanese Kerria add interest to the winter landscape.

Jasmine
Jasminum

Features: fragrant flowers, habit
Habit: deciduous; trailing shrubs or woody climbers
Height: 3–40' (1–12 m) **Spread:** 4–15' (1.2–4.5 m)
Planting: container; spring **Zones:** 6–10

Bring the sweet smell of a tropical island to your garden with jasmine. Make the most of the scent by growing a plant near a deck or patio, and bring cuttings indoors to enjoy in a fresh arrangement. Make a jasmine the focal point of a fragrant theme garden by training one up a trellis near other sweet-smelling favorites such as lilac, honeysuckle and roses.

GROWING

Jasmines grow well in **full sun** or **partial shade.** The soil should be **fertile** and **well drained.** These drought-tolerant plants adapt to most soil conditions.

Prune jasmines after they finish flowering. Thin out shoots on climbing plants as needed to train them to grow where you want them to. On shrubby plants, thin out one-third of the oldest growth each year.

TIPS

Climbing jasmines can be trained to grow up trellises, walls, fences, arbors or even over shrubs. Lilacs and forsythias are good choices because they flower early in the season and then provide little interest afterward. Shrubby jasmines can be grown in a shrub or mixed border. Both types can be grown in planters—a good idea in regions where these plants aren't hardy, because the whole plant can be moved indoors to a bright window or sheltered porch out of the winter cold.

J. nudiflorum (this page)

RECOMMENDED

J. nudiflorum (Winter Jasmine) is a spreading, mounding plant with slender, trailing branches that root where they touch the ground. It grows 3–10' (1–3 m) tall and spreads 4–10' (1.2–3 m). In winter and early spring, this species bears unscented yellow flowers. (Zones 6–9.)

J. officinale (Common White Jasmine) is a twining climber that can be trained to form a trailing shrub. It can grow up to 40' (12 m) tall as a climber, but it can be kept as a large shrub 10–15' (3–4.5 m) in height and spread. It can also be grown as a houseplant in a bright window. From summer to early fall it bears fragrant white flowers. (Zones 8–10.)

PESTS & PROBLEMS

Problems are rarely serious, but jasmines may be affected by root rot, leaf spot, viruses, aphids, scale insects or mealybugs.

The familiar jasmine scent is derived from the essential oil of J. officinale, *used for perfumes, food flavoring and aromatherapy.*

Juniper

Juniperus

Features: variety of color, size and habit; foliage
Habit: evergreen; conical or columnar trees,
rounded or spreading shrubs, prostrate groundcovers
Height: 0.5–70' (0.2–21 m) **Spread:** 1–25' (0.3–7.5 m)
Planting: B & B, container; spring, fall **Zones:** 2–9

Often wrongly accused of being boring, the hard-to-kill, versatile junipers have the beauty of diversity. So many forms, colors and textures are available that there seems to be a juniper for just about every landscaping dilemma. The tall, narrow forms of the upright junipers serve as exclamation points in a mixed border or perennial garden, and the low, ground-hugging junipers grow into weed-blocking carpets. Some junipers even become small evergreen trees, suitable for space-limited gardens.

GROWING

Junipers prefer **full sun,** but tolerate light shade. Ideally the soil should be of **average fertility** and **well drained,** but these plants tolerate most conditions.

Though these evergreens rarely need pruning, they tolerate it well. They can be used for topiary and can be trimmed in summer as required to maintain their shape or limit their size.

TIPS

With the wide variety of junipers available, there are endless uses for them in the garden. They make prickly barriers and hedges, and they can be used in borders, as specimens or in groups. The larger species can be used to form windbreaks, while the low-growing species can be used in rock gardens and as groundcovers.

J. horizontalis
J. communis 'Hornibrookii'

The prickly foliage gives some gardeners a rash. It is a good idea to wear long sleeves and gloves when handling junipers. Juniper 'berries' are **poisonous** if eaten in quantity.

RECOMMENDED

J. chinensis (Chinese Juniper) is a conical tree or spreading shrub. It grows 50–70' (15–21 m) tall and spreads 15–20' (4.5–6 m). Many cultivars

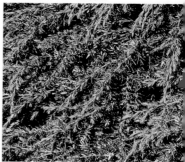

J. sabina (below)

J. squamata

have been developed from this species. **'Hetzii'** is a large, upright, spreading shrub that may reach 5–15' (1.5–4.5 m) in height, with an equal spread. **'Pfitzeriana'** is a wide-spreading shrub that grows 5–10' (1.5–3 m) tall, with an equal spread. 'Hetzii' and 'Pfitzeriana' still appear in many gardens, but they are beginning to be passed over in favor of the new, attractive, more reasonably sized cultivars derived from them. **'Hetzii Columnaris'** forms an attractive, narrow pyramid about 20' (6 m) tall. **'Pfitzeriana Compacta'** is a dwarf form that grows about 4' (1.2 m) tall, with an equal or greater spread. **Var.** *sargentii* (Sargent Juniper) is a low-growing, spreading variety. It grows only 12–24" (30–60 cm) tall, but can spread to 9' (2.7 m). (Zones 3–9.)

J. communis (Common Juniper) is a native species that is widespread over the Northern Hemisphere. It grows in two distinct forms, as a spreading shrub or as a small, columnar tree. The size varies; plants may reach 2–20' (0.5–6 m) in height and

Junipers come in all shapes and sizes and can suit almost any garden. Grow them in the sun to avoid open, straggly growth.

3–15' (1–4.5 m) in width. **'Hornibrookii'** is a low
shrub up to 20" (50 cm) tall, spreading 4' (1.2 m)
or more. It is silvery green in summer but may
turn brownish in winter. (Zones 2–6.)

J. conferta (Shore Juniper) is a dense, bushy,
prostrate shrub. It grows 12–24" (30–60 cm) tall
and spreads 9' (2.7 m) or more. **'Blue Pacific'** is
an attractive, heat-tolerant groundcover with a
dense, trailing habit and blue-green needles.
'Emerald Sea' is more salt and cold tolerant; it
forms a wide-spreading, dense, emerald green
mat. (Zones 5–9.)

J. horizontalis (Creeping Juniper) is a prostrate,
creeping groundcover that is native to the Rocky
Mountains and to boreal regions across North
America. It grows 12–24" (30–60 cm) tall and
spreads up to 8' (2.5 m). This juniper is attractive
when grown on top of rock walls, where it can
cascade down. The foliage is blue-green and takes
on a purple hue in winter. **'Bar Harbor'** grows

J. horizontalis (this page)

*The blue 'berries'
(actually fleshy
cones) are used to
flavor meat dishes
and to give gin its
distinctive character.
They also make a
nice addition to
potpourri.*

12" (30 cm) tall and spreads 6–10' (1.8–3 m). The foliage turns a distinct purple in winter. This cultivar is a good choice for coastal gardens. **'Wiltonii'** ('Blue Rug') is very low growing, with trailing branches and silvery blue foliage. It grows 4–6" (10–15 cm) tall and spreads 6–8' (1.8–2.5 m). (Zones 3–9.)

J. procumbens (Japanese Garden Juniper) is a wide-spreading, stiff-branched, low shrub. It grows 12–36" (30–90 cm) tall and 6–15' (1.8–4.5 m) wide. **'Nana'** is a dwarf, compact, mat-forming shrub. It grows 12–24" (30–60 cm) tall and spreads 6–12' (1.8–3.5 m). (Zones 4–9.)

J. sabina (Savin Juniper) is a variable, spreading to erect shrub. It grows 4–15' (1.2–4.5 m) tall and may spread 5–20' (1.5–6 m). The cultivar **'Broadmoor'** is a low spreader with erect branchlets. It grows 24–36" (60–90 cm) tall and spreads up to 10' (3 m). (Zones 4–7.)

J. communis 'Hornibrookii'

J. conferta 'Emerald Sea'

J. scopulorum (Rocky Mountain Juniper) is a rounded or spreading tree or shrub, native to western North America. It grows 30–50' (9–15 m) tall and spreads 3–20' (1–6 m). **'Skyrocket'** is a very narrow, columnar tree with gray-green needles. It grows up to 20' (6 m) tall, but spreads only 12–24" (30–60 cm). **'Tolleson's Weeping'** has arching branches and pendulous, silvery blue, string-like foliage. It grows about 20' (6 m) tall and spreads 10' (3 m). It is sometimes grafted to create a small, weeping standard tree. This cultivar can be used in a large planter. (Zones 3–7.)

J. squamata (Singleseed Juniper) forms a prostrate or low, spreading shrub or a small, upright tree. It grows up to 30' (9 m) tall and spreads 3–25' (1–7.5 m). It is rarely grown in favor of the cultivars. **'Blue Carpet'** forms a low groundcover with blue-gray needles. It grows 8–12" (20–30 cm) high and spreads 4–5' (1.2–1.5 m). **'Blue Star'** is a compact, rounded shrub with silvery blue needles. It grows 12–36" (30–90 cm) tall and spreads 3–4' (0.9–1.2 m). (Zones 4–8.)

PESTS & PROBLEMS
Although junipers are tough plants, occasional problems may be caused by aphids, bagworm, bark beetles, canker, caterpillars, cedar-apple rust, leaf miners, mites, scale insects and twig blight.

J. scopulorum 'Skyrocket'

Juniper was used traditionally to purify homes affected by sickness and death.

Kalmia
Mountain Laurel
Kalmia latifolia

Features: foliage, late-spring to mid-summer flowers
Habit: large, dense, bushy, evergreen shrub
Height: 3–15' (1–4.5 m) **Spread:** 3–15' (1–4.5 m)
Planting: spring, fall **Zones:** 4–9

A more delicate, less vigorous relative of rhododendrons, and one that also loves the cool west coast, Kalmia has been described as the most beautiful blooming shrub in the world. It may also be one of the most finicky. Still, meeting its unique soil and light requirements is a challenge worth attempting, because the clusters of bell-shaped blooms are so exquisite that examining one up close always makes me proud to have Kalmia in the garden.

Kalmia's ridged, star-like flower buds look as if they were created with a cake-decorating tool.

GROWING

Kalmia prefers **light or partial shade,** but it tolerates full sun if the soil remains consistently moist. The soil should be of **average to high fertility, moist, acidic** and **well drained.** A mulch of leaf mold or pine needles will protect the roots of this drought-sensitive plant from drying out.

Little pruning is required, but spent flowerheads can be removed in summer and awkward shoots removed as needed.

TIPS

Use Kalmia in a shaded part of a shrub or mixed border, in a woodland garden or combined with other acid- and shade-loving plants such as rhododendrons.

Do not make a tea with or otherwise ingest Kalmia **flowers or foliage,** which are extremely **poisonous**.

RECOMMENDED

K. latifolia grows 7–15' (2–4.5 m) tall, with an equal spread. It has glossy green leaves and pink or white flowers. Cultivars are more commonly grown. **'Alpine Pink'** has a very dense habit and dark pink buds that open to light pink flowers. **'Elf'** is a dwarf cultivar that grows to 36" (90 cm) in height and width. It has pink buds, white flowers and quite small leaves. **'Ostbo Red'** is an old cultivar with bright red buds and light pink flowers, and **'Silver Dollar'** has large white flowers.

'Ostbo Red'

PESTS & PROBLEMS

Kalmia suffers from no serious problems, but it can be affected by borers, lace bugs, leaf blight, leaf gall, leaf spot, powdery mildew, scale insects and weevils.

Katsura-Tree

Cercidiphyllum japonicum

Features: summer and fall foliage, habit
Habit: rounded or spreading, often multi-stemmed, deciduous tree
Height: 10–70' (3–21 m) **Spread:** 10–70' (3–21 m)
Planting: B & B, container; spring **Zones:** 4–8

A lovely specimen, the first weeping Katsura-tree I ever met was perfectly positioned in the curve of a perennial garden with bulbs blooming at her feet, pendulous branches arching like a waterfall to the ground. Give this tree a frame of empty space around the branches, and then call attention to the tint of red in the golden autumn leaves. Plant rusty-colored 'Autumn Joy' sedum nearby or a groundcover of crimson-berried cotoneaster to echo the color of the heart-shaped leaves.

GROWING

Katsura-tree grows equally well in **full sun** or **partial shade.** The soil should be **fertile, humus rich, neutral to acidic, moist** and **well drained.** This tree will become established more quickly if watered regularly during dry spells for the first year or two.

Pruning is unnecessary. Damaged branches can be removed as needed.

TIPS

Katsura-tree is useful as a specimen or shade tree. The species is quite large and is best used in large gardens. The cultivar 'Pendula' is quite wide spreading, but can be used in a smaller garden than the species.

This tree is native to eastern Asia, and the delicate foliage blends well into Japanese-style gardens.

RECOMMENDED

C. japonicum grows 40–70' (12–21 m) tall, with an equal or sometimes greater spread. It is a slow-growing tree that takes a long time to exceed 40' (12 m). The heart-shaped, blue-green foliage turns yellow and orange in fall and develops a spicy scent. **'Pendula'** is one of the most elegant weeping trees available. It is usually grafted to a standard and grows 10–25' (3–7.5 m) tall, with an equal or greater spread. Mounding, cascading branches sweep the ground, giving the entire tree the appearance of a waterfall tumbling over rocks. Ungrafted specimens of 'Pendula' may grow as tall as the species; they vary in the degree to which the branches droop and sweep the ground. They are attractive, but not always as dramatic as the grafted specimens.

When in fall color, the leaves of Katsura-tree emit a spicy aroma.

C. japonicum *is the largest native deciduous tree in Japan and China, growing as tall as 130' (40 m) in the wild.*

'Pendula'

Kinnikinnick
Bearberry
Arctostaphylos uva-ursi

Features: late-spring flowers, fruit, foliage
Habit: low-growing, mat-forming, evergreen shrub
Height: 4–6" (10–15 cm) **Spread:** 18–48" (45–120 cm)
Planting: container; spring, fall **Zones:** 2–7

*T*his evergreen groundcover is something of a character in the garden, so the amusing name rings true. Kinnikinnick never seems to have a bad season, with its white spring blooms, red fall berries and evergreen foliage. It skips happily over the ground wherever it is planted, weaving under trees, spilling from rockeries and retaining walls and making a colorful carpet in woodland gardens.

GROWING
Kinnikinnick grows well in **full sun** or **partial shade.** The soil should be of **average to high fertility, acidic** and **moist.** Generally no pruning is required.

TIPS
Kinnikinnick can be used as a groundcover or can be included in a rock garden. It is a good plant for coastal gardens because it is tolerant of salty seaside conditions.

Once established, Kinnikinnick is a vigorous, wide-spreading grower but it can be slow to get started. Use mulch to keep the weeds down while the plant is becoming established.

RECOMMENDED

*A. **uva-ursi*** is a native shrub with white flowers that appear in late spring, followed by berries that ripen to bright red. It grows 4–6" (10–15 cm) tall and spreads 18–20" (45–50 cm). The cultivars share the white flowers and red fruit but also have leaves that turn bright red in winter. **'Vancouver Jade'** is a low-growing plant with arching stems. It grows 6" (15 cm) high and spreads 18" (45 cm). This cultivar is resistant to the leaf spot that may afflict these plants. **'Wood's Compact'** spreads about 36–48" (90–120 cm).

PESTS & PROBLEMS

Possible problems include bud and leaf galls as well as fungal diseases of the leaves, stems and fruit.

'Vancouver Jade'

'Kinnikinnick' is said to be an Algonquian term meaning 'smoking mixture,' reflecting that traditional use for the leaves.

Kiwi

Actinidia

Features: early-summer flowers,
edible fruit, habit
Habit: woody, climbing, deciduous vines
Height: 15–30' (4.5–9 m) **Spread:** indefinite
Planting: spring, fall **Zones:** 3–8

*A*mong the most enthusiastic vines, kiwis are for those who think they don't have a green thumb—the growing energy these plants possess often rubs off on the gardener. Put all that foliage and growth to work in your garden, and use a kiwi on a huge screen for privacy or over a large pergola for shade. Watch it swallow a small arbor with exuberant growth within a single season.

These species make good substitutes for A. chinensis (A. deliciosa)*, the commercially available brown, hairy-skinned kiwi. The fruits of* A. arguta *and* A. kolomikta *are hairless and high in Vitamin C, potassium and fiber.*

GROWING

Kiwi vines grow best in **full sun.** The soil should be **fertile** and **well drained.** These plants require **shelter** from strong winds.

Prune in late winter. Plants can be trimmed to fit the area they've been given, or, if greater fruit production is desired, side shoots can be cut back to two or three buds from the main stems.

TIPS

These vines need a sturdy structure to twine around. Pergolas, arbors and sufficiently large and sturdy fences provide good support. Given a trellis against a wall, a tree or some other upright structure, kiwis will twine upwards all summer. Don't be afraid to prune them back. They can also be grown in containers.

RECOMMENDED

A. arguta (Hardy Kiwi, Bower Actinidia) grows 20–30' (6–9 m) high, but can be trained to grow lower through the judicious use of pruning shears. The leaves are dark green and heart shaped. White flowers are followed by smooth-skinned, greenish-yellow, edible fruit.

A. kolomikta (Variegated Kiwi Vine, Kolomikta Actinidia) grows 15–20' (4.5–6 m) high. The green leaves are strongly variegated with pink and white, and some of the leaves may be entirely white. White flowers are followed by smooth-skinned, greenish-yellow, edible fruit.

PESTS & PROBLEMS

Kiwis are occasionally afflicted with fungal diseases, but these are not a serious concern.

To produce fruit, male and female kiwi plants must be grown together. Containers are often sold with plants of both sexes in the same pot.

A. arguta

Larch

Larix

Features: summer and fall foliage, cones, habit
Habit: pyramidal, deciduous conifers
Height: 30–100' (9–30 m) **Spread:** 12–40' (3.5–12 m)
Planting: B & B, container; early spring **Zones:** 1–7

A golden larch amidst a grove of evergreens is an arresting sight when autumn turns the needles of this deciduous conifer golden yellow. For this reason plant any larch where it has a dark backdrop, perhaps on the edge of a wooded area, and add a red-berried groundcover such as Kinnikinnick or a cotoneaster under the spreading branches for an autumn festival of color.

GROWING

Larches grow best in **full sun.** The soil should be of **average fertility, acidic, moist** and **well drained.** Though tolerant of most conditions, these trees don't like dry or chalky soils. Pruning is rarely required.

TIPS

Larches make interesting specimen trees. They are among the few needled trees that lose their foliage each year. In fall the needles turn golden yellow before dropping, and in winter the cones stand out on the bare branches.

Larches are good trees for attracting birds to the garden.

RECOMMENDED

L. decidua (European Larch) is a large, narrow, pyramidal tree. It grows 70–100' (21–30 m) tall and spreads 12–30' (3.5–9 m). **'Pendula'** has a weeping habit and is usually grafted to a standard. Specimens vary greatly from the bizarre to the elegant. (Zones 3–6.)

L. kaempferi (Japanese Larch) grows 50–100' (15–30 m) tall and spreads 15–40' (4.5–12 m). It has pendulous branchlets. The summer color of the needles is more blue than that of the European Larch. Fall color is excellent. (Zones 4–7.)

L. laricina (Tamarack) is an open, pyramidal tree with drooping branchlets. It is very tolerant of moist soils because it naturally grows in bogs. It grows 30–80' (9–25 m) tall and spreads 15–30' (4.5–9 m). (Zones 1–5.)

PESTS & PROBLEMS

Problems may be caused by aphids, case bearers, caterpillars, needle blight, rust and sawflies.

Be prepared to reassure your neighbors that your larch is not dying when it loses its needles in fall.

L. laricina (above), *L. decidua* 'Pendula' (below)

Leucothoe
Rainbow Bush
Leucothoe

Features: spring flowers, summer foliage **Habit:** upright, bushy, evergreen shrubs
Height: 3–6' (1–1.8 m) **Spread:** 3–10' (1–3 m)
Planting: container; spring **Zones:** 5–9

*I*f ever a shrub seemed touched with nature's paintbrush, 'Rainbow' leucothoe is the one. The shiny, pointed leaves are splotched and splattered as if the pink, rose and purple colors were truly flung from an artist's brush. I display mine against a plain wall on the shaded, north side of the house, where the handsome foliage stands out proudly. When used in a woodland or shade garden, the always healthy evergreen leaves provide form and texture, especially during the winter months. Use leucothoes with rhododendrons, as a background for azaleas or as understory plants for maples and tall evergreens.

Be sure to give leucothoes moist, well-drained soil and shelter from the direct sun to ensure optimum performance.

GROWING

Leucothoes grow well in **light shade, partial shade** or **full shade.** The soil should be **fertile, acidic, humus rich** and **moist.**

Pruning is rarely needed. Old plants can be rejuvenated by cutting them back to within 6" (15 cm) of the ground.

TIPS

Leucothoes make excellent foliage plants. Include them in woodland gardens and shaded borders.

RECOMMENDED

L. davisiae (Western Leucothoe, Sierra Laurel) is an upright, suckering, evergreen shrub that is native to Oregon and California. It grows about 36" (90 cm) tall and spreads 5' (1.5 m). In early summer this species bears white flowers in upright clusters. (Zones 8–9.)

L. fontanesiana (Drooping Leucothoe) is an upright, evergreen shrub with arching branches. It grows 3–6' (1–1.8 m) tall and spreads 3–10' (1–3 m). The white flowers are borne in drooping clusters. The cultivar **'Rainbow'** (Rainbow Bush) is one of the most commonly used leucothoes. It grows 5' (1.5 m) tall and spreads 6' (1.8 m). The green leaves are mottled with cream and pink. Note that the foliage color can fade in full sun. (Zones 5–8.)

Cut the colorful foliage and use it in indoor arrangements.

L. fontanesiana (this page)

PESTS & PROBLEMS

Possible problems include leaf spot, powdery mildew, leaf gall, lace bugs and scale insects. Root rot may occur in very wet soil. Tip growth may turn black and die in harsh or windy locations.

Lilac

Syringa

Features: late-spring to early-summer flowers, habit
Habit: rounded or suckering, deciduous shrubs or small trees
Height: 4–30' (1.2–9 m) **Spread:** 4–25' (1.2–7.5 m)
Planting: B & B, container; late winter, early spring **Zones:** 3–8

*T*he name itself conjures up such fragrant memories that it is now synonymous with soft purple and with sweet scents, reminding us of old-fashioned gardens and Sunday rides in the country. But make way for the new lilacs, as compact, bushy forms turn heads and noses in contemporary gardens and tidy entryway designs. Pair lilacs with summer-blooming buddleia or butterfly bush, or use one as the focal point in a fragrant theme garden with daphne, roses and honeysuckle.

GROWING

Lilacs grow best in **full sun.** The soil should be **fertile, humus rich** and **well drained.** These plants tolerate open, windy locations, and the improved air circulation helps keep powdery mildew at bay. Clear up leaves in fall to help discourage overwintering pests.

Most lilacs need little pruning. Deadhead as much as possible to keep plants neat. On established French Lilac plants, one-third to one-half of the growth can be cut right back each year after flowering. This treatment will make way for vigorous young growth and prevent the plants from becoming leggy and unattractive.

TIPS

Include lilacs in a shrub or mixed border or use them to create an informal hedge. Japanese Tree Lilac can be used as a specimen tree.

The wonderfully fragrant flowers have inspired the development of eight or nine hundred cultivars of S. vulgaris.

S. vulgaris (this page)

S. reticulata 'Ivory Silk' (this page)

RECOMMENDED

S. meyeri (Meyer Lilac) is a compact, rounded shrub that grows 4–8' (1.2–2.5 m) tall and spreads 4–12' (1.2–3.5 m). It bears fragrant pink or lavender flowers in late spring and early summer. (Zones 3–7.)

S. microphylla (Littleleaf Lilac) is an upright, broad-spreading shrub. It grows 6' (1.8 m) tall and spreads 9–12' (2.7–3.5 m). It bears fragrant, lilac-pink flowers in early summer and sometimes again in fall. This is a very neat shrub with small, tidy leaves and attractive, airy clusters of flowers. (Zones 4–8.)

S. reticulata (Japanese Tree Lilac) is a rounded large shrub or small tree that grows 20–30' (6–9 m) tall and spreads 15–25' (4.5–7.5 m). It bears white flowers in early summer. This species and its cultivars are resistant to the troublesome powdery mildew, scale insects and borers. **'Ivory Silk'** has a more compact habit and produces more flowers than the species. It grows 10–12' (3–3.5 m) tall and spreads 6' (1.8 m). (Zones 3–7.)

S. vulgaris (French Lilac, Common Lilac) is the plant most people think of when they think of lilacs. It grows 8–22' (2.5–7 m) tall, spreads 6–22' (1.8–7 m) and bears fragrant, lilac-colored flowers in late spring and

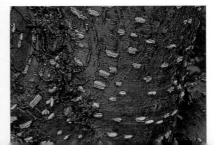

early summer. This suckering, spreading shrub has an irregular habit, but consistent maintenance pruning will keep it neat and in good condition. Many cultivars are available, of which the following are but a few examples. **'Alba'** has white single flowers. **'Belle de Nancy'** has pink double flowers. **'Charles Joly'** has magenta double flowers. **'Mme Lemoine'** has large, white double flowers. **'President Lincoln'** has very fragrant, blue single flowers.

PESTS & PROBLEMS

Powdery mildew, leaf spot, borers, caterpillars, scale insects and root-knot nematodes are all possible troublemakers for lilacs.

For the best flowering, plant lilacs where they will get some frost.

Magnolia
Magnolia

Features: flowers, fruit, foliage, habit, bark
Habit: upright to spreading, deciduous or evergreen shrubs or trees
Height: 10–60' (3–18 m) **Spread:** 10–50' (3–15 m)
Planting: B & B, container; winter, early spring **Zones:** 3–9

Sweet-smelling Southern belle of the flower garden, the evergreen Southern Magnolia and its spectacular blooms have inspired poets and artists for generations. Young gardeners may wait impatiently for the fine, fat buds of the early-blooming Star Magnolia to open and announce the end of winter, but more mature gardeners learn to enjoy this tree longer by appreciating the soft fur, pointed shape and dramatically slow opening of the buds themselves. Use double-flowering 'Angélique' tulips at the base of a spring-blooming magnolia to underscore the elegance and formality of its large blooms.

GROWING

Magnolias grow well in **full sun** or **partial shade.** The soil should be **fertile, humus rich, acidic, moist** and **well drained.** A summer mulch will help keep the roots cool and the soil moist. Very little pruning is needed. When plants are young, thin out a few branches to encourage an attractive habit. Avoid transplanting; if necessary, do so in early spring.

TIPS

Magnolias are used as specimens and the smaller species in borders.

Avoid planting magnolias where the morning sun will encourage the blooms to open too early in the season. The blossoms can be damaged by cold, wind and rain.

RECOMMENDED

M. denudata (Yulan Magnolia) is a spreading, deciduous tree 20–30' (6–9 m) tall, with an equal spread. White flowers appear in spring before the leaves emerge. (Zones 5–9.)

M. grandiflora (Southern Magnolia) is a dense, broad, pyramidal, evergreen tree. It grows 20–60' (6–18 m) tall, with a spread of 50' (15 m). Fragrant white flowers appear in mid-spring. **'Little Gem'** is a more upright, compact tree, with smaller flowers. It grows 20' (6 m) tall and spreads 10' (3 m). (Zones 7–9.)

M. stellata

Despite their often fuzzy coats, magnolia flower buds are frost sensitive in cold winter climates.

M. x *loebneri* (Loebner Magnolia) is an upright, rounded, deciduous shrub or small tree. It grows 20–30' (6–9 m) tall, with an equal spread. It bears fragrant white flowers in midspring. **'Ballerina'** grows 15–20' (4.5–6 m) tall. The very fragrant flowers have about 30 long, narrow petals, giving the blossoms a fluffy appearance. **'Merrill'** is a densely branched tree. It grows to the same height as the species, but is rarely as wide. (Zones 5–9.)

M. sieboldii (Oyama Magnolia) is a spreading, deciduous shrub or tree. It generally grows 10–15' (3–4.5 m) tall, but can reach 25' (7.5 m). It spreads up to 30' (9 m). Fragrant white flowers last from late spring to late summer. (Zones 6–9.)

M. x *soulangeana* (Saucer Magnolia) is a rounded, spreading, deciduous shrub or tree. It grows 20–30' (6–9 m) tall, with an equal spread. Pink, purple or white flowers emerge

M. x *soulangeana*

in mid- to late spring. **'Alexandrina'** is an upright tree. Its flower petals are pink on the outside and white on the inside. **'Brozzonii'** has white flowers with a pinkish-purple tinge on the base of the petals. (Zones 5–9.)

M. stellata (Star Magnolia) is a compact, bushy or spreading, deciduous shrub or small tree. It grows 10–20' (3–6 m) tall and spreads 10–15' (3–4.5 m). Many-petalled, fragrant white flowers appear in early to mid-spring. The species is hardy in Zones 4–9. **'Centennial'** is a vigorous, upright cultivar that is cold hardy to Zone 3. Its white flowers have 28 to 32 petals.

PESTS & PROBLEMS
Possible problems affecting magnolias include leaf spot (common in coastal regions), canker, dieback, treehoppers, powdery mildew, scale insects, snails, thrips and weevils.

M. x *soulangeana* (left & below)

Maple

Acer

Features: foliage, bark, fruit, fall color, form, flowers
Habit: small, multi-stemmed, deciduous trees or large shrubs
Height: 6–50' (1.8–15 m)
Spread: 10–40' (3–12 m)
Planting: B & B, container; preferably spring
Zones: 2–9

Maples are attractive all year long. In spring the flowers, though not showy, are delicate and pretty. In summer the attractive foliage comes in many forms and colors and is accented by the winged fruits, called *samaras*, which hang in clusters and often ripen to a brilliant red. The renowned vibrant fall leaf color ranges from yellow and orange to red and purple. In winter the bark, which is sometimes exfoliating, and the artistic branch structures provide interest while the garden lies dormant.

The sap of A. saccharum is used to make the famous, and delicious, maple syrup, but other maples can also be tapped for the sweet sap.

GROWING

Generally maples do well in **full sun** or **light shade,** though this varies from species to species. The soil should be **fertile, moist,** high in **organic** matter and **well drained.**

Pruning is largely up to you. Maples can be allowed to grow naturally, with dead, damaged or diseased branches removed at any time. These trees respond well to pruning, however, and can even be used to create bonsai specimens. The amount of pruning depends on how much time you have and on what purpose the tree will serve in the garden. Informal and naturalistic gardens will require less pruning, while a formal garden may demand more effort. In general, pruning should take place in mid-summer to late fall.

A. japonicum (above)
A. palmatum var. *atropurpureum* (below)

TIPS

Maples can be used as specimen trees or as large elements in shrub or mixed borders. Some are useful as understory plants bordering wooded areas; others can be grown in pots

on patios or terraces. Few Japanese gardens are without the attractive smaller maples, which are often used for bonsai.

RECOMMENDED

The following are small maple species, suitable for most gardens.

A. circinatum (Vine Maple, Oregon Vine Maple) is a Pacific Northwest native that closely resembles *A. palmatum*. It grows naturally as an understory tree or shrub in damp areas and along stream banks. It often becomes a multi-stemmed tree 10–20' (3–6 m) in height, with a greater spread. This maple is elegant in form and texture, with bright red-green bark and lovely layered foliage. The fall color ranges from golden, in the shade, to fire-engine red, in open sites. (Zones 6–9.)

A. ginnala (Amur Maple) is a tree that is both attractive and extremely hardy; it can withstand winter temperatures as low as −50° F (−46° C). It also adapts to many soil types and a wide pH range. This species grows 15–25' (4.5–7.5 m) tall,

A. palmatum var. *atropurpureum* (above), *A. palmatum* (below)

with an equal or greater spread. It can be grown as a large, multi-stemmed shrub or it can be pruned to form a small tree. Amur Maple responds well to pruning and in cold climates is often used in place of the tender Japanese Maple (*A. palmatum*) in Japanese-style gardens. This tree has attractive dark green leaves, bright red samaras and smooth bark with distinctive vertical striping. The fall foliage is often a brilliant crimson. The color develops best in full sun, but the tree will also grow well in light shade. This is a popular tree for patios and terraces because it can be grown in a large planter. (Zones 2–8.)

A. palmatum (above & center)

A. japonicum (Fullmoon Maple, Japanese Maple) grows about 30' (9 m) tall, with a spread usually equal to or greater than the height. This tree dislikes very hot and very cold weather, making it an excellent candidate for the mild coastal climate. It has good fall color, with the foliage turning shades of yellow, orange and red. The best fall color is found on the cultivar **'Vitifolium.'** It has leaves that turn variegated shades of purple, red and orange. (Zones 5–7.)

Maple wood is hard and dense and is used for fine furniture construction and for some musical instruments.

A. japonicum (below)

A. palmatum (Japanese Maple) is considered by many gardeners to be one of the most beautiful and versatile trees available. Though many cultivars and varieties are quite small, the species itself generally grows 15–25' (4.5–7.5 m) tall, with an equal or greater spread. With enough space this tree may even reach 50' (15 m). Because it leafs out early in spring, this tree can be badly damaged or killed where late-spring frosts are common.

Two distinct groups of cultivars have been developed from *A. palmatum* varieties. Types without dissected leaves, derived from ***A. p.* var. *atropurpureum,*** are grown for their purple foliage, though many lose their purple coloring as summer progresses. Two that keep their color are **'Bloodgood'** and **'Moonfire,'** both of which grow to about 15' (4.5 m) tall. Types with dissected leaves, derived from ***A. p.* var. *dissectum,*** have foliage so deeply lobed and divided that it appears fern-like or even thread-like. The leaves can be green, as in the cultivar **'Waterfall,'** or red, as in **'Red Filigree Lace.'** These trees are generally small, growing to 6–10' (1.8–3 m) tall.

A. palmatum (this page)

Other cultivars are available that don't belong to either of these two groups, such as the popular **'Sangokaku'** (Coralbark Maple). It grows 20' (6 m) tall and spreads 15' (4.5 m). The stems of this plant can be salmon pink or bright red. The foliage is bright yellow. This cultivar makes a striking statement when planted against a house. (Zones 5–8.)

ALTERNATE SPECIES
The following species are attractive and desirable, but they can be difficult and expensive to obtain.

A. ginnala (above)

A. buergeranum (Trident Maple) can grow 20–35' (6–10 m) tall, with an equal spread. It is drought and heat tolerant, but may suffer winter damage if temperatures drop below −20° F (−29° C). This species prefers full sun and acidic soil. The bark develops scales that flake off, revealing lighter bark beneath. The fall color ranges from yellow to red. (Zones 5–9.)

A. griseum (Paperbark Maple) is attractive and adaptable to many conditions. It grows slowly to 20–35' (6–10 m) tall, with a width half or equal the height. Paperbark Maple is popular because of its orange-brown bark that peels and curls away from the trunk in papery strips. Unfortunately this species is difficult to propagate, making it very expensive, when it is even available. (Zones 4–8.)

A. palmatum var. dissectum (center)

PROBLEMS & PESTS
The maples discussed here are more disease and pest resistant than many other species. Leaf scorch can be prevented by watering the trees during hot, dry spells.

The wings of maple samaras act like miniature helicopter rotors and help in dispersal.

A. palmatum

Mock-Orange
Philadelphus

Features: early-summer flowers
Habit: rounded, deciduous shrubs with arching branches
Height: 1.5–12' (0.5–3.5 m) **Spread:** 1.5–12' (0.5–3.5 m)
Planting: spring, fall **Zones:** 3–8

I smelled my first mock-orange before I ever saw it. It was planted near the fenceline of a deserted house in the country, and when I discovered the pure white blooms amidst the brambles and weeds, I was much impressed with the survival skills of such a delicate-looking shrub. It was this same spirit of survival that made mock-oranges favorites of pioneer farmers.

GROWING
Mock-oranges grow well in **full sun, partial shade** or **light shade.** The soil should be of **average fertility, humus rich, moist** and **well drained.**

On established plants, remove one-third of the old wood each year, after flowering. Overgrown shrubs can be rejuvenated by cutting them right back to within 6" (15 cm) of the ground. Established mock-oranges transplant readily, although they have a huge mass of woody roots in relation to the amount of top growth.

TIPS

Include mock-oranges in shrub or mixed borders or in woodland gardens. Use them in groups to create barriers and screens.

RECOMMENDED

P. coronarius (Sweet Mock-orange) is an upright, broadly rounded shrub with fragrant white flowers. It grows 8–12' (2.5–3.5 m) tall, with an equal width. **'Aureus'** has bright yellow young foliage that matures to yellow-green. It grows 8' (2.5 m) tall and spreads 5' (1.5 m). **'Variegatus'** has leaves with creamy white margins. It grows 8' (2.5 m) tall and spreads 6' (1.8 m). (Zones 4–8.)

P. lewisii (Wild Mock-orange) is a vigorous native species that is variable in size. Abundant clusters of fragrant white flowers appear in late spring.

P. **'Nachez'** grows 8–10' (2.5–3 m) tall and 4–8' (1.2–2.5 m) wide. It bears slightly fragrant white flowers in late spring.

'Nachez' (above), *P.* x *virginalis* 'Minnesota Snowflake' (below)

P. **'Snowdwarf'** is a compact shrub with arching branches. It grows 18–36" (45–90 cm) tall and spreads 18" (45 cm). The fragrant white flowers appear in summer.

P. x *virginalis* **'Minnesota Snowflake'** is a hardy, dense, upright shrub. It grows 8' (2.5 m) tall and spreads 8–10' (2.5–3 m). It bears fragrant, white double flowers in midsummer. (Zones 3–7.)

PESTS & PROBLEMS

Mock-oranges may be affected by fungal spots, gray mold, powdery mildew, rust and scale insects, but these problems are rarely serious.

Ninebark

Physocarpus

Features: mid-spring or early-summer flowers, fruit, bark, foliage
Habit: upright, sometimes suckering, deciduous shrubs
Height: 2–10' (0.5–3 m) **Spread:** 2–15' (0.5–4.5 m)
Planting: spring, fall **Zones:** 2–10

*T*he name 'ninebark' describes the peeling, flecked bark that reveals layers of shiny brown skin beneath. You may not find nine layers of bark exposed, but the bare, flaking branches are especially interesting in the winter months. With their dry, beaked fruiting pods, these shrubs work well in front of maples or other trees with spectacular autumn color. Pair ninebarks with equally adaptable, easy-to-grow spireas.

The inflated seed pods give rise to the name Physocarpus, *from* physa *('bladder') and* carpos *('fruit').*

GROWING
Ninebarks grow well in **full sun** or **partial shade.**
The best leaf coloring develops in a sunny location. The soil should be **fertile, acidic, moist** and
well drained.

Little pruning is required, but you can remove
one-third of the old growth each year after flowering is finished to encourage vigorous new
growth.

TIPS
Ninebarks can be included in a shrub or mixed
border, or in a woodland or naturalistic garden.

RECOMMENDED
P. capitatus (Pacific Ninebark) is an upright
shrub that is native to the Pacific Northwest. It
grows about 10' (3 m) tall, with an equal spread.
The young leaves are hairy and sticky. In mid-
spring this shrub bears dense, rounded clusters
of tiny, creamy white flowers, followed by reddish
bunches of inflated seed pods. (Zones 6–10.)

P. monogynus (Mountain Ninebark) is a compact, upright shrub. It grows 24–36" (60–90 cm)
tall, with an equal spread. It bears white or light
pink flowers in late spring and early summer.
The fruits ripen to reddish green in late summer.
(Zones 5–8.)

P. opulifolius (Common Ninebark) is a suckering
shrub with long, arching branches and exfoliating
bark. It grows 5–10' (1.5–3 m) tall and spreads
6–15' (1.8–4.5 m). Light pink flowers in early
summer are followed by fruits that ripen to reddish green. (Zones 2–7.)

PESTS & PROBLEMS
Occasional problems with leaf spot, fire blight
and powdery mildew may occur.

*The exfoliating bark of these shrubs adds
interest to the winter landscape.*

P. opulifolius (this page)

Oak

Quercus

Features: summer and fall foliage, bark, habit, acorns
Habit: large, rounded, spreading, deciduous trees
Height: 30–120' (9–36 m)
Spread: 10–100' (3–30 m)
Planting: B & B, container; spring, fall **Zones:** 3–9

*I*n a roadside field near my home stands a single old oak tree, branches open wide like welcoming arms. Driving past one summer day, I noticed a family had spread out a blanket and were eating a picnic lunch in the perfect shade of that huge tree. Large, open parks and gardens are the best places to plant oak trees, and generations to come will appreciate the legacy you leave. The mighty oak tree grows tall and wide, so give it room to reach out its arms.

GROWING

Oaks grow well in **full sun** or **partial shade.** The soil should be **fertile, moist** and **well drained.** No pruning is needed. These trees can be difficult to establish. Transplant them only while they are young.

TIPS

Oaks are large trees best suited as specimens or groves in parks and large gardens. Do not disturb the ground around the base of an oak; these trees are very sensitive to changes in grade.

Oak acorns are generally **not edible.** Acorns of certain species are edible but usually must be processed first to leach out the bitter tannins.

RECOMMENDED

Q. alba (White Oak) is a rounded, spreading tree with peeling bark. It grows 50–100' (15–30 m) tall, with an equal spread. The leaves turn purple-red in fall.

Q. garryana (Garry Oak, Oregon White Oak) is a rounded, slow-growing tree that is native to much of the Pacific Northwest. It grows up to 80' (25 m) tall and may spread almost as wide, but it is much smaller on rocky sites. The branches have a pleasing gnarled appearance that is especially striking in winter. The acorns of this species are edible, but bitter. (Zones 3–8.)

Q. robur (English Oak) is a rounded, spreading tree. It grows 40–120' (12–36 m) tall and spreads 40–80' (12–25 m). The fall color is golden yellow. Also available are narrow, columnar cultivars that will grow in a smaller garden than the species. Most grow 60' (18 m) tall but spread only 10–15' (3–4.5 m). (Zones 3–8.)

Q. rubra (Red Oak) is a rounded, spreading tree that grows 60–75' (18–23 m) tall, with an equal spread. The fall color ranges from yellow to red-brown. This species prefers a moist, acidic soil. The roots are shallow, so be careful not to damage them if you cultivate the ground around the tree. (Zones 4–9.)

PESTS & PROBLEMS

The many possible problems are rarely serious: borers, canker, caterpillars, leaf gall, leaf miners, leaf rollers, leaf skeletonizers, leaf spot, powdery mildew, rust, scale insects, twig blight and wilt.

Be aware that, in California, Coast Live Oak (*Q. agrifolia*), California Black Oak (*Q. kelloggii*) and Tan Oak (*Lithocarpus densiflorus*) are dying in large numbers from 'sudden oak death.' Caused by a *Phytophthora* fungus, the disease is spreading.

Q. alba (above), *Q. robur* (below)

Oregon-Grape
Oregon Grapeholly
Mahonia aquifolium

Features: spring flowers, summer fruit, late-fall and winter foliage
Habit: upright, suckering, evergreen shrub
Height: 2–6' (0.5–1.8 m) **Spread:** 2–6' (0.5–1.8 m)
Planting: B & B, container; spring, fall **Zones:** 5–9

Birdsong will fill the garden when the berries are ripe on the Oregon-grape, and the glossy, holly-like leaves make a fine backdrop for the warm yellow and orange colors of fall. Use this native shrub around the bases of large trees or mixed with evergreen huckleberries and ferns for a lush Northwest look.

GROWING

Oregon-grape prefers **light to partial shade** but tolerates full sun if the soil is moist. The soil should be of **average fertility, humus rich, moist** and **well drained.** Provide **shelter** from winter winds to prevent the foliage from drying out. Awkward shoots can be removed in early summer. Deadheading will keep the plant looking neat but will prevent the attractive, edible fruit from forming.

TIPS

Use low-growing plants as ground-covers. All plants can be used in shrub or mixed borders and in woodland gardens.

The juicy berries are edible, but very tart. They can be eaten fresh or used to make jellies, juices or wine.

RECOMMENDED

M. aquifolium is a Pacific Northwest native and the state flower of Oregon. It grows 3–6' (1–1.8 m) tall, with an equal spread. Bright yellow flowers appear in spring and are followed by clusters of purple or blue berries. The foliage turns a bronze-purple color in late fall and winter. **'Compactum'** is a low, mounding shrub with bronze foliage. It grows 24–36" (60–90 cm) tall, with an equal spread.

PESTS & PROBLEMS

Rust, leaf spot, gall and scale insects may cause occasional problems. Plants in exposed locations may develop leaf scorch in winter.

Try this attractive plant as a hedge or windbreak.

Pieris
Lily-of-the-Valley Shrub
Pieris japonica

Features: colorful new growth, late-winter to spring flowers
Habit: compact, rounded, evergreen shrub
Height: 3–12' (1–3.5 m) **Spread:** 3–10' (1–3 m)
Planting: B & B, container; spring, fall **Zones:** 5–8

I was once asked to recommend a shrub that didn't lose it leaves, bloomed spring through summer, didn't need pruning and rarely had pest problems. *Pieris japonica* fits the bill and adds fragrance to the garden as a bonus. The new leaves of 'Mountain Fire' are peach-colored and look smashing paired with a Coralbark Maple or 'Apricot Beauty' tulips.

GROWING

Pieris grows equally well in **full sun** and **partial shade.** The soil should be of **average fertility, acidic, humus rich, moist** and **well drained.** Gardeners outside the mildest coastal areas should provide a sheltered location protected from the hot sun and drying winds.

Remove spent flowers once flowering is complete. Prune out awkward shoots at the same time.

TIPS

Pieris can be used in a shrub or mixed border, in a woodland garden or as a specimen. Try group-ing it with rhododendrons and other acid-loving plants. With its year-round good looks, this is a great shrub to use in a protected entryway.

All parts of Pieris plants, and even honey made from the nectar, are extremely **poisonous.** Children have died from eating the leaves.

RECOMMENDED

P. japonica grows 8–12' (2.5–3.5 m) tall and spreads 6–10' (1.8–3 m). It bears white flowers in long, pendulous clusters at the ends of the branches. **'Mountain Fire'** has bright red new growth that matures to chestnut brown. The flowers are white. **'Variegata'** also has white flowers but its green leaves have creamy white margins. **'Valley Rose'** has dark green foliage and pink flowers. Several dwarf cultivars grow about 36" (90 cm) tall and wide.

PESTS & PROBLEMS

Canker, lace bugs, nematodes and root rot can cause occasional problems. Plants may suffer dieback if exposed to too much wind.

The flower buds of Pieris form in late summer in the year before flowering and provide an attractive show all winter.

'Mountain Fire' (above)

Pine

Pinus

Features: foliage, bark, cones, habit
Habit: upright, columnar or spreading, evergreen trees
Height: 8–130' (2.5–40 m) **Spread:** 15–60' (4.5–18 m)
Planting: B & B, container; spring, fall **Zones:** 2–8

The scent of pine trees in the air and the sound of the wind in the branches stir memories for me of summer in the mountains and Christmas on the farm. Including a large or dwarf pine in the garden adds texture and an interesting winter form. Put these trees to work as windbreaks, or take advantage of the dark green needles and underplant with pale flowers such as Japanese Anemone or with gray-leaved plants such as artemisia and lamb's ears.

GROWING

Pines grow best in **full sun.** These trees adapt to most **well-drained** soils, but do not tolerate polluted urban conditions.

Generally little or no pruning is required. Hedges can be trimmed in mid-summer. Pinch up to one-half the length of the 'candles,' the fully extended but still soft new growth, to shape the plant or to regulate growth.

TIPS

Pines can be used as specimen trees, as hedges or to create windbreaks. Smaller cultivars can be included in shrub or mixed borders.

These trees are not heavy feeders. Fertilizing will encourage rapid new growth that is weak and susceptible to pest and disease problems.

RECOMMENDED

P. bungeana (Lacebark Pine) is a columnar or bushy tree. It grows 30–50' (9–15 m) tall and spreads 15–35' (4.5–10 m). Its main attraction is the bark, which flakes off in rounded scales, leaving the trunk mottled with patches of cream, brown and red. (Zones 4–8.)

P. cembra (Swiss Stone Pine) has a dense, columnar habit. It grows 30–70' (9–21 m) tall and spreads 15–25' (4.5–7.5 m). This slow-growing pine is resistant to white pine blister rust. (Zones 3–7.)

P. mugo (this page)

P. ponderosa (this page)

P. densiflora (Japanese Red Pine) is a broad, spreading tree. It grows 40–80' (12–25 m) tall and spreads 15–60' (4.5–18 m). This generally hardy tree dislikes strong winter winds. (Zones 4–7.)

P. flexilis (Limber Pine) is a broad, conical tree that is native to the Rocky Mountains and California. It grows 30–70' (9–21 m) tall and spreads 15–35' (4.5–10 m). This species is sometimes trained to form a bonsai. (Zones 3–7.)

P. monticola (Western White Pine), a species native to British Columbia, Montana and California, is a narrowly conical tree that becomes columnar at maturity. It grows 80–130' (25–40 m) tall and spreads 20–25' (6–7.5 m). This species is susceptible to white pine blister rust. (Zones 4–8.)

P. mugo (Mugo Pine) is a low, rounded, spreading shrub or tree. It grows 10–20' (3–6 m) tall and spreads 15–20' (4.5–6 m). **Var. *pumilliio*** is dense and prostrate, growing up to 8' (2.5 m) tall. Its slow growth and small size make this variety a good choice for planters and rock gardens. (Zones 2–7.)

P. parviflora (Japanese White Pine) is conical or columnar when young and matures to a spreading crown. It grows 20–70' (6–21 m) tall and spreads 20–50' (6–15 m). This species is used to create bonsai. It is a good choice for coastal gardens. (Zones 4–8.)

P. ponderosa (Ponderosa Pine, Western Yellow Pine) is a conical, columnar or spreading tree that is native from the southern interior of British Columbia south to northern Mexico. It grows 80–120' (25–36 m) tall and spreads 20–30' (6–9 m). This species has striking orange-brown bark with black fissures. It is extremely heat and drought tolerant. (Zones 5–8.)

Most pines' seeds are edible ('pine nuts'), though many are too small to bother with.

P. strobus (Eastern White Pine) is a slender, conical tree with soft, plumy needles. It grows 50–120'
(15–36 m) tall and spreads 20–40' (6–12 m). It is
sometimes grown as a hedge. **'Compacta'** is a
dense, rounded, slow-growing form. **'Fastigiata'**
is an attractive, narrow, columnar form that
grows up to 70' (21 m) tall. **'Pendula'** has long,
ground-sweeping branches. It must be trained to
form an upright leader when young to give it
some height and shape. (Zones 3–8.)

P. thunbergiana (Japanese Black Pine) can be
trained to form a small, rounded, conical tree
15–25' (4.5–7.5 m) tall, with an equal spread. Left
to its own devices, it will grow up to 100' (30 m)
tall. It responds well to pruning and can be used
to create bonsai. (Zones 5–8.)

PESTS & PROBLEMS

Blight, blister rust, borers, caterpillars, cone rust,
leaf miners, mealybugs, pitch canker, sawflies,
scale insects and tar spot can all cause problems.
The European pine-shoot moth attacks pines
with needles in clusters of two or three.

P. strobus (above), *P. flexilis* (below)

*Pines are more
diverse and widely
adapted than all
other conifers.*

Plane-Tree
London Plane
Platanus x *acerifolia*

Features: bark, fall foliage
Habit: broad, rounded or pyramidal, deciduous tree
Height: 70–100' (21–30 m) **Spread:** 65–80' (20–25 m)
Planting: B & B, container in spring, fall; bare-root in spring **Zones:** 4–8

I once thought the Plane-tree's name referred to the fact that this tree does not make a spectacle of itself with its small, greenish spring flowers—but then I noticed the attention-grabbing bark (and the spelling). The bark peels off in irregular patches, revealing different shades of color as the tree matures. That feature, and the tree's ability to survive the worst city pollution, makes it a popular choice for lining streets in cities around the world. 'Plane' is actually derived from the Greek word for 'broad,' referring to the beautiful, wide, maple-like leaves.

GROWING

Plane-tree grows well in **full sun. Any soil conditions** are tolerated. This tree even thrives in compacted soil with poor air circulation. The roots can lift and damage pavement, so plant away from pavement edges.

Pruning is rarely required. Plane-tree can, however, withstand heavy pruning and can be used as a very large hedge.

TIPS

This large tree is best suited to parks, streetsides and spacious gardens.

RECOMMENDED

P. x *acerifolia* is a large tree with wide, spreading branches. It is grown for its tolerance of adverse conditions and its attractive exfoliating bark. The flaking patches leave the smooth bark mottled with different colors. In fall the leaves turn golden brown. **'Bloodgood'** is a popular, quick-growing, drought-tolerant cultivar that has some resistance to anthracnose.

PESTS & PROBLEMS

Originally this tree had few, if any, serious problems. Its overuse as a street tree, however, has made it more vulnerable to some diseases. Anthracnose blight and canker stain are the two most serious problems. Other possible problems include borers, branch canker, caterpillars, mites, powdery mildew and scale insects.

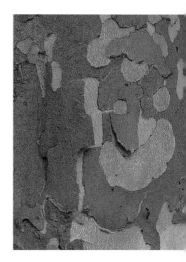

Plane-tree is the dominant street and park tree in London, England.

This young tree will broaden, becoming rounder as it matures.

Potentilla
Shrubby Cinquefoil
Potentilla fruticosa

Features: flowers, foliage **Habit:** mounding, deciduous shrub
Height: 12–40" (30–100 cm) **Spread:** 24–48" (60–120 cm)
Planting: container; spring, fall **Zones:** 2–8

For color all summer, even in the hottest parts of the garden, this is your shrub. After killing three rose plants in a hot spot next to the driveway, I finally threw in the trowel and was rescued by Potentilla. Grow this tough shrub with other drought-resistant bloomers such as 'Autumn Joy' sedum or 'Summer Pastels' yarrow. Underplant with spring bulbs so that by the time daffodil or tulip foliage is yellowing, Potentilla's leaves have returned to hide the unsightly mess. Neither the spring bulbs nor Potentilla likes a lot of summer water, and the twiggy branches challenge squirrels that try to raid the bulbs.

GROWING

Potentilla prefers **full sun** but will tolerate partial or light shade. The soil should, preferably, be of **poor to average fertility** and **well drained.** Most conditions are tolerated by this plant, including sandy or clay soil and wet or dry conditions. Established plants are drought tolerant. Too much fertilizer or too rich a soil will encourage weak, floppy, disease-prone growth.

On mature plants, prune up to one-third of the old wood each year to keep the growth neat and vigorous. Though they will tolerate more severe pruning, these plants look best if left to grow as informal mounds and rounded shrubs.

TIPS

Potentilla is useful in a shrub or mixed border. The smaller cultivars can be included in rock gardens and on rock walls. On slopes that are steep or awkward to mow, Potentilla can prevent soil erosion and reduce the time spent maintaining the lawn. Potentilla can even be used to form a low, informal hedge.

Potentilla will tolerate excess lime in the soil and can handle extreme cold very well. Try this small shrub as a low-maintenance alternative to turfgrass.

'Abbotswood' (above), 'Tangerine' (below)

'Tangerine' (above)

'Abbotswood' (below)

If your Potentilla's flowers fade in the bright sun or in hot weather, try moving the plant to a more sheltered location. A cooler location that still gets lots of sun or a spot with some shade from the hot afternoon sun may be all your plant needs to keep its color. Yellow-flowered plants are the least likely to be affected by heat and sun.

RECOMMENDED

There are many, many cultivars of *P. fruticosa*. The following are a few of the more popular and interesting.

'Abbotswood' is one of the best white-flowered cultivars. It grows 30–36" (75–90 cm) tall and spreads up to 48" (120 cm).

'Goldfinger' has large yellow flowers. It grows up to 40" (100 cm) tall, with an equal spread.

'Princess' ('Pink Princess') has light pink flowers that fade to white in hot weather. It grows about 36" (90 cm) tall, with an equal spread.

'Red Ace' has brick red or orange-red flowers with yellow undersides to the petals. It grows 12–36" (30–90 cm) tall and spreads about 24–36" (60–90 cm). This cultivar has the best color when grown in light or partial shade. It is well suited to the cooler coastal summers, because it tends to wilt and die young during the hot summers in much of the rest of North America.

'Tangerine' has orange flowers that bleach to yellow if the plant is exposed to too much direct sunlight, so plant in partial or light shade. This cultivar grows 18–24" (45–60 cm) tall and spreads 36–48" (90–120 cm).

'Yellow Gem' has bright yellow flowers. It is a low, mounding, spreading cultivar that grows 12–18" (30–45 cm) tall and spreads up to 36" (90 cm).

PESTS & PROBLEMS
Though infrequent, occasional problems with mildew, fungal leaf spot or spider mites are possible.

Potentilla varieties offer a rainbow of possible colors: white, yellow, pink, orange and red.

Redbud

Cercis

Features: spring flowers, fall foliage
Habit: rounded or spreading, multi-stemmed, deciduous trees or shrubs
Height: 6–30' (1.8–9 m) **Spread:** 6–35' (1.8–10 m)
Planting: B & B, container; spring, fall **Zones:** 4–9

I've always had trouble growing sweetpeas, but redbuds are the perfect substitute, with branches full of sweetpea-like blooms and lovely fall foliage to boot. The spring buds open on leafless branches, giving these trees or shrubs an artistic, Japanese look that really suits contemporary gardens. If your goal is to have year-round color in the garden, redbuds will fill the bloom gap between early-spring plums and cherries and late-spring dogwoods and crabapples.

GROWING

Redbuds grow well in **full sun, partial shade** or **light shade.** The soil should be a **fertile, deep loam** that is **moist** and **well drained.**

Pruning is rarely required. Growth of young plants can be thinned to encourage an open habit at maturity. Awkward branches can be removed after flowering. These plants have tender roots and do not like being transplanted.

TIPS

Redbuds can be used as specimen trees, in shrub or mixed borders and in woodland gardens.

RECOMMENDED

C. canadensis (Eastern Redbud) is a spreading, multi-stemmed tree that grows 20–30' (6–9 m) tall and spreads 25–35' (7.5–10 m). It bears red, purple or pink flowers in mid-spring, before the leaves emerge. The young foliage is bronze, fading to green over the summer and turning bright yellow in fall. **Var.** *alba* has white flowers. **'Forest Pansy'** has purple or pink flowers and reddish-purple foliage that fades to green over the summer. The best foliage color is produced when this shrub is cut back hard in early spring, but plants cut back this way will not produce flowers.

C. chinensis (Chinese Redbud) is a dense, rounded, multi-stemmed shrub or tree that grows 6–15' (1.8–4.5 m) tall, with an equal width. It bears pink or purple flowers from early to mid-spring. This species performs best in partial shade. (Zones 6–9.)

PESTS & PROBLEMS

Blight, canker, caterpillars, dieback, downy mildew, leafhoppers, leaf spot, scale insects, weevils and verticillium wilt are potential problems for redbuds.

'Redbud' describes the pointed flower buds, which are slightly deeper in color than the flowers.

C. canadensis (this page)

Select a redbud from a locally grown source. Plants from seeds produced in the south are not hardy in the north.

Redwood
Coast Redwood
Sequoia sempervirens

Features: foliage, bark, cones, habit **Habit:** columnar or conical, evergreen tree
Height: 5–100' (1.5–30 m) **Spread:** 5–30' (1.5–9 m)
Planting: container; spring, fall **Zones:** 6–9

A mature Redwood is nothing short of magnificent, and so beloved
are these majestic giants that one homeowner opted to tear down
his garage to give space to the tree he had planted as a seedling
years before. The deep red bark grows richer with age. If you have the room,
this tree is an unparalleled investment in ever-growing beauty.

GROWING

Redwood grows well in **full sun** or **light shade.** The soil should be of **average fertility, moist** and **well drained.** Pruning is rarely required.

TIPS

Redwood makes a stunning specimen tree. Never underestimate its potential size—this giant is not for the average garden. Lack of water in summer will slow the tree's growth. The smaller cultivars can be used as windbreaks, as hedges and in shrub or mixed borders.

Unlike most coniferous trees, Redwood will sprout new shoots from the base if cut down.

RECOMMENDED

S. sempervirens is a tall, columnar or conical tree, native to the coastal regions of Oregon and California and hardy in Zones 7–9. It grows 70–100' (21–30 m) tall in cultivation but can grow three times as tall in the wild. In gardens it spreads

about 20–30' (6–9 m). **'Adpressa'** is a smaller, slower-growing cultivar that is hardier than the species, to Zone 6. It grows 20–30' (6–9 m) tall and spreads 10–20' (3–6 m). **'Prostrata'** is a dwarf, spreading cultivar. It grows 5' (1.5 m) tall and spreads 5–10' (1.5–3 m). This cultivar has a tendency to revert to the upright form, so watch for and remove any strongly upright growth.

Redwoods are the tallest conifers in the world; the record-holding tree is a towering 365' (110 m).

Rhododendron Azalea

Rhododendron

Features: late-winter to early-summer flowers, foliage, habit
Habit: upright, mounding, rounded, evergreen or deciduous shrubs
Height: 2–12' (0.5–3.5 m) **Spread:** 2–12' (0.5–3.5 m)
Planting: B & B, container; spring, fall **Zones:** 3–9

*P*acific Northwest gardeners are guilty of taking for granted the beautiful foliage and flowers of rhododendrons and their azalea relatives. Visitors from central North America gush over the huge, abundant, colorful blossoms and equally photogenic leaves. Group these plants together with camellias, viburnums and Pieris, and underplant with shade-tolerant groundcovers such as Lamium, Ajuga and saxifrages for carefree color. And don't forget to say a word or two of heartfelt thanks!

GROWING

Rhododendrons prefer **partial shade** or **light shade,** but they tolerate full sun in a site with adequate moisture. A location sheltered from strong winds is preferable. The soil should be **fertile, humus rich, acidic, moist** and **well drained.** Rhododendrons are sensitive to high pH, salinity and winter injury.

Shallow planting with a good mulch is essential, as is excellent drainage. In heavy soils, elevate the crown of rhododendrons 1" (2.5 cm) above soil level when planting to ensure surface drainage of excess water.

Dead and damaged growth can be removed in mid-spring. Spent flower clusters should be removed if possible. Grasp the base of the cluster between your thumb and forefinger and twist to remove the entire cluster. Be careful not to damage the new buds that form directly beneath the flowerheads.

TIPS

Take advantage of these gorgeous shrubs almost anywhere in the garden. Use them in shrub or mixed borders, in woodland gardens, as specimen plants, in group plantings, as hedges and informal barriers, in rock gardens or in planters on a shady patio or balcony.

The **flowers and foliage** of *Rhododendron* species are **poisonous,** as is honey produced from the nectar.

R. calophytum

'Rhododendron' translates as 'rose tree'—an apt description of these beautiful plants.

RECOMMENDED

R. calophytum is a distinctive, evergreen, early-blooming large shrub or small tree up to about 20' (6 m) tall and wide. The white or pale pink flowers each have a crimson spot in the throat. (Zones 6–9.)

R. catawbiense (Catawba Rhododendron, Mountain Rosebay) is a large, rounded, evergreen species. It grows 6–10' (1.8–3 m) tall, with an equal spread. Clusters of reddish-purple flowers appear in late spring. **'Album'** has light purple buds and white flowers. **'Christmas Cheer'** is an early bloomer with light pink flowers. **'Cilpinense'** has white flowers flushed with pink. (Zones 4–8.)

R. **'Dora Amateis'** is a compact, evergreen rhododendron 24" (60 cm) tall, with an equal spread. In mid-spring, it bears white flowers flushed with pink. (Zones 6–9.)

R. **Exbury Hybrids** are rounded, upright, deciduous rhododendrons. They grow 8–12' (2.5–3.5 m) tall and spread 6–12' (1.8–3.5 m). The flower color varies from cultivar to cultivar. **'Dawn's Chorus'** has pink buds and white flowers with pink veins. **'Firefly'** has red flowers. **'Gold Dust'** has fragrant, bright yellow flowers. (Zones 5–7.)

R. **Knap Hill Hybrids** are rounded, upright, deciduous rhododendrons that grow 8–12' (2.5–3.5 m) tall and spread 6–12' (1.8–3.5 m). The flower color varies with the cultivar. **'Altair'** has fragrant, creamy white flowers.

'**Cockatoo**' has fragrant, pink-yellow flowers. '**Fireball**' is a vigorous plant with bronze new foliage that matures to dark green. The flowers are orange-red. (Zones 5–7.)

R. **Kurume Hybrids** are deciduous, dwarf azaleas, often used for bonsai and mass plantings. They grow 24–36" (60–90 cm) tall, with an equal spread. The color of the spring flowers varies with the cultivar. '**Hino-Crimson**' has a dense habit and red flowers. '**Rosebud**' is a compact, low-growing plant with rose pink flowers. (Zones 5–8.)

R. **Northern Lights Hybrids** are broad, rounded, deciduous azaleas. They grow about 5' (1.5 m) tall and spread about 4' (1.2 m). These hybrids are very cold hardy. '**Apricot Surprise**' has yellow-orange flowers.

Northern Lights Hybrid

Rhododendrons and azaleas are generally grouped together. Extensive breeding and hybridizing are making it more and more difficult to apply one label or the other.

'**Golden Lights**' has fragrant, yellow flowers. '**Orchid Lights**' is a bushy, compact plant with light purple flowers. '**Rosy Lights**' has fragrant, dark pink flowers. '**Spicy Lights**' has fragrant, light orange-red flowers. '**White Lights**' has fragrant, white flowers. (Zones 3–7.)

R. **PJM Hybrids** are compact, rounded, dwarf, evergreen rhododendrons. They grow 3–6' (1–1.8 m) tall, with an equal spread. These hybrids are weevil resistant. '**Elite**' has pink-purple flowers. '**Regal**' has a more spreading habit and pink flowers. '**Victor**' is compact and slow growing; it has pink flowers. (Zones 4–8.)

R. yakushimanum (Yakushima Rhododendron) is a dense, mounding, evergreen rhododendron. It grows 36" (90 cm) tall, with an equal spread. Rose red buds open to reveal

PJM Hybrid (above)

white flowers in mid-spring. The underside of the foliage is soft and fuzzy. This rhododendron is resistant to root weevils. (Zones 5–9.)

PESTS & PROBLEMS

Rhododendrons planted in good conditions, with well-drained soil, suffer few problems. When plants are stressed, however, aphids, caterpillars, lace bugs, leaf galls, leafhoppers, petal blight, powdery mildew, root rot, root weevils, rust, scale insects, vine weevils and whiteflies can cause problems.

The native R. macrophyllum (Pacific Rhododendron, California Rosebay) is the state flower of Washington.

Rockrose

Cistus

Features: foliage, summer flowers **Habit:** upright, rounded, evergreen shrub
Height: 1.5–6' (0.5–1.8 m) **Spread:** 1.5–6' (0.5–1.8 m)
Planting: container; spring, fall **Zones:** 8–10

The rose-like flowers that appear despite poor, rocky soil give rock-roses their name. A still more apt epithet would be 'toughrose' because these shrubs will bloom even near the ocean. The evergreen foliage is a surprise bonus, and if you grab a leaf and crush it between your fingers you'll be delighted with the fragrance that is released. Grow rockroses with succulents, such as sedums, and with other sun-lovers that don't demand much water.

GROWING

Rockroses grow best in a **sheltered** site in **full sun.** The soil should be of **poor to average fertility** and **well drained.** These plants are drought tolerant once established.

Young plants can be pinched to shape them and to encourage bushy growth. These shrubs respond poorly to hard pruning.

TIPS

Rockroses are used in shrub or mixed borders, on sunny banks, against warm walls and in planters.

These plants can look unattractive when they become old and leggy. It is best to remove such specimens rather than try to rejuvenate them because they can't be cut back and don't transplant easily.

RECOMMENDED

C. laurifolius (Rockrose) grows 3–6' (1–1.8 m) tall, with an equal spread. It has blue-green foliage and bears white flowers with yellow centers in summer. The growth is stiff and upright.

C. x *purpureus* (Orchidspot Rockrose) forms a rounded mound 18–36" (45–90 cm) tall, with an equal spread. The flowers, borne in clusters, are dark pink with purple spots at the bases. (Zones 9–10.)

Certain Cistus *species produce an aromatic resin that was used by the Greeks and Romans for perfume and incense.*

These short-lived shrubs have an extended flowering period, sometimes all year long, although they dislike high humidity.

C. laurifolius (this page)

Rose-of-Sharon
Hibiscus
Hibiscus syriacus

Features: mid-summer to fall flowers **Habit:** bushy, upright, deciduous shrub
Height: 8–12' (2.5–3.5 m) **Spread:** 6–10' (1.8–3 m)
Planting: B & B, container; spring, fall **Zones:** 5–9

*T*he biggest mystery about Rose-of-Sharon is why it isn't used more often. Easy-going, with large, impressive blooms at the end of summer when everything else is fading, this hibiscus looks as if it belongs on a tropical island instead of a northwestern September garden. Our grandparents were wise to the ways of this plant, and you can still see tree-size specimens blooming in older neighborhoods. I've seen more than a few neglected Rose-of-Sharon plants surviving in front of abandoned homes. Underplant with Bluebeard and hardy purple asters for a refreshing fall display in purples, blues and pinks.

GROWING

Rose-of-Sharon prefers **full sun** and tolerates part shade. The soil should be **humus rich, moist** and **well drained.** Pinch young plants to encourage bushy growth.

Young plants can be trained to form a tree by selectively pruning out all but the strongest stem. The flowers form on the current year's growth; prune back tip growth in late winter or early spring for larger but fewer flowers.

TIPS
Rose-of-Sharon is best used in shrub or mixed borders.

This plant develops unsightly legs as it matures. Plant low, bushy perennials or shrubs around the base to hide the bare stems.

The leaves emerge late in spring and drop early in fall. Planting Rose-of-Sharon along with evergreen shrubs will make up for the short period of green.

RECOMMENDED
H. syriacus is an erect, multi-stemmed shrub that bears dark pink flowers from mid-summer to fall.

'Blue Bird' (above), 'Diana' (below)

It can be trained to form a small, single-stemmed tree. Many cultivars are available. **'Aphrodite'** bears rose pink flowers with dark red centers. **'Blue Bird'** bears large blue flowers with red centers. **'Diana'** bears large white flowers. **'Helene'** has white flowers with red petal bases.

PESTS & PROBLEMS
Rose-of-Sharon can be afflicted with aphids, bacterial blight, caterpillars, fungal leaf spot, mealybugs, mites, root rot, rust, scale insects, stem rot, verticillium wilt and viruses.

Russian Olive

Elaeagnus

Features: fragrant summer flowers, summer foliage, fruit
Habit: rounded, spreading, deciduous trees or shrubs
Height: 6–20' (1.8–6 m) **Spread:** 6–20' (1.8–6 m)
Planting: B & B, container; spring, fall **Zones:** 2–8

*T*hese tough shrubs or trees thrive even in the windswept cold winters and hot summers of parts of our region, and the silver-gray leaves make a terrific backdrop for the yellow summer blooms. These are the plants to use when poor growing conditions present a challenge, and they can even be pruned into a formal shape, masquerading as rare and unusual specimen trees in a perennial garden or shrub border. Use plants with purple foliage near a Russian olive for a lovely color contrast. The 'Royal Purple' Smoketree and Burgundy Barberry will thrive in the same dry soil.

GROWING

Russian olives grow best in **full sun.** Preferably, the soil should be a **well-drained, sandy loam** of **average to high fertility.** These plants adapt to poor soil because they can fix nitrogen from the air. They also tolerate salty and dry conditions.

These trees or shrubs tolerate hard pruning. One-third of the old growth can be removed each year from multi-stemmed specimens.

TIPS

Russian olives are used in shrub or mixed borders, as hedges and screens and as specimen plants. The fruits are edible but dry and mealy.

RECOMMENDED

E. angustifolia (Russian Olive) is a rounded, spreading tree. It grows 12–20' (3.5–6 m) tall, with an equal spread. The fragrant, yellow summer flowers are often obscured by the foliage, as is the silvery yellow fruit. The main attractions of this species are its tolerance of adverse conditions and its narrow, silver-gray leaves.

E. angustifolia (this page)

E. multiflora (Cherry Eleagnus) is a wide-spreading, rounded shrub with somewhat arching branches. It grows 6–10' (1.8–3 m) tall, with an equal spread. The bright red fruits are hidden by the silvery green foliage. (Zones 5–7.)

PESTS & PROBLEMS

In stressful conditions these plants are susceptible to canker, dieback, fungal leaf spot, nematodes, root rot and rust.

Silverbell

Halesia

Features: late-spring to early-summer flowers, summer and fall foliage
Habit: spreading, rounded, deciduous trees or large shrubs
Height: 20–40' (6–12 m) **Spread:** 20–35' (6–10 m)
Planting: B & B, container; spring, fall **Zones:** 5–9

*S*et a lounge chair under a silverbell in bloom and look up into the face of heaven. The delicate, hanging flowers seem to display an artist's attention to detail, and these trees go on to add fall color and winter fruit. Use silverbells to add excitement to woodland gardens or as taller companions to rhododendrons and azaleas. Ferns and columbine planted beneath a silverbell canopy will add to the airy feeling of enchantment.

GROWING

Silverbells grow well in **full sun, partial shade** or **light shade.** The soil should be **fertile, humus rich, neutral to acidic, moist** and **well drained.** Pruning is rarely required.

TIPS

Silverbells make attractive, small specimen trees. They can also be used in a woodland garden or as backdrop plants in a shrub or mixed border. Narrow ridges or wings run down the length of each fruiting capsule, two or four depending on the species, giving rise to the specific epithets *diptera* ('two-winged') and *tetraptera* ('four-winged').

RECOMMENDED

H. tetraptera (*H. carolina*) (Snowdrop Tree, Carolina Silverbell) is a rounded, spreading tree. It grows 25–40' (7.5–12 m) tall and spreads 25–35' (7.5–10 m). The white flowers appear in spring before the leaves emerge. Fall color is yellow. **'Rosea'** has pink flowers. The intensity of the pink can vary greatly from plant to plant; some flowers are just tinged with pink and others are a much deeper hue. Purchase young plants while they are in flower to be sure of getting the desired color. (Zones 5–8.)

ALTERNATE SPECIES

H. diptera (Two-wing Silverbell) is similar to but slightly smaller than *H. tetraptera*. Early-summer white flowers are followed by two-winged capsules. The fall color is yellow. (Zones 5–9.)

PESTS & PROBLEMS

Occasional problems with root rot, wood rot and scale insects are possible.

H. tetraptera (this page)

For the best effect, place these plants against an evergreen backdrop. Try underplanting a silverbell with a rhododendron.

The fruiting capsules of these plants are interesting and hang from the branches almost all winter.

Skimmia

Skimmia japonica

Features: foliage, spring flowers, fruit
Habit: low-growing or upright, spreading, evergreen shrub
Height: 1.5–10' (0.5–3 m) **Spread:** 2–10' (0.5–3 m)
Planting: container; spring, fall **Zones:** 6–9

For a mow-free zone in the shade, Skimmia can't be beat, and some of the tidiest natural landscapes I've seen have woven Vine Maple, rhododendrons and Skimmia together in a lovely carpet of green. The red berries and bright green foliage have always made me think of Christmas, even though this cheerful color combo appears in summer. The stiff, waxy green leaves hold up well to slugs and rainstorms.

GROWING

Skimmia grows best in **light shade** or **full shade.** The soil should be of **average fertility, humus rich, moist** and **well drained.** This plant tolerates neglect and pollution.

Pruning is rarely necessary. Gardeners not concerned with fruit can remove the spent flowers. Awkward or asymmetrical growth can be removed in early spring or after flowering is complete.

TIPS

Skimmia can be used in shaded borders and woodland gardens. The fruits may cause mild stomach upset if eaten.

RECOMMENDED

S. japonica (Japanese Skimmia) is a rounded, upright or creeping shrub. It generally grows 3–4' (0.9–1.2 m) tall, but can grow up to 10' (3 m). The spread is equal to the height. Clusters of fragrant white, pink or red flowers appear in mid- to late spring. Both a male and a female plant are required for the female to develop bright red berries in summer. **Subsp. *reevesiana*** (Reeves Skimmia) is a low-growing plant with a loose, open habit. It grows 18–36" (45–90 cm) tall with a spread of 24–36" (60–90 cm). Fragrant male and female flowers are borne on the same plant so only one plant is required for fruit to set. This subspecies is hardy in Zones 6–8.

PESTS & PROBLEMS

Mites can be a problem on plants under drought stress. Leaves of mite-infested plants turn yellow and develop a scorched appearance. Scale insects and aphids can be troublesome on occasion.

subsp. *reevesiana*

Skimmia's bright red fruit and glossy green leaves make this plant a prickle-less, non-invasive substitute for holly.

Smoketree

Cotinus coggygria

Features: early-summer flowers, summer and fall foliage
Habit: bushy, rounded, spreading, deciduous tree or shrub
Height: 10–20' (3–6 m) **Spread:** 10–15' (3–4.5 m)
Planting: container; spring, fall **Zones:** 4–8

Named for the smoky look of the flower clusters that emerge in summer, this small tree or large shrub should have a place of honor in any garden on the merits of the majestic foliage alone. The purple leaves of the 'Royal Purple' Smoketree contrast with silver-gray lamb's ears in my own garden, and neither plant minds the rocky, dry soil. Smoketree can also be used as an accent plant in a perennial garden—cut it to the ground each spring to keep it shrubby, or train it as a tree and encourage a clematis vine to hop aboard and twine happily through the open, spreading branches.

GROWING

Smoketree grows well in **full sun** or **partial shade.** It prefers soil of **average fertility** that is **moist** and **well drained,** but it will adapt to all but very wet soils. In gardens near the coast it's a good idea to grow Smoketree in rocky soils to encourage good drainage and prevent root rot.

Where pruning is concerned, this is an all-or-nothing plant. Long, lanky growth develops from pruning cuts. It can be cut back to the ground each spring to maintain low, shrubby growth, but larger shrubs and tree specimens shouldn't be pruned at all.

TIPS

Smoketree can be used in a shrub or mixed border, as a single specimen or in groups. It is a good choice for a rocky hillside planting.

RECOMMENDED

C. coggygria grows 10–15' (3–4.5 m) tall, with an equal spread. It bears large, puffy plumes of flowers that start out green and gradually turn a pinky gray. The green foliage turns red, orange and yellow in fall. **'Daydream'** develops many pink plumes. The habit is more dense than that of the species. **'Flame'** develops into a small, bushy tree or large shrub with purple-pink plumes. It can grow up to 20' (6 m) tall. The fall color is a brilliant red. **'Royal Purple'** (Purple Smoketree) has dark purple foliage and purple-gray flowers.

PESTS & PROBLEMS

Verticillium wilt and powdery mildew are possible problems. Purple-leaved plants are more likely to be affected by powdery mildew.

The much-branched flower clusters, usually dull purple and hairy, produce an effect of puffs of smoke over the foliage.

'Royal Purple' (this page)

Snowbell

Styrax

Features: late-spring to early-summer flowers, foliage, habit
Habit: upright, rounded, spreading or columnar, deciduous trees or shrubs
Height: 6–40' (1.8–12 m) **Spread:** 6–30' (1.8–9 m)
Planting: B & B, container; early spring **Zones:** 4–9

Many gardeners call Japanese Snowbell the most beautiful flowering tree in the world. These must be gardeners who spend time gazing upward at the dangling flower bells and dark green leaves. Even when the flowers are gone it's easy to admire snowbells for their delicate, shapely appearance and reasonable size. These are perfect trees to build a white theme garden around. Use white-flowered azaleas, Candytuft and impatiens as ladies-in-waiting ready to take over once the snowbell finishes her show of blooms.

GROWING

Snowbells grow well in **full sun, partial shade** or **light shade,** in a spot that is **sheltered** from the rain. The soil should be **fertile, humus rich, neutral to acidic, moist** and **well drained.**

Pruning is not generally required. Simply remove damaged branches as needed. To encourage a tree form rather than a shrub form, trim side branches to the trunk.

TIPS

Snowbells can be used in a shrub or mixed border or in a woodland garden. As trees, they make interesting specimens near an entryway or patio.

RECOMMENDED

S. japonica (Japanese Snowbell) is a graceful, upright tree with arching, spreading branches. It grows 20–30' (6–9 m) tall, with an equal spread. White flowers dangle from the undersides of the branches in late spring. (Zones 5–8.)

S. obassia (Fragrant Snowbell) is a broad, columnar tree. It grows 20–40' (6–12 m) tall and spreads 20–30' (6–9 m). In early summer, white flowers appear in long clusters at the branch ends. (Zones 4–8.)

ALTERNATE SPECIES

S. americanus (American Snowbell) forms a neat, rounded shrub 6–10' (1.8–3 m) tall, and up to 8' (2.5 m) wide. It bears nodding white flowers along the stems in early and mid-summer. This species is not as commonly available at garden centers. (Zones 6–9.)

S. japonica (this page)

Plant a Japanese Snowbell next to your patio so you can admire the beautiful flowers while sipping a cool drink.

Snowberry
Coralberry
Symphoricarpos

Features: foliage, fall and winter fruit, habit
Habit: rounded or spreading, deciduous shrubs
Height: 2–6' (0.5–1.8 m) **Spread:** 3–12' (1–3.5 m)
Planting: B & B, container; spring, fall **Zones:** 3–7

The winter I first noticed the lovely white berries on these easy-to-grow shrubs, I wondered how I could have missed appreciating them earlier. Now I can spot snowberries yards away. Although I'll always think of them as wild native shrubs, I see them being harnessed and put to work in the city, where their suckering roots bind soil on hillsides and where their quick-growing, shrubby forms make adaptable screens.

GROWING

Snowberries prefer **partial or light shade** but tolerate full sun. These plants adapt to any soil that is **fertile** and **well drained** and can handle pollution, drought and exposure.

Little pruning is required. On established plants one-third of the old growth can be removed each year, in early spring.

These low-maintenance shrubs spread readily and are good for filling in gaps in shady areas.

TIPS

Snowberries can be used in shrub or mixed borders, in woodland gardens or as screens or informal hedges. The low, spreading 'Hancock' can be used as a groundcover.

The berries are **not edible** and should be left for the birds.

RECOMMENDED

S. albus (Common Snowberry) is a rounded, suckering native shrub with arching branches. It grows 3–6' (1–1.8 m) tall, or sometimes taller, with a spread usually equal to the height. The small, delicate pinkish-white summer flowers are rather inconspicuous but still attractive. The clusters of white berries that follow are interesting and persist through fall and early winter.

Symphoricarpos translates as 'together to bear fruit,' referring to the clustered berries.

S. x chenaultii (Chenault Snowberry) is a low, spreading shrub, with gently arching branches. It grows 3–6' (1–1.8 m) tall, with an equal spread. The fruits are red but are smaller and less noticeable than those of *S. albus*. **'Hancock'** is a very low, spreading cultivar. It grows 24" (60 cm) high and spreads up to 12' (3.5 m). The arching branches develop an attractive, layered appearance. (Zones 4–7.)

S. x chenaultii berries exhibit a distinct two-tone effect, with increasing amounts of red on sun-exposed fruit.

PESTS & PROBLEMS

Snowberries are occasionally afflicted with anthracnose or powdery mildew.

S. albus (this page)

Spirea

Spiraea

Features: summer flowers, habit
Habit: round, bushy, deciduous shrubs
Height: 2–10' (0.5–3 m) **Spread:** 2–12' (0.5–3.5 m)
Planting: container; spring, fall **Zones:** 3–9

The first spirea I fell in love with was called 'Little Princess,' and her petite form and pretty pink flowers made her as cute as a newborn baby when we first met at the nursery. Like any princess, however, she soon became queen sized—and demanded more pruning than I was willing to give. I've learned a healthy respect for the vigorous growth of these plants, but they still warm my heart with their adaptability and dependable blooming. They are also the noisiest shrubs in my garden, surrounded by bees happily humming all summer long as the flower clusters come and go.

Pruning is necessary to keep spireas tidy and graceful in form. The tight, shrubby types require less pruning than the larger, more open forms, which may require heavy renewal pruning in spring.

GROWING

Spireas prefer **full sun.** Provide protection from the hottest sun in the eastern and southern regions to help prevent foliage burn. The soil should be **fertile, acidic, moist** and **well drained.**

Pruning is dependent on the flowering time for any given species. Those that bloom in spring and early summer usually form their flowers the previous year. These plants should be pruned immediately after flowering is complete. Cut out one-third of the old growth to encourage new, young growth.

Plants that flower later in summer or in fall generally form flowers during the current year. These can be cut back to within 12" (30 cm) of the ground in early spring, as the buds begin to swell, to encourage lots of new growth and flowers later in the season.

TIPS

Spireas are used in shrub or mixed borders, in rock gardens and as informal screens and hedges.

S. japonica 'Shibori' (this page)

Under a magnifying glass the flowers of these shrubs in the rose family indeed resemble tiny roses.

S. japonica 'Goldmound'

S. x billiardii

RECOMMENDED

S*. x *billiardii (Billiard Spirea) is an upright shrub, up to 6' (1.8 m) tall, that suckers and may spread widely. Dense, narrow clusters of purple-pink flowers appear in summer. (Zones 4–8.)

S*. x *bumalda (*S. japonica* 'Bumalda') is a low, broad, mounded shrub with pink spring or early-summer flowers. It is rarely grown in favor of the many cultivars, which also have pink flowers. **'Anthony Waterer'** grows 3–4' (0.9–1.2 m) tall and spreads 4–5' (1.2–1.5 m). The new foliage is reddish, turning blue-green over summer and red again in fall. **'Goldflame'** grows 24–36" (60–90 cm) tall and spreads 2–4' (0.6–1.2 m). The new foliage emerges red and matures to yellow-green, with red, orange and yellow fall color. **'Limemound'** grows about 36" (90 cm) tall and spreads about 6' (1.8 m). The stems are red and the foliage is yellow with good fall color. (Zones 3–8.)

S. douglasii (Hardhack) is an erect, suckering shrub that is native to western North America. This vigorous species grows up to 7' (2 m) tall and spreads up to 5' (1.5 m). Pink to deep rose flower clusters

appear in early and mid-summer. This species can grow well in wet places in the garden. (Zones 5–8.)

S. japonica (Japanese Spirea) forms a clump of erect stems. It grows 4–6' (1.2–1.8 m) tall and spreads up to 5' (1.5 m). Pink or white flowers are borne in mid- and late summer. There are many varieties, cultivars and hybrids. **Var. *albiflora*** (*S. albiflora*) (Japanese White Spirea) is a low, dense, mounding shrub. It grows 24–36" (60–90 cm) tall, with an equal spread, and bears white flowers in early summer. **'Goldmound'** has bright yellow foliage and bears pink flowers in late spring and early summer. **'Little Princess'** forms a dense mound 18" (45 cm) tall and 3–6' (1–1.8 m) wide. The flowers are rose pink. **'Shibori'** ('Shirobana') grows 24" (60 cm) tall and wide. Both pink and white flowers appear on the same plant. (Zones 4–9.)

S. nipponica (Nippon Spirea) is an upright shrub with arching branches. It grows 4–8' (1.2–2.5 m) tall, with an equal spread. White flowers appear in mid-summer. **'Snowmound'** (Snowmound Nippon Spirea) is grown more commonly than the species. The spreading, arching branches are covered with flowers in early summer. It grows 3–5' (0.9–1.5 m) tall, with an equal spread. (Zones 4–8.)

S. x vanhouttei (Bridal Wreath Spirea, Vanhoutte Spirea) is a dense, bushy shrub with arching branches. It grows 6–10' (1.8–3 m) tall and spreads 10–12' (3–3.5 m). White flowers are borne in clusters in early summer. (Zones 3–8.)

PESTS & PROBLEMS
Aphids, dieback, fire blight, leaf spot, powdery mildew, scale insects and weevils can cause occasional problems.

S. x vanhouttei

Spruce

Picea

Features: foliage, cones, habit **Habit:** conical or columnar, evergreen trees
Height: 3–80' (1–25 m) **Spread:** 3–20' (1–6 m)
Planting: B & B, container; spring, fall **Zones:** 2–9

The Dwarf Alberta Spruce are the most sentimental shrubs in my garden. They were given as living gifts when my children were born and grew slowly over the years until—as with my children—I noticed one day what handsome specimens they had become. Tidy, compact and slower growing than other evergreens, spruce form the backbone of the winter garden. Use the compact, blue forms together with a burgundy beech or other purple-leaved plant for a lovely contrast of foliage color.

Spruce is the traditional Christmas tree in Europe.

GROWING

Spruce grow best in **full sun.** The soil should be **deep, moist, well drained** and **neutral to acidic.** These trees generally don't like hot, dry or polluted conditions. Pruning is rarely needed.

Spruce trees are best grown from smaller stock as they dislike being transplanted when large.

TIPS

Spruce are used as specimen trees. The dwarf and slow-growing cultivars can also be used in shrub or mixed borders and for bonsai.

Oil-based pesticides such as dormant oil can take the blue out of your blue-needled spruces.

RECOMMENDED

P. abies (Norway Spruce) is a fast-growing, pyramidal tree with dark green needles. It grows 70–80' (21–25 m) tall and spreads about 20' (6 m). This species is wind resistant. **'Nidiformis'** (Nest Spruce) is a slow-growing, low, compact, mounding form. It grows about 3–4' (0.9–1.2 m) tall and spreads 3–5' (0.9–1.5 m). (Zones 2–8.)

P. breweriana (Weeping Spruce, Brewer Spruce) is a columnar tree with drooping branchlets up to 36" (90 cm) long. It can grow 30–50' (9–15 m) tall and spread 10–12' (3–3.5 m). (Zones 4–9.)

P. abies (above), *P. abies* 'Nidiformis' (below)

P. glauca (White Spruce) is native to Alaska, most of Canada and the northeastern U.S. This conical tree with blue-green needles grows 40–60' (12–18 m) tall and spreads 10–20' (3–6 m). It can grow up to 160' (48 m) tall in the wild. **'Conica'** (Dwarf White Spruce, Dwarf Alberta Spruce) is a dense, conical, bushy shrub. It grows 6–20' (1.8–6 m) tall and spreads 3–8' (1–2.5 m). This cultivar works well in planters. (Zones 2–6.)

P. abies 'Pendula'

P. abies

P. omorika (Serbian Spruce) is a slow-growing, narrow, spire-like tree with upward-arching branches and drooping branchlets. Two white stripes run the length of each needle. This tree grows 30–50' (9–15 m) tall and spreads 10–15' (3–4.5 m). (Zones 4–8.)

P. pungens (Colorado Spruce) is a conical or columnar tree with stiff, blue-green needles and dense growth. This hardy, drought-tolerant tree grows 30–60' (9–18 m) tall, with a spread of 10–20' (3–6 m). **Var. *glauca*** (Colorado Blue Spruce) is similar to the species, but with blue-gray needles. Some smaller cultivars have been developed from this variety. **'Hoopsii'** grows up to 60' (18 m) tall. It has a dense, pyramidal form and even more blue-white foliage than var. *glauca*. **'Mission Blue'** is a broad-based, compact form 4–8' (1.2–2.5 m) tall, with bold blue foliage. (Zones 2–8.)

PESTS & PROBLEMS

Possible problems include aphids, caterpillars, gall insects, needle cast, nematodes, rust, sawflies, scale insects, spider mites and wood rot. Aphid damage is common on spruce in the Pacific Northwest in late winter. The damage shows up in summer as branches appear to be very dry and branch tips may die. In February, use a strong spray from a garden hose to dislodge the pests or use insecticidal soap.

Stradivarius used spruce to make his renowned violins, and the resonant, lightweight but tough wood is still preferred for violins, guitars, harps and the sounding boards of pianos.

P. pungens var. *glauca* 'Hoopsii'

P. pungens var. *glauca* 'Mission Blue'

Stewartia

Stewartia

Features: mid-summer flowers, summer and fall foliage, exfoliating bark
Habit: broad, conical or rounded, deciduous trees
Height: 20–80' (6–25 m) **Spread:** 20–40' (6–12 m)
Planting: B & B, container; spring, fall **Zones:** 5–9

These easy-going trees rival dogwoods as my favorite plants for four seasons of interest. Their blooms appear in summer, after the more common spring-flowering trees have finished their show, and the brilliant fall color that follows can't be ignored. The shaggy bark peels or flakes off, creating a mottled trunk that is particularly striking in winter. These trees make good specimens for areas such as the front yard or near a patio, where year-long interest will be most appreciated.

GROWING

Stewartias grow well in **full sun** or **light shade.** The soil should be of **average to high fertility, humus rich, neutral to acidic, moist** and **well drained.** These plants need some **shelter** from strong winds. Pruning is rarely required.

These trees do not transplant easily. The suggested maximum plant size is 4–5' (1.2–1.5 m).

TIPS

Stewartias are used as specimen trees and in group plantings. They make good companions for rhododendrons and azaleas because they enjoy the same growing conditions.

Don't be concerned if the bark doesn't put on a display when you first plant a stewartia, because it can take several years for the flaking to develop. Branches less than 2" (5 cm) in diameter don't exfoliate.

RECOMMENDED

S. monadelpha (Tall Stewartia) can be shrubby and multi-stemmed, or narrowly conical and single-stemmed. It grows 20–30' (6–9 m) tall, with an equal spread. It can grow up to 80' (25 m) tall in ideal conditions. The mid-summer flowers are hidden by the leaves, but the bright red fall color and the exfoliating bark are worthy features.

S. pseudocamellia (Japanese Stewartia) is a broad, columnar or pyramidal tree. It grows 20–40' (6–12 m) tall, with an equal spread. Attractive white flowers with showy yellow

S. monadelpha (this page)

stamens appear in mid-summer. The leaves turn yellow, orange and red in fall. The bark is scaly and exfoliating, leaving the trunk mottled with gray, orange, pink and red-brown. (Zones 5–8.)

Stewartias are rarely affected by pests or diseases.

Sumac

Rhus

Features: summer and fall foliage, summer flowers, late-summer to fall fruit, habit
Habit: bushy, suckering, colony-forming, deciduous shrubs
Height: 6–25' (1.8–7.5 m) **Spread:** equal to or greater than height
Planting: container; spring, fall **Zones:** 2–9

The sumacs well deserve their antler analogies. Especially in winter, the many angular, forked branches do look like the antlers of a majestic stag. The branches of *R. typhina* are also covered with a fine, dense fur that is much like antler velvet. The summer flowers of sumacs are followed by conical clusters of fuzzy, round, deep red fruit. The real show comes in fall, when these shrubs become a blaze of scarlet. Sumacs seem to shout for attention and will ramble right up onto your lap if you don't notice the suckers taking over your yard.

GROWING

Sumacs develop the best fall color in **full sun** but tolerate partial shade. The soil should be **moist, well-drained** and of **average fertility.**

These plants can become invasive in the garden. Remove suckers that come up where you don't want them. Cut out some of the oldest growth each year and allow some suckers to grow in to replace it. If the colony is growing in your lawn, you can mow down any plants that pop up out of bounds while they are still young.

TIPS

Sumacs can be used to form a specimen group in a shrub or mixed border, in a woodland garden or on a sloping bank. Both male and female plants are required for fruit to form.

Be sure to wear gloves if pulling up suckers, to avoid getting the odd, oniony smell all over your hands.

The fruits are edible. To create a refreshing beverage that tastes like pink lemonade, soak the ripe fruits in cold water overnight and then strain and sweeten to taste.

RECOMMENDED

R. glabra (Smooth Sumac) is a native shrub that forms a bushy, suckering colony. It grows 10–15' (3–4.5 m) tall, with an equal or greater spread. Green summer flower spikes are followed, on female plants, by fuzzy, red fruit. The foliage turns brilliant shades of orange, red and purple in fall.

R. typhina (this page)

R. typhina (Staghorn Sumac) is a suckering shrub with velvety branches. It grows 15–25' (5–7.5 m) tall and spreads 25' (7.5 m) or more. Fuzzy, yellow flowers are followed by hairy, red fruit. **'Dissecta'** ('Laciniata') has finely cut leaves that give the plant a lacy, graceful appearance. It is more compact than the species, growing 6' (1.8 m) high and spreading 10' (3 m). (Zones 3–8.)

PESTS & PROBLEMS

Blister, canker, caterpillars, dieback, leaf spot, powdery mildew, scale insects, wood rot and verticillium wilt can afflict these shrubs.

Sunrose
Rockrose
Helianthemum

Features: late-spring to mid-summer flowers, summer foliage
Habit: low, spreading, evergreen or semi-evergreen shrubs
Height: 12" (30 cm) **Spread:** 12–18" (30–45 cm)
Planting: container; spring **Zones:** 5–9

Rock gardens are known for their quick-draining soil, and a rock garden built around arborvitae often has soil that is sandy as well as rocky. These conditions are difficult for many flowering plants, but perfect for sunroses. The gray foliage seems to blend in with the stones, and the spreading habit of these shrubs helps block out any pesky weeds that try to invade the rockery. Pair this bloomer with ornamental grasses, which look best with a contrasting form growing in front of their upright, spiky blades.

GROWING

As the name implies, sunroses prefer **full sun.** The soil should be of **average fertility, neutral to alkaline** and **well drained.** Provide winter protection in the colder regions.

Once the spring blooming flush is finished, shear plants back to within an inch of the previous year's growth and expect a second flush in fall.

TIPS

Sunroses can be used in a rock garden, in planters, as groundcovers or at the front of a border.

RECOMMENDED

H. **'Rhodanthe Carneum'** ('Wisely Pink') is a low, rounded, spreading shrub with gray-green foliage. It grows 12" (30 cm) tall and spreads 12–18" (30–45 cm). Pink flowers with yellow centers last from late spring to mid-summer.

'Rhodanthe Carneum' (this page)

H. **'Wisely White'** is a rounded, spreading shrub with gray-green foliage. It grows 12" (30 cm) tall and spreads 18" (45 cm). The creamy white flowers have yellow centers. (Zones 6–8.)

Each lovely sunrose bloom lasts a single day.

Sweetbox

Sarcococca

Features: early-spring flowers, fruit, foliage
Habit: dense, suckering, evergreen shrubs
Height: 1.5–6' (0.5–1.8 m) **Spread:** 3–6' (1–1.8 m)
Planting: container; spring **Zones:** 6–9

Cold, rainy winters in the Pacific Northwest are bearable in part because we can grow sweetboxes so easily. Come February, a breath of sweet air from these vanilla-scented shrubs announces the end of another dreary winter. I use one of these shade-loving evergreens near the front door so that visitors will smell the vanilla fragrance and think I am busy baking. A sweetbox makes an excellent hedge along the north side of a house.

GROWING

Sweetboxes grow well in **partial, light or full shade.** The soil should be of **average fertility, humus rich, moist** and **well drained.** These plants are drought tolerant. Deadhead sweetboxes after flowering is complete. Fruit production is usually quite sporadic and the plants will look neater if trimmed back. Remove winter-damaged growth in mid-spring.

TIPS

Sweetboxes can be used in a shady border, as groundcovers, in a woodland garden, as low hedges or combined with ericaceous plants (plants in the heather family), such as rhododendrons.

RECOMMENDED

S. hookeriana (Sweetbox, Himalayan Sarcococca) is a dense, bushy, suckering shrub with glossy evergreen foliage. It grows 4–6' (1.2–1.8 m) tall, with an equal or greater spread. Fragrant flowers appear in early to mid-spring. Some dark blue fruits may form, if spent flowers are not removed. **Var. humilis** is a dwarf, clump-forming shrub that grows 18–24" (45–60 cm) tall and spreads 36" (90 cm). In early spring, it bears fragrant white flowers tinged with pink.

S. hookeriana var. *humilis* (this page)

S. rusticifolia (Fragrant Sarcococca) is a dense, bushy shrub with arching shoots. It grows 36" (90 cm) tall, with an equal spread. It bears clusters of fragrant white flowers in early spring, followed by red fruits. **Var. chinensis,** more commonly available than the species, is similar but has narrower leaves.

These easy-care plants rarely present problems with pests or diseases.

Thornless Honeylocust

Gleditsia triacanthos var. *inermis*

Features: summer and fall foliage, habit, fall seed pods
Habit: rounded, spreading, deciduous tree
Height: 15–100' (4.5–30 m) **Spread:** 15–70' (4.5–21 m)
Planting: B & B, container; spring, fall **Zones:** 3–8

The fall color of this elegant tree brings to mind the golden warmth of honey, and after the foliage falls you'll hear natural wind chimes when the long, narrow seed pods shake and rattle in the winter wind. Use Thornless Honeylocust as a focal point for a fall theme garden with Burning Bush euonymus and red-berried cotoneaster or Kinnikinnick.

GROWING

Thornless Honeylocust prefers **full sun.** The soil should be **fertile** and **well drained.** This tree adapts to most soil types.

No pruning is required. Stake and pinch young plants to establish a good branching pattern.

TIPS

Use Thornless Honeylocust as a specimen tree. Though it is often used as a street tree, this species is a poor choice for that purpose because the vigorous roots can break up pavement and sidewalks. Also, mass plantings (such as along a street) may lead to problems because the roots interconnect and can quickly transmit diseases from one tree to another.

The stunning beauty of a golden Thornless Honeylocust in fall almost makes up for the nuisance the tiny leaflets create. They get into every imaginable place and may need to be swept up because they slip between the tines of a rake. They do however, disintegrate quickly on soil or lawn.

'Sunburst'

The twisted, hanging pods of Thornless Honeylocust contain a sweet, edible pulp. Do not, however, confuse this species with the poisonous Black Locust (Robinia pseudoacacia) *or Kentucky Coffee Tree* (Gymnocladus dioica).

RECOMMENDED

G. triacanthos var. inermis is a spreading, rounded tree. It grows up to 100' (30 m) tall and spreads up to 70' (21 m). The fall color is a warm golden yellow. The flowers are inconspicuous, but the long, pea-like pods that develop in late summer persist into fall and sometimes still dangle from the branches after the leaves have fallen. This variety is thornless and many cultivars have been developed from it. **'Elegantissima'** is dense, shrubby, compact and slow growing. It grows 15–25' (4.5–7.5 m) tall and spreads up to about 15' (4.5 m). **'Sunburst'** is fast growing and broad spreading. It grows 30–40' (9–12 m) tall and spreads 25–30' (7.5–9 m). The foliage emerges a bright yellow in spring and matures to light green over the summer.

PESTS & PROBLEMS

Aphids, borers, canker, caterpillars, heart rot, leaf spot, mites, powdery mildew, tar spot and webworm can cause problems.

This adaptable, quick-growing tree provides very light shade, making it a good choice for lawns.

Viburnum

Viburnum

Features: flowers, summer and fall foliage, fruit, habit
Habit: bushy or spreading, evergreen or deciduous shrubs
Height: 2–15' (0.5–4.5 m) **Spread:** 2–15' (0.5–4.5 m)
Planting: bare-root, B & B, container; spring, fall **Zones:** 2–10

*I*t is the richly textured foliage that has always attracted me to viburnums, and many varieties have the rabbit-soft fur beneath the leaves that makes these shrubs so pettable. Add to this the fragrant flowers and striking blue or red berries and you have a decidedly handsome shrub. Viburnums add color and texture to woodland and shade gardens and look lovely in the shade of tall evergreens, or as background plants for blooming azaleas.

GROWING

Viburnums grow well in **full sun, partial shade** or **light shade.** The soil should be of **average fertility, moist** and **well drained.** Viburnums tolerate both alkaline and acidic soils.

These plants will look neatest if deadheaded, but this practice will of course prevent fruits from forming. Fruiting is better when more than one plant of a species is grown.

TIPS

Viburnums can be used in borders and woodland gardens. They are a good choice for plantings near swimming pools.

The edible but very tart fruits of *V. opulus* and *V. trilobum* are popular for making jellies, pies and wine. They can be sweetened somewhat by freezing or letting the frost nip them.

RECOMMENDED

V. x burkwoodii (Burkwood Viburnum) is a rounded shrub that is evergreen in warm climates. It grows 8–10' (2.5–3 m) tall and spreads 8' (2.5 m). Clusters of pinkish-white flowers appear in mid- to late spring and are followed by red fruits that ripen to black. (Zones 4–8.)

V. carlesii (Korean Spice Viburnum) is a dense, bushy, rounded, deciduous shrub. It grows 4–8' (1.2–2.5 m)

V. opulus (this page)

tall, with an equal spread. White or pink, spicy-scented flowers appear in mid- to late spring. The fruits are red, ripening to black. The foliage may turn red in fall. **'Aurora'** has dark pink flower buds. (Zones 5–8.)

V. davidii (David Viburnum) is a low, rounded, compact, evergreen shrub. It grows 3–5' (0.9–1.5 m) tall, with an equal spread. White spring flowers are followed by metallic blue fruit. This species and its cultivars are not self-fertile, so two different plants (sometimes sold as 'male' and 'female') must be present for fruit to set. Protect these plants from strong winds. (Zones 7–9.)

V. opulus (this page)

Many species of birds are attracted to viburnums for the edible fruit and the shelter they provide.

Try V. davidii *or* V. tinus *as a hedge.*

V. farreri (Fragrant Viburnum) is an upright, bushy, deciduous shrub 8–12' (2.5–3.5 m) tall and 6–10' (1.8–3 m) in spread. The very fragrant white or pink flowers appear in late winter or early spring, followed by red fruit. The fall color is reddish purple. Pruning will keep this species from becoming too leggy. (Zones 5–8.)

V. opulus (European Cranberrybush, Guelder-rose) is a rounded, spreading, deciduous shrub. It grows 8–15' (2.5–4.5 m) tall and spreads 8–12' (2.5–3.5 m). The flower clusters consist of an outer ring of showy sterile flowers surrounding the inner fertile flowers, giving the plant a lacy look when in bloom. The fall foliage and fruit are red. **'Nanum'** ('Compactum') is dense and slow growing, reaching 2–5' (0.5–1.5 m) in height and spread. (Zones 3–8.)

V. plicatum (Japanese Snowball Viburnum) is a bushy, upright, deciduous shrub with arching stems. It grows 10–15' (3–4.5 m) tall and spreads 12–15' (3.5–4.5 m). Ball-like clusters of flowers appear in late spring. Fall color is reddish purple. **Var. *tomentosum*** (Doublefile Viburnum) has graceful, horizontal branching that gives the shrub a layered effect. It grows 8–10' (2.5–3 m) tall and spreads 9–12' (2.7–3.5 m). The leaves are fuzzy underneath. Clusters of inconspicuous fertile flowers surrounded by showy sterile flowers blanket the branches. Several cultivars have been developed from this variety. **'Lanarth'** has showier flowerheads with larger sterile flowers. **'Mariesii'** has more distinctly layered branches. (Zones 5–8.)

V. sargentii (Sargent Viburnum) is a large, bushy, deciduous shrub. It grows 10–15' (3–4.5 m) tall, with an equal spread. The early-spring flowers consist of clusters of inconspicuous fertile flowers surrounded by showy sterile flowers. Fall color is yellow, orange and red. **'Onondaga'** has purple-stemmed, inconspicuous flowers ringed with showy, sterile, white flowers. The purple-green foliage turns red in fall. (Zones 3–7.)

V. tinus (Laurustinus) is an evergreen shrub with dark green, leathery leaves. It grows 6–12' (1.8–3.5 m) tall, with an equal spread. Pink buds open to white flowers that bloom most of the summer. This species makes a good hedge plant. (Zones 7–10.)

V. trilobum (American Cranberrybush, High-bush Cranberry) is a dense, rounded shrub that is native to much of central North America. It grows 8–15' (2.5–4.5 m) tall, with a spread of 8–12' (2.5–3.5 m). Early-summer clusters of showy sterile and inconspicuous fertile flowers are followed by edible red fruit. The fall color is red. **'Compactum'** is a smaller, more dense shrub that grows 5–6' (1.5–1.8 m) in height and width. Flowers and fruit resemble those of the species. (Zones 2–7.)

V. opulus

PESTS & PROBLEMS
Aphids, dieback, downy mildew, gray mold, leaf spot, mealybugs, powdery mildew, scale insects, treehoppers, verticillium wilt, weevils and wood rot can affect viburnums.

V. x *burkwoodii*

V. opulus 'Nanum'

V. plicatum 'Mariesii'

Virginia Creeper
Boston Ivy
Parthenocissus

Features: summer and fall foliage, habit
Habit: clinging, woody, deciduous climbers
Height: 30–70' (9–21 m) **Spread:** indefinite
Planting: container; spring, fall **Zones:** 3–9

Brick walls were made to showcase Virginia creepers, particularly in fall, when the warm colors of the brick complement the fiery orange and scarlet display. Let a Virginia creeper adorn any garden that needs a look of wild abandon. This enthusiastic climber is sure to get away from all but the most persistent pruners, and once Virginia is let loose, away she goes to light a wild fire of color each fall.

GROWING

These vines grow well in any light from **full sun** to **full shade.** The soil should preferably be **fertile** and **well drained.** The plants will adapt to clay or sandy soils.

These vigorous growers may need to be trimmed back frequently to keep them where you want them.

TIPS

Virginia creepers can cover an entire building, given enough time. They do not require support because they have clinging rootlets that can adhere to just about any surface—even smooth wood, vinyl or metal.

Give the plants lots of space and let them cover a wall, fence or arbor. Note, though, that when a vine is pulled off, the sticky ends leave little marks that can be hard to remove or even paint over. The **fruits** of Virginia creepers are **poisonous.**

RECOMMENDED

These species are very similar, except for the shape of the leaves.

P. quinquefolia (Virginia Creeper, Woodbine) is a clinging, woody climber that can grow 30–50' (9–15 m) tall. The dark green foliage turns flame red in fall. Each leaf is divided into five leaflets.

P. tricuspidata (Boston Ivy, Japanese Creeper) is also a clinging, woody climber. It grows 50–70' (15–21 m) tall. The three-lobed leaves turn red in fall. (Zones 4–8.)

PESTS & PROBLEMS

Aphids, bacterial leaf scorch, black rot, canker, dieback, downy mildew, grape leaf beetle, leafhoppers, leaf skeletonizers, leaf spot, powdery mildew, scab and scale insects can cause trouble.

P. quinquefolia (this page)

These vines can be used as groundcovers.

The ability of Virginia creepers to cover the sides of buildings can help keep buildings cool in the summer heat. Cut the plants back to keep windows and doors accessible.

Weigela

Weigela

Features: late-spring to early-summer flowers, foliage, habit
Habit: upright or low, spreading, deciduous shrubs
Height: 2–9' (0.5–2.7 m) **Spread:** 4–12' (1.2–3.5 m)
Planting: bare-root, container; spring, fall **Zones:** 3–8

*E*veryone loves a weigela in bloom, especially hummingbirds and children. The trumpet-shaped flowers are enchanting, and English picture books often show them used as caps for garden fairies. Any gardener who could benefit from the magic of fairies and the company of hummingbirds should find space for a weigela.

Weigelas are some of the longest-blooming shrubs—the main flush of blooms lasts six weeks and sporadic flowers appear all summer.

GROWING

Weigelas prefer **full sun** but tolerate partial shade. The soil should be **fertile** and **well drained.** These plants will adapt to most well-drained soil conditions.

Once flowering is finished, cut flowering shoots back to strong buds or branch junctions. One-third of the old growth can be cut back to the ground at the same time.

TIPS

Weigelas can be used in shrub or mixed borders, in open woodland gardens and as informal barrier plantings.

RECOMMENDED

W. florida is a spreading shrub with arching branches. It grows 6–9' (1.8–2.7 m) tall and spreads 8–12' (2.5–3.5 m). Dark pink flowers in clusters appear in late spring and early summer. **'Variegata'** is a compact plant that grows about 5' (1.5 m) tall, with an equal spread. The flowers are pale pink and the leaves have creamy white margins. (Zones 5–8.)

The following may be listed as cultivars of *W. florida.*

W. **'Minuet'** is a compact, spreading shrub. It grows 24–36" (60–90 cm) tall and spreads 4' (1.2 m). The dark pink flowers have yellow throats. (Zones 3–7.)

W. **'Red Prince'** is an upright shrub. It grows 5–6' (1.5–1.8 m) tall and spreads about 5' (1.5 m). Bright red flowers appear in early summer, with a second flush in late summer. (Zones 4–7.)

PESTS & PROBLEMS

Scale insects, twig-knot nematodes, twig dieback and verticillium wilt are possible, but usually not serious, problems.

'Variegata'

Hummingbirds will be especially attracted to weigelas with long, red flowers. This shrub's name honors German botanist Christian Weigel (1748–1831).

Winter Currant
Red-Flowering Currant, Blood Currant
Ribes sanguineum

Features: spring flowers, fruit, foliage
Habit: upright, deciduous shrub with arching stems
Height: 6–10' (1.8–3 m) **Spread:** 6–10' (1.8–3 m)
Planting: container; spring, fall **Zones:** 5–8

*T*his graceful shrub is one of many Northwest natives that are, ironically, more appreciated in European gardens than right here at home. Discover its appeal for yourself. Gorgeous clusters of red to pinkish flowers hang from the branches in spring, attracting attention along with hummingbirds. After blooming, the shrub's attractive foliage makes a perfect backdrop for your summer flowers.

GROWING

Winter Currant grows well in **full sun** or **partial shade.** The soil should be of **average fertility, moist** and **well drained.** This plant is drought tolerant.

One-third of the growth can be removed each year after flowering. Flowering shoots can be cut back to a strong bud or branch after flowering unless fruit is desired. Hedges can be trimmed back after flowering.

TIPS

Winter Currant can be used as a specimen, in a shrub or mixed border, on the edge of a woodland garden or as an informal hedge. The species tends to become leggy under too much shade.

Male and female flowers appear on separate plants. Male flowers are generally showier. Plants of both sexes are needed if fruits are desired.

The berries are edible but not tasty.

RECOMMENDED

R. sanguineum is native to the Pacific Northwest. It is an upright, rounded shrub with arching branches, reaching 6–10' (1.8–3 m) in height, with an equal spread. Striking clusters of dark pink flowers dangle from the branches in spring, followed by dark blue fruit on female plants in summer. **'White Icicle'** grows 6–8' (1.8–2.5 m) tall, with an equal spread. It has showy white flowers. This cultivar is more shade tolerant than the species.

PESTS & PROBLEMS

Anthracnose, aphids, caterpillars, dieback, downy mildew, leaf spot, powdery mildew, rust and scale insects can cause problems. Some species of currants are banned in many communities because they are alternate hosts for white pine blister rust, a devastating fungal disease of pines.

'White Icicle'

Try training 'White Icicle' to grow up a trellis against a wall.

Winterhazel

Corylopsis

Features: early to mid-spring flowers   **Habit:** spreading, deciduous shrubs
Height: 4–10' (1.2–3 m)   **Spread:** 4–10' (1.2–3 m)
Planting: B & B, container; spring, fall   **Zones:** 5–9

---

*D*angling like golden earrings, winterhazel flowers perfume the air just when we need relief from winter most. Open and casual in form, this shrub will blend beautifully with rhododendrons and native Vine Maple in the woodland garden. Placing this appealing bloomer at the end of a path will inspire you to bundle up and take an early spring walk in the garden.

GROWING

Winterhazels grow best in **partial or light shade** and in **fertile, moist** and **well-drained** soil. These plants will require winter protection in colder areas of the region.

Remove awkward shoots right after flowering has finished.

TIPS

Use winterhazels in shady borders, woodland gardens and group plantings.

Cutting a few branches in December and putting them in a vase indoors will force them into early bloom.

RECOMMENDED

C. pauciflora (Buttercup Winterhazel, Butterfly Winterhazel, Fragrant Winterhazel) is a rounded, spreading shrub. It grows 4–10' (1.2–3 m) tall and spreads 4–8' (1.2–2.5 m). Short, tassel-like clusters of fragrant, dangling, bright yellow flowers appear in early to mid-spring. (Zones 6–9.)

C. spicata (Spike Winterhazel) is an open, wide-spreading shrub that grows 4–10' (1.2–3 m) tall and spreads 6–10' (1.8–3 m). It bears pale yellow flowers in tassels 6" (15 cm) long in mid-spring. (Zones 5–8.)

The attractive, fragrant flowers appear before the foliage in spring. These easy-care shrubs are rarely affected by pests or diseases.

C. spicata

Wisteria

Wisteria

Features: late-spring flowers, foliage, habit
Habit: twining, woody, deciduous climbers
Height: 20–50' (6–15 m) or more
Spread: indefinite
Planting: container; spring, fall
Zones: 4–9

When wisterias are in bloom, nothing else matters. Wisteria hysteria takes over as the huge flower clusters hang in gorgeous majesty, blocking all thoughts of other plants from a gardener's mind. Venture closer to observe the blossoms and the sweet scent only adds to the allure. In my garden, a wisteria merited not just a trellis to grow on, but an entire house-like structure, a sturdy pergola that can be expanded as the years go by and I become ever more enamored with this spectacular vine.

GROWING

Wisterias grow well in **full sun** or **partial shade.** The soil should be of **average fertility, moist** and **well drained.** Vines grown in too fertile a soil will produce lots of vegetative growth but very few flowers. Avoid planting wisteria near a lawn where fertilizer may leach over to your vine.

The first two or three years will be used to establish a main framework of sturdy stems. Once the vine is established, side shoots can be cut back in late winter to within three to six buds of the main stems. Trim the entire plant back in mid-summer if the growth is becoming rampant. Grown on a large, sturdy structure, wisteria can simply be left to its own devices, but be prepared for it to escape once it runs out of room.

To propagate wisteria, bend a length of vine down and bury it in a pot of good potting soil. Hold the branch in place with a rock if required. The buried section will root and can then be cut from the main plant. The roots have taken when you can no longer pull the buried section up out of the pot with a gentle tug.

TIPS

These vines require something to twine around, such as a trellis or other sturdy structure. You can also train a wisteria to form a small tree. Try to select a permanent site; wisterias don't like being moved once established.

These vigorous vines may send up suckers and can root wherever branches touch the ground. Regular pruning will prevent your wisteria from getting out of hand.

All parts of wisteria plants, especially the **seeds,** are **poisonous.**

RECOMMENDED

W. floribunda (Japanese Wisteria) grows 25–50' (7.5–15 m) tall, or taller. Long, pendulous clusters of fragrant blue, purple, pink or white flowers appear in late spring before the leaves emerge. Long, bean-like pods follow.

W. sinensis (this page)

W. sinensis (Chinese Wisteria) can grow 20–30' (6–9 m) tall, or taller. It bears long, pendant clusters of fragrant blue-purple flowers in late spring. **'Alba'** has white flowers. (Zones 5–8.)

PESTS & PROBLEMS

Aphids, crown gall, dieback, leaf miners, leaf spot, mealybugs and virus diseases may cause occasional problems.

You may need to treat your wisteria very badly to get the best blooms. If you have a reluctant bloomer, try pruning the roots and withholding food and water.

Witch-Hazel
Hamamelis

Features: flowers, foliage, habit
Habit: spreading, deciduous shrubs or small trees
Height: 10–20' (3–6 m) **Spread:** 10–20' (3–6 m)
Planting: B & B, container; spring, fall **Zones:** 3–9

A winter walk brought me nose to branch with a collection of witch-hazel in a city arboretum, and the remarkable fragrance is still on my mind. The naked winter form of this shrub is enchanting even before the mysteriously twisted flowers emerge. A little pruning turns the shrub into a tidy small tree—the perfect focal point for an otherworldly winter garden, with hellebores and crocuses casting a spell beneath the skirts of the blooming witch-hazel.

GROWING
Witch-hazels grow best in a **sheltered** spot under **full sun** or **light shade.** The soil should be of **average fertility, neutral to acidic, moist** and **well drained.**

Pruning is rarely required. Remove awkward shoots once flowering is complete.

TIPS

Witch-hazels work well individually or in groups. They can be used as specimen plants, in shrub or mixed borders or in woodland gardens. As small trees, they are ideal for space-limited gardens.

The unique flowers have long, narrow, crinkled petals that give the plant a spidery appearance when in bloom. If the weather gets too cold, the petals will roll up, protecting the flowers and extending the flowering season.

RECOMMENDED

H. x intermedia is a vase-shaped, spreading shrub. It grows 10–20' (3–6 m) tall, with an equal spread. Fragrant clusters of yellow, orange or red flowers appear in mid- to late winter. The leaves turn attractive

H. virginiana

Flowering branches of H. japonica *are often cut and used as interior decoration.*

H. x intermedia 'Arnold Promise'

shades of orange, red and bronze in fall. **'Arnold Promise'** has large, fragrant, bright yellow or yellow-orange flowers. **'Diane'** ('Diana') has dark red flowers in late winter and good fall color of yellow, orange and red. **'Jelena'** has a horizontal, spreading habit. The fragrant flowers are coppery orange and the fall color is orange-red. **'Pallida'** is a more compact plant, growing to 12' (3.5 m) tall and wide. Its flowers are bright yellow. (Zones 5–9.)

H. japonica (Japanese Witch-hazel) is an open, wide-spreading tree. It grows 10–15' (3–4.5 m) tall, with an equal or greater spread. Yellow flowers appear in mid- to late winter, and the fall color is also yellow. The angular branches form an attractive criss-cross pattern. (Zones 5–9.)

H. mollis (Chinese Witch-hazel) is a rounded, spreading shrub that is more dense and compact than the other species. The branches lie in an attractive zig-zag pattern. This species grows 10–15' (3–4.5 m) tall, with an equal spread.

H. virginiana (this page)

It bears very fragrant yellow flowers in mid- to late winter. The fall color may be orange or yellow. (Zones 5–9.)

H. virginiana (Common Witch-hazel) is a large, rounded, spreading shrub or small tree. It grows 12–20' (3.5–6 m) or more in height, with an equal spread. Yellow fall flowers are often hidden by the foliage that turns yellow at the same time, but this species is attractive nonetheless. (Zones 3–8.)

PESTS & PROBLEMS
Aphids, leaf rollers, leaf spot, powdery mildew, scale insects and wood rot are possible, but rarely serious, problems.

A witch-hazel extract was used traditionally as a general remedy for burns and skin inflammations. Today it is often sold as a mild astringent in facial products.

H. virginiana (this page)

Yew

Taxus

Features: foliage, habit, red seed cups
Habit: evergreen; conical or columnar trees or bushy or spreading shrubs
Height: 2–70' (0.5–21 m) **Spread:** 4–30' (1.2–9 m)
Planting: B & B, container; spring, fall **Zones:** 4–8

Yews are the stately soldiers of the landscape, stable and reliable, adding strong bones and good posture to the garden structure. Use them to mark walls or entrances for garden rooms, or to accent the corner of a house or the curve in a garden path. Left to their own devices, yews grow into large, attractive trees, but they withstand any amount of pruning and can be kept to almost any size and shape, making them popular for hedges and topiary.

GROWING

Yews grow well in any light conditions from **full sun** to **full shade.** The soil should be **fertile, moist** and **well drained.** These trees tolerate coastal, dry and polluted conditions, and soils of any acidity. They dislike excessive heat, however, and on the hot south or southwest side of a building they may suffer needle scorch.

Hedges and topiary can be trimmed back in summer and fall. New growth will sprout from hard prunings. Even mature wood will sprout new growth if exposed.

TIPS

Yews can be used in borders or as specimens, hedges, topiary and groundcovers.

Male and female flowers are borne on separate plants. Both must be present for the attractive red arils (seed cups) to form.

T. cuspidata

*All parts of yews are **poisonous,** except the pleasant-tasting, fleshy red cup that surrounds the inedible hard seed.*

T. baccata

T. baccata (all photos)

Taxol, a drug for treating ovarian, breast and other cancers, was originally derived from the bark of the native T. brevifolia *(Western Yew).*

RECOMMENDED

T. baccata (English Yew) is a broad, conical tree with attractive, flaking bark. It grows 30–70' (9–21 m) tall and spreads 15–30' (4.5–9 m). The foliage can become discolored in winter. The species is hardy in Zones 6–8. Among the many cultivars, **'Fastigiata'** (Irish Yew) is a columnar, female cultivar grown for its attractive, upright habit. It grows 15–30' (4.5–9 m) tall and spreads 5–10' (1.5–3 m). **'Repandens'** is a wide-spreading, mounding shrub with greater cold hardiness than the species, to Zone 5. It grows 2–4' (0.6–1.2 m) tall and spreads 12–15' (3.5–4.5 m).

T. cuspidata (Japanese Yew) is a slow-growing, broad, columnar or conical tree. It grows 30–50' (9–15 m) tall and spreads 20–30' (6–9 m). **'Nana'** is a compact, spreading cultivar that may grow 3–6' (0.9–1.8 m) tall and 4–10' (1.2–3 m) wide. (Zones 4–7.)

T. x *media* (English Japanese Yew), a cross between the other two species, has the vigor of the English Yew and the cold-hardiness of the Japanese Yew. It forms a rounded, upright tree or shrub 2–25' (0.5–7.5 m) in height, depending on the cultivar. **'Densiformis'** is a wide, dense, rounded shrub. It grows 3–4' (0.9–1.2 m) tall and spreads 6–8' (1.8–2.5 m). **'Hicksii'** is an open, columnar tree that grows 15–25' (4.5–7.5 m) tall and spreads 5–10' (1.5–3 m). This narrow, upright yew is a good choice in colder climates. (Zones 4–7.)

PESTS & PROBLEMS

Black vine weevils, dieback, mealybugs, mites, needle blight, root rot and scale insects are possible but not serious problems. A wash with soapy water during hot weather will help control mites. Be sure to rinse plants well.

The tough wood of T. baccata *was traditionally valued for carving and for making longbows. Robin Hood is said to have made his bow from this wood.*

Yucca
Adam's Needle
Yucca filamentosa

Features: summer flowers, foliage, habit
Habit: rounded rosette of long, stiff, spiky, evergreen leaves
Height: 24–36" (60–90 cm); up to 6' (1.8 m) in flower
Spread: 24–36" (60–90 cm)
Planting: spring, fall **Zones:** 5–9

This spiky plant looks as though it belongs in a desert. When used as a specimen in an urn or large pot, it makes a real exclamation point. Use the yellow and green varieties to add foliage color as well as texture in a perennial garden, or to call attention to large boulder outcrops or groups of smooth stones. Add a touch of the desert to your personal oasis with Yucca.

GROWING

Yucca grows best in **full sun.** Any **well-drained** soil is suitable. This drought-tolerant plant grows best in areas of low humidity.

Pruning is not needed, but the flower spikes can be removed when flowering is finished.

The striking white flowers are edible raw or cooked and are said to taste like Belgian endive. Try adding them to a salad.

TIPS

Yucca is used as a specimen, usually in groups or in planters, to give a garden a southern appearance. In pots, planters and urns this plant also makes a strong architectural statement.

RECOMMENDED

Y. filamentosa has long, stiff, finely serrated, pointed leaves with threads that peel back from the edges. It is the most frost-hardy *Yucca* species available. **'Bright Edge'** has leaves with yellow margins. **'Golden Sword'** has leaves with yellow centers and green margins.

PESTS & PROBLEMS

Cane borers, fungal leaf spot and scale insects can cause problems.

Yucca fruits are rarely seen in cultivation. The Yucca moth, which pollinates the flowers, is uncommon outside the plant's natural range in the southeastern U.S.

'Bright Edge' (this page)

OTHER TREES & SHRUBS TO CONSIDER

Bald Cypress

BALD CYPRESS
Taxodium distichum

Deciduous or semi-evergreen, conical coniferous tree 50–130' (15–40 m) tall and 20–30' (6–9 m) in spread. Becomes more open and asymmetrical with age. Bright green foliage turns orangy brown in fall. In or near swampy areas tree forms gnome-like 'knees' (*pneumatophores*); these knobby roots poke up out of the water and allow the roots to breathe.

Bald Cypress prefers **full sun** or **partial shade** and **moist, acidic** soil but will adapt to different soil conditions, even dry soils. Alkaline soils can cause the foliage to turn yellow (chlorotic). Bald Cypress has a deep taproot but transplants easily when young. Use as a large specimen tree individually or in groups; it looks especially good near lakes and streams. (Zones 4–9.)

Camperdown Elm

CAMPERDOWN ELM
Ulmus glabra 'Camperdownii'

Deciduous, shrubby form grafted onto a 6–7' (2 m) standard to form a domed, weeping tree with ground-sweeping branches. Can grow 20–25' (6–7.5 m) tall, with an equal spread. Attractive bare branches provide winter interest.

Camperdown Elm prefers **full sun** and **moist, well-drained** soil. This cultivar is susceptible to Dutch Elm Disease and the many other problems that afflict elms, but it is more resistant than most species. It makes a striking specimen, more suitable for a small garden than many larger trees. (Zones 4–7.)

EUROPEAN HORNBEAM
Carpinius betulus

Deciduous, broadly conical to oval tree with no central leader; grows 30–50' (9–15 m) tall and spreads 20–40' (6–12 m). Female flowers have large, conspicuous, three-lobed bracts that provide a nice summer feature. Cultivars have different forms, such as the popular upright 'Fastigiata' and the less common, weeping 'Pendula.'

European Hornbeam prefers **full sun** to **partial shade** and **cool, moist** conditions. Many soil types are acceptable as long as they are **well drained**. This tree provides dense shade and can be used as a specimen. It is very effective as a screen or hedge because it tolerates heavy pruning. It will also adapt well to a large planter. (Zones 5–9.)

FALSE ARBORVITAE
Thujopsis dolabrata

Evergreen, pyramidal tree 20–70' (6–21 m) tall and 15–30' (4.5–9 m) wide. Shiny green foliage resembles that of *Thuja* but consists of much larger scales. The dwarf, rounded cultivar **'Nana'** grows about 36" (90 cm) tall.

Grow False Arborvitae in **full sun** and **fertile, humus-rich, moist** and **well-drained** soil. It grows quickly and easily from cuttings. This species is not susceptible to the pest problems that afflict *Thuja* and doesn't suffer from winter desiccation. It is a beautiful tree to use as a specimen in a large garden. (Zones 5–8.)

False Arborvitae can be difficult to find at garden centers. Ask somebody who already has a mature tree if you can take cuttings.

European Hornbeam

False Arborvitae

HEDGE BAMBOO
Bambusa multiplex

Technically a member of the grass family, Hedge Bamboo is at home with trees and shrubs. It can grow 10–50' (3–15 m) tall and can spread indefinitely. Strong, arching, yellow, often striped hollow stems bear narrow, leafy branches.

Hedge Bamboo prefers **full sun** to **partial shade, humus-rich** soil and **humid** conditions. For best results plant in a **sheltered** location. Use it in frost-free areas for a unique hedge or windbreak or try it in a large planter. A barrier in the soil may be needed to stop this plant from spreading excessively. (Zones 8–10.)

Hedge Bamboo

Japanese Pagoda-Tree

JAPANESE PAGODA-TREE
Sophora japonica

Deciduous, dense, rounded, wide-spreading tree 50–100' (15–30 m) tall, with an equal spread; has a symmetrical, layered appearance. Fragrant white flowers are produced in summer, followed by pea-like fruit pods resembling strings of beads. The seeds are **poisonous**. 'Pendula' is a dramatic, weeping cultivar 10' (3 m) tall, with an equal spread.

Japanese Pagoda-tree grows best in **full sun** with **well-drained, moderately fertile** soil. It adapts to most conditions and tolerates polluted urban environments. A beautiful and worthwhile specimen or shade tree, but best reserved for parks and large properties where it will have enough space to reach its full potential. (Zones 4–9.)

Japanese Pagoda-tree looks at home in any garden style, from Victorian to contemporary, but it is especially attractive in gardens with an Eastern influence.

LINDEN
Tilia

Deciduous. Several species commonly grown; all are large, rounded or columnar or pyramidal trees 70–100' (21–30 m) tall, spreading 50–80' (15–25 m). Bracted clusters of creamy, fragrant flowers are borne in summer. Two commonly grown species are Littleleaf Linden (*T. cordata*) and Bigleaf Linden (*T. platyphyllos*).

Lindens prefer **full sun** to **partial shade** with **moist, well-drained, neutral to slightly alkaline** soil. These trees adapt to most conditions, making them popular street trees. They also make good specimen or shade trees. Avoid areas with strong winds and ensure adequate water during dry periods. (Zones 3–8.)

Linden

Monkey Puzzle Tree

MONKEY PUZZLE TREE
Araucaria araucana

Evergreen, broadly pyramidal coniferous tree 50–80' (15–25 m) tall and 20–30' (6–9 m) wide. Whorled branches give a tiered appearance and are densely packed with overlapping, stiff, sharp-pointed, triangular leaves that persist for many years. Lower branches drop as the tree ages. Huge cones, up to 12" (30 cm) long, are produced only on female trees.

Monkey Puzzle Tree prefers **full sun** to **partial shade** with **moist, well-drained** soil of **average fertility**. Periods of drought are tolerated. This unique, exotic tree can be used as a specimen in larger areas but is very impractical for smaller gardens. Use where close contact with the armored branches can be avoided until the lower branches drop. (Zones 7–10.)

SILK TREE
Albizia julibrissin

Deciduous, fast-growing but short-lived, multi-stemmed, vase-shaped small tree or large shrub 20–35' (6–10 m) tall and wide. Foliage is fern-like and flowers are fluffy and light to deep pink. Common name comes from the long, showy stamens that resemble strands of pink silk.

Silk Tree prefers **full sun** with **well-drained** soil of **poor to average fertility**. It can withstand drought, high wind, high pH and high soil salinity. Grown for the foliage and flowers, this plant can add a tropical touch to your garden. (Zones 6–10.)

SWEET GUM
Liquidambar styraciflua

Silk Tree

Sweet Gum

Deciduous tree with an open habit and broad, rounded form; grows 60–80' (18–25 m) tall and spreads 40–60' (12–18 m). Young twigs and branches have corky ridges along their lengths. Maple-like foliage is showy in fall; leaves turn vivid shades of orange, red, pink and purple. Variegated-leaved cultivars are available. Round, spiny fruits may persist and provide winter interest.

Sweet Gum prefers **full sun** and **neutral to slightly acidic, fertile, moist** soil with lots of room for root growth. Though it prefers moist conditions, it is drought tolerant. Try Sweet Gum as a specimen or as part of a mixed woody grouping. It also makes a nice light shade tree. The spiny fruits can be hazardous to bare feet when they drop. A fruitless cultivar with rounded leaves, called **'Rotundiloba,'** has apparently been developed. (Zones 5–9.)

Sweet Gum is so named because the cut bark exudes a sweet, fragrant, amber-colored liquid used to make perfumes.

TULIP TREE
Liriodendron tulipifera

Deciduous, round-oval tree 70–100' (21–30 m) or more tall and 35–50' (10–15 m) wide. Leaves turn golden yellow in fall. A large, fast-growing tree that needs lots of space to grow. Common name comes from the yellow-green, tulip-shaped flowers, often hidden in the high branches.

Tulip Tree grows best in **full sun** to **partial shade** with **fertile, moist, well-drained** soil. It prefers a slightly acidic soil, but will tolerate a range of pH levels. In drought conditions the inner leaves may drop prematurely. This tree dislikes being transplanted once established. Use in a large garden as a specimen, individually or grouped. (Zones 4–10.)

WEEPING WILLOW
Salix alba 'Tristis'

Deciduous, rounded tree 30–50' (9–15 m) tall with an equal spread. Delicate, flexible, weeping branches sweep the ground. Long, narrow leaves emerge early in spring and turn bright yellow before dropping late in fall.

Tulip Tree (flower, above)

Weeping Willow

Weeping Willow prefers **full sun** with **well-drained** but **moist** soil and lots of room for roots to spread. It suffers in shallow, alkaline soil. This graceful, elegant tree can be used as a specimen or shade tree. It is displayed to best advantage next to a lake, river or other water source. A beautiful tree, but not without problems; the roots can be destructive, breaking into pipes and through foundations, and twigs and leaves drop constantly. (Zones 4–9.)

Weeping Willow is one of the first deciduous trees to leaf out, and one of the last to drop its leaves. The golden branches provide winter interest.

TREE HEIGHT LEGEND: Short: < 25' (7. 5 m) • Medium: 25–50' (7.5–15 m) • Tall: > 50' (15 m)

SPECIES by Common Name	FORM						FOLIAGE							
	Tall Tree	Med. Tree	Short Tree	Shrub	Groundcover	Climber	Evergreen	Deciduous	Variegated	Blue/White	Purple/Red	Yellow/Gold	Dark green	Light green
Abelia				•	•		•	•					•	
Aralia			•	•				•	•				•	
Arborvitae	•	•	•	•			•			•		•	•	
Arbutus	•	•	•				•						•	
Barberry				•			•	•	•		•	•	•	
Beautyberry				•				•						
Beech	•	•						•	•		•	•	•	
Birch	•	•						•						
Bluebeard				•				•				•		•
Bog Rosemary				•	•		•						•	
Boxwood				•			•						•	
Broom				•	•			•						
Butterfly Bush			•	•				•					•	•
California Lilac				•	•		•	•						
Cedar	•	•	•	•	•		•			•		•		•
Clethra				•				•					•	
Cotoneaster			•	•	•		•						•	
Daphne				•	•		•		•			•	•	
Dawn Redwood	•							•					•	
Deutzia				•				•						
Dogwood			•	•				•					•	•
Douglas-fir	•		•				•						•	
Dove Tree		•	•					•				•		•
Elder			•	•				•			•	•	•	
English Ivy					•	•	•	•	•			•	•	
Enkianthus			•	•				•						
Euonymus			•	•	•	•	•	•	•			•	•	•
False Cypress	•	•	•	•			•			•			•	•
Fir	•	•	•	•			•			•			•	•
Firethorn				•		•	•						•	
Flowering Cherry	•	•	•	•				•			•		•	•
Flowering Crabapple		•	•			•		•					•	•

| | FEATURES | | | | | | | BLOOMING | | | | | | |
Form	Flowers	Foliage	Bark	Fruit/Cones	Scent	Spines	Fall Color	Winter	Spring	Summer	Fall	Zones	Page Number	SPECIES by Common Name
•	•	•					•		•	•	•	5–9	72	Abelia
	•	•		•		•				•		4–9	74	Aralia
•		•	•	•	•							2–9	76	Arborvitae
•	•	•	•	•						•	•	7–9	80	Arbutus
	•	•		•		•	•		•			6–9	82	Barberry
		•					•					6–10	86	Beautyberry
•		•	•	•			•					4–9	88	Beech
•	•	•	•				•		•			2–9	92	Birch
	•	•			•					•		5–9	96	Bluebeard
	•	•							•	•		2–8	98	Bog Rosemary
•		•										4–9	100	Boxwood
•	•								•	•		3–9	104	Broom
•	•	•							•	•	•	4–9	106	Butterfly Bush
•	•	•							•	•		7–9	110	California Lilac
•		•	•	•								5–9	112	Cedar
	•	•			•		•			•		3–9	114	Clethra
•	•	•		•			•			•		4–9	116	Cotoneaster
	•	•			•			•	•		•	4–8	120	Daphne
•		•	•	•			•					5–9	124	Dawn Redwood
	•								•	•		5–9	126	Deutzia
•	•	•	•	•			•		•	•		2–9	128	Dogwood
•		•	•	•								4–9	132	Douglas-fir
•	•		•						•			6–8	134	Dove Tree
	•	•		•			•		•	•		3–9	136	Elder
•		•					•					5–10	138	English Ivy
	•						•		•	•		4–8	140	Enkianthus
•		•	•				•					4–9	142	Euonymus
•		•	•	•								4–9	146	False Cypress
•		•		•								3–7	152	Fir
•	•	•		•		•				•		5–9	154	Firethorn
•	•		•	•	•		•	•	•		•	2–9	158	Flowering Cherry
•	•			•	•				•			4–8	164	Flowering Crabapple

TREE HEIGHT LEGEND: Short: < 25' (7. 5 m) • Medium: 25–50' (7.5–15 m) • Tall: > 50' (15 m)

SPECIES by Common Name	FORM							FOLIAGE							
	Tall Tree	Med. Tree	Short Tree	Shrub	Groundcover	Climber		Evergreen	Deciduous	Variegated	Blue/White	Purple/Red	Yellow/Gold	Dark green	Light green
Flowering Quince				•					•						
Forsythia				•					•						•
Fothergilla				•					•	•					•
Fringe Tree			•	•					•						•
Ginkgo	•	•							•						•
Goldenchain Tree			•			•			•						
Grape						•			•			•		•	
Hawthorn			•						•					•	
Hazel			•	•					•						
Heather				•	•			•						•	
Hemlock	•	•	•	•				•						•	•
Holly	•	•	•	•				•		•			•	•	
Horsechestnut	•	•							•						
Huckleberry				•	•			•	•					•	•
Hydrangea			•	•	•	•			•					•	•
Incense-cedar	•	•						•		•			•	•	
Japanese Acuba				•				•		•					
Japanese Kerria				•					•	•			•		•
Jasmine				•	•	•			•					•	
Juniper	•	•	•	•	•	•		•			•		•	•	•
Kalmia				•				•						•	
Katsura-tree	•	•	•						•						•
Kinnikinnick					•			•						•	
Kiwi						•			•	•				•	
Larch	•	•							•		•				•
Leucothoe				•				•		•				•	
Lilac		•	•	•					•					•	
Magnolia		•	•	•				•	•					•	
Maple		•	•	•					•	•		•	•	•	
Mock-orange				•					•				•		•
Ninebark				•					•						•
Oak	•	•							•					•	

	FEATURES							BLOOMING						SPECIES by Common Name
Form	Flowers	Foliage	Bark	Fruit/Cones	Scent	Spines	Fall Color	Winter	Spring	Summer	Fall	Zones	Page Number	
	•			•	•	•			•			4–9	168	Flowering Quince
	•								•			4–9	170	Forsythia
	•				•		•		•			4–9	174	Fothergilla
•			•		•					•		4–9	176	Fringe Tree
•		•	•				•					3–9	178	Ginkgo
•	•				•				•	•		5–8	180	Goldenchain Tree
•		•					•					5–9	182	Grape
•	•	•	•			•	•		•	•		3–8	184	Hawthorn
•	•	•	•	•					•			3–9	188	Hazel
•	•	•			•			•	•	•		5–7	190	Heather
•		•		•								3–8	192	Hemlock
•		•		•		•			•			4–9	196	Holly
•		•								•		3–8	200	Horsechestnut
	•	•							•	•		2–9	202	Huckleberry
•	•						•			•	•	3–9	204	Hydrangea
•		•		•								5–8	210	Incense-cedar
		•		•								6–9	212	Japanese Acuba
•	•	•							•	•		4–9	214	Japanese Kerria
•	•				•			•	•	•	•	6–10	216	Jasmine
•		•		•		•						2–9	218	Juniper
	•	•							•	•		4–9	224	Kalmia
•		•			•		•					4–8	226	Katsura-tree
•	•	•		•			•		•			2–7	228	Kinnikinnick
•	•	•		•						•		3–8	230	Kiwi
•		•		•			•					1–7	232	Larch
	•	•							•			5–9	234	Leucothoe
•	•				•				•	•		3–8	236	Lilac
•	•	•	•	•					•	•		3–9	240	Magnolia
•		•	•	•	•		•		•			2–9	244	Maple
	•				•				•	•		3–8	250	Mock-orange
	•	•	•	•					•	•		2–10	252	Ninebark
•		•	•	•			•					3–9	254	Oak

TREE HEIGHT LEGEND: Short: < 25' (7. 5 m) • Medium: 25–50' (7.5–15 m) • Tall: > 50' (15 m)

SPECIES
by Common Name

Species	Tall Tree	Med. Tree	Short Tree	Shrub	Groundcover	Climber	Evergreen	Deciduous	Variegated	Blue/White	Purple/Red	Yellow/Gold	Dark green	Light green
Oregon-grape				•	•		•						•	
Pieris				•			•		•		•		•	
Pine	•	•	•	•			•						•	
Plane-tree	•							•					•	•
Potentilla				•				•						•
Redbud		•	•	•				•						
Redwood	•	•	•	•			•						•	
Rhododendron				•			•	•					•	
Rockrose				•			•				•			
Rose-of-Sharon			•	•				•						
Russian Olive			•	•				•		•				•
Silverbell		•	•	•				•						•
Skimmia				•			•						•	
Smoketree			•	•				•			•		•	
Snowbell		•	•	•				•					•	
Snowberry			•		•			•		•				•
Spirea				•				•		•		•		
Spruce	•	•	•	•			•			•			•	
Stewartia	•	•	•					•						
Sumac			•	•				•					•	
Sunrose			•		•		•	•		•				•
Sweetbox			•		•		•						•	
Thornless Honeylocust	•	•	•					•				•		•
Viburnum		•	•				•	•					•	•
Virginia Creeper					•	•		•			•		•	
Weigela				•				•						
Winter Currant				•				•						•
Winterhazel				•				•						
Wisteria					•			•						
Witch-hazel			•	•				•					•	•
Yew	•	•	•	•	•		•						•	
Yucca				•			•		•					•

Form	Flowers	Foliage	Bark	Fruit/Cones	Scent	Spines	Fall Color	Winter	Spring	Summer	Fall	Zones	Page Number	SPECIES by Common Name
	●	●		●			●		●			5–9	256	Oregon-grape
	●	●			●			●	●			5–8	258	Pieris
●		●	●	●								2–8	260	Pine
●		●	●				●					4–8	264	Plane-tree
	●	●							●	●	●	2–8	266	Potentilla
	●						●		●			4–9	270	Redbud
●		●	●	●								6–9	272	Redwood
●	●	●			●			●	●	●		3–9	274	Rhododendron
	●	●			●					●		8–10	280	Rockrose
	●			●						●	●	5–9	282	Rose-of-Sharon
●	●	●		●	●					●		2–8	284	Russian Olive
	●	●		●			●		●	●		5–9	286	Silverbell
	●	●		●	●				●			6–9	288	Skimmia
●	●	●					●			●		4–8	290	Smoketree
●	●	●			●				●	●		4–9	292	Snowbell
●		●		●						●		3–7	294	Snowberry
●	●	●					●		●	●		3–9	296	Spirea
●		●		●	●	●						2–9	300	Spruce
●	●	●	●				●			●		5–9	304	Stewartia
●	●	●		●			●			●		2–9	306	Sumac
●	●	●							●	●		5–9	308	Sunrose
	●	●		●	●				●			6–9	310	Sweetbox
●		●		●			●					3–8	312	Thornless Honeylocust
●	●	●		●	●		●	●	●	●		2–10	314	Viburnum
●		●					●					3–9	318	Virginia Creeper
●	●	●							●	●		3–8	320	Weigela
	●	●		●					●			5–8	322	Winter Currant
	●				●				●			5–9	324	Winterhazel
●	●	●		●	●				●			4–9	326	Wisteria
●	●	●			●		●	●	●		●	3–9	328	Witch-hazel
●		●	●									4–8	332	Yew
●	●	●			●				●			5–9	336	Yucca

GLOSSARY

B & B: abbreviation for balled-and-burlapped stock, i.e., plants that have been dug out of the ground and have had their rootballs wrapped in burlap

Bonsai: the art of training plants into miniature trees and landscapes

Candles: the new, soft spring growth of needle-leaved evergreens such as pine, spruce and fir

Crown: the part of a plant at or just below the soil where the stems meet the roots; also, the top of a tree, including the branches and leaves

Cultivar: a cultivated plant variety with one or more distinct differences from the species; e.g., *Hedera helix* is a botanical species, of which 'Gold-Heart' is a cultivar distinguished by leaf variegation

Deadhead: to remove spent flowers in order to maintain a neat appearance, encourage a longer blooming period and prevent the plant from expending energy on fruit production

Dieback: death of a branch from the tip inwards; usually used to describe winter damage

Dormancy: an inactive stage, often coinciding with the onset of winter

Double flower: a flower with an unusually large number of petals, often caused by mutation of the stamens into petals

Dripline: the area around the bottom of a tree, directly under the tips of the farthest-extending branches

Dwarf: a plant that is small compared to the normal growth of the species; dwarf growth is often cultivated by plant breeders

Espalier: the training of a tree or shrub to grow in two dimensions

Gall: an abnormal outgrowth or swelling produced as a reaction to sucking insects, other pests or diseases

Genus: a category of biological classification between the species and family levels; the first word in a Latin name indicates the genus, e.g., *Pinus* in *Pinus contorta*

Girdling: a restricted flow of water and nutrients in a plant caused by something tied tightly around a trunk or branch, or by an encircling cut

Grafting: a type of propagation in which a stem or bud of one plant is joined onto the rootstock of another plant of a closely related species

Heartwood: the wood in the center of a stem or branch consisting of old, dense, non-functional conducting tissue

Hybrid: a plant resulting from natural or human-induced cross-breeding between varieties, species, or genera; often sterile, but may be more vigorous than either parent and have attributes of both

Inflorescence: a flower cluster

Leader: the dominant upward growth at the top of a tree; may be erect or drooping

Nodes: the places on the stem from where leaves grow; when cuttings are planted, new roots grow from the nodes under the soil

pH: a measure of acidity or alkalinity (the lower the pH, the higher the acidity); the pH of soil influences availability of nutrients for plants

Procumbent, prostrate: terms used to describe plants that grow along the ground

Rootball: the root mass and surrounding soil of a container-grown or dug-out plant

Rhizome: a modified stem that grows underground, horizontally

Single flower: a flower with a single ring of typically four or five petals

Species: simply defined as a group of organisms that can interbreed to yield fertile offspring; the fundamental unit of biological classification

Standard: a shrub or small tree grown with an erect main stem; accomplished either through pruning and training, or by grafting the plant onto a tall, straight stock

Subspecies (subsp.): a naturally occurring, regional form of a species, often geographically isolated from other subspecies but still potentially interfertile with them

Sucker: a shoot that comes up from a root, often some distance from the plant; it can be separated to form a new plant once it develops its own roots

Topiary: the training of plants into geometric, animal or other unique shapes

Variegation: describes foliage that has more than one color, often patched or striped or bearing differently colored leaf margins

Variety (var.): a naturally occurring variant of a species; below the level of subspecies in biological classification

FURTHER READING

Cavendish Gardens. 1999. *Handbook of Pruning and Training.* Cavendish Books, Vancouver, British Columbia.

Editors of Sunset Books and Sunset Magazine. 1995. *Sunset Western Garden Book.* Sunset Publishing Corporation, Menlo Park, California.

Ellis, B. W. and F. M. Bradley, eds. 1996. *The Organic Gardener's Handbook of Natural Insect and Disease Control.* Rodale Press, Emmaus, Pennsylvania.

Kruckeberg, A. R. 1982. *Gardening with Native Plants of the Pacific Northwest.* University of Washington Press, Seattle.

Pettinger, A. 1996. *Native Plants in the Coastal Garden: A Guide for Gardeners in British Columbia and the Pacific Northwest.* Whitecap Books, Vancouver, British Columbia.

Thompson, P. 1992. *Creative Propagation: A Grower's Guide.* Timber Press, Portland, Oregon.

INDEX

More Garden Delights from Lone Pine

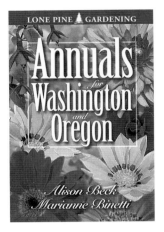

Plenty of photographs accompany clear, easy-to-follow gardening advice for growing 281 favorite annuals. This indispensable guide includes tips on when to plant, growing from seed, optimal growth conditions, common pests and problems and much more.

Annuals for Washington & Oregon
by Alison Beck & Marianne Binetti
Lone Pine Publishing
ISBN 1-55105-160-5
Softcover • Color photos • Pictorial guide
256 pages • $18.95 US

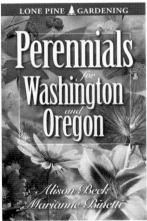

Featuring 434 favorite perennials, this guide offers practical advice on planting, propagating, blooming periods, choosing the best plants for your garden conditions and more. The book is beautifully illustrated with 537 color photographs and includes a reference chart with a wealth of valuable information at your fingertips.

Perennials for Washington & Oregon
by Alison Beck & Marianne Binetti
Lone Pine Publishing
ISBN 1-55105-162-1
Softcover • Color photos • Pictorial guide
352 pages • $18.95 US

Available at bookstores or
order toll-free
(800) 518-3541